Russia in Manchuria

Manchuria, the name given to China's North-eastern provinces by foreign powers, has been contested by China, Russia and Japan in particular over many centuries. This book surveys the history of Manchuria, focusing particularly on the Russian and Soviet perspective. It outlines early colonisation of the region and examines the importance of the Chinese Eastern Railway, a branch of the Trans-Siberian Railway, and the remarkable railway city of Harbin for consolidating the Russian presence in the region and for developing the region's economy. It goes on to consider twentieth century developments, including the Japanese invasion and the puppet state of Manchukuo. Throughout, the book reflects on the nature of empire, especially Russian/Soviet imperialism and its similarities to and differences from other nations' imperial ventures.

Paul Dukes was Emeritus Professor of Russian History at the University of Aberdeen.

Routledge Studies in the History of Russia and Eastern Europe

For a full list of available titles please visit: https://www.routledge.com/Routledge-Studies-in-the-History-of-Russia-and-Eastern-Europe/book-series/SE0329

30 Everyday Soviet Utopias
The Planning, Design and the Aesthetics of Developed Socialism
Anna Alekseyeva

31 Tourism and Travel during the Cold War
Negotiating Tourist Experiences across the Iron Curtain
Sune Bechmann Pedersen and Christian Noack

32 Soviet Women – Everyday Lives
Melanie Ilic

33 Late Tsarist Russia, 1881–1913
Beryl Williams

34 Duelling, the Russian Cultural Imagination, and Masculinity in Crisis
Amanda DiGioia

35 Russian Peasant Bride Theft
John Bushnell

36 The Soviet Union and Global Environmental Change
Modifying the Biosphere and Conceptualising Society-Nature Interaction
Jonathan D. Oldfield

37 Russia in Manchuria
A Problem of Empire
Paul Dukes

38 Soviet and Post-Soviet Lithuania
Generational Experiences
Edited by Laima Žilinskienė and Melanie Ilic

39 Muslim Reformers and the Bolsheviks
The Case of Daghestan
Naira Sahakyan

Russia in Manchuria
A Problem of Empire

Paul Dukes

LONDON AND NEW YORK

First published 2022
by Routledge
2 Park Square, Milton Park, Abingdon, Oxon OX14 4RN

and by Routledge
605 Third Avenue, New York, NY 10158

Routledge is an imprint of the Taylor & Francis Group, an informa business

© 2022 Paul Dukes

The right of Paul Dukes to be identified as author of this work has been asserted by him in accordance with sections 77 and 78 of the Copyright, Designs and Patents Act 1988.

All rights reserved. No part of this book may be reprinted or reproduced or utilised in any form or by any electronic, mechanical, or other means, now known or hereafter invented, including photocopying and recording, or in any information storage or retrieval system, without permission in writing from the publishers.

Trademark notice: Product or corporate names may be trademarks or registered trademarks, and are used only for identification and explanation without intent to infringe.

British Library Cataloguing-in-Publication Data
A catalogue record for this book is available from the British Library

Library of Congress Cataloging-in-Publication Data
A catalog record has been requested for this book

ISBN: 978-0-367-75216-3 (hbk)
ISBN: 978-0-367-75267-5 (pbk)
ISBN: 978-1-003-16176-9 (ebk)

DOI: 10.4324/9781003161769

Typeset in Times New Roman
by Deanta Global Publishing Services, Chennai, India

Contents

Epigraph: 'Lines on Harbin'		vii
List of figures		viii
Preface		x
Acknowledgement		xii
A note on names		xiii

1 Introduction to Manchuria: Early empire   1

Introduction to Manchuria 1
Early empire 7
From crisis to advance 10
From expansion to withdrawal 13
Conclusion 15
Notes 16

2 Empire before the railway, 1689–1892   18

Russia and China 18
The Great Game of empire 22
The new imperialism 29
Conclusion 33
Notes 33

3 The arrival of the railway and war with Japan, 1892–1906   36

The Trans-Siberian railway: Nicholas II and his bureaucracy 36
War between Japan and China: the Chinese Eastern Railway 39
The Boxer challenge and response 41
Towards war between Russia and Japan 44
The Russo-Japanese War, 1904–5, and after 47
Conclusion 52
Notes 53

4 To the First World War and Russian Revolution, 1906–18   56

Relations between Russia, Japan and China 56
Developments in Harbin 61

The Mongolian question 64
The arrival of war and revolution 68
The Russian Revolution and international relations 71
Conclusion 73
Notes 74

5 **Soviet Russia, Imperial Japan and the USA: Harbin, 1918–29**   77

The Paris Conference: revolution, civil war and intervention in the Far East 77
The Washington Conference: Harbin and North Manchuria 82
The press in Harbin 84
Ideology in Harbin 88
New diplomacy? 91
Conclusion 94
Notes 94

6 **Conflict with China: Manchukuo and the Second World War, 1929–45**   97

Conflict with China 97
Manchukuo and the Lytton Commission 100
Reactions to Manchukuo 104
From border clashes to the Second World War 111
Conclusion 113
Notes 114

7 **The Soviet invasion, the Chinese Revolution and the Korean War, 1945–56**   117

The Soviet invasion 117
Postwar readjustment 123
The Chinese Revolution 127
The Korean War and withdrawal 131
Conclusion 134
Notes 135

8 **Conclusion: Empire and after – Manchuria past, present, future**   137

Russia and China 137
Empire and after 140
Manchuria past 144
Manchuria present 148
Conclusion 153
Notes 154

Index   157

Epigraph: 'Lines on Harbin'

Dear city, proud and well-built,
The day will come,
When they won't remember, that you were fashioned
By a Russian hand.

Let us not avert our eyes
From such a bitter fate;
Remember, old man historian,
Remember us.

You will look for what has been forgotten,
You will write some mournful pages,
And to the Russian cemetery
A tourist will drop by.

He will take with him a dictionary
And read the epitaphs ...
And so our little lamp will be extinguished,
Its flickering flame worn out.

Arsenii Nesmelov, 'Stikhi o Harbine,' G. V. Melikhov, *Man'chzhuriia: dalekaia i blizkaia* (Moscow: Nauka, 1991), p. 188. John J. Stephan, author of *The Russian Fascists: Tragedy and Farce in Exile, 1925–1945* (London: Hamish Hamilton, 1978) informs me that Nesmelov was a party bard laureate under the name of Nikolai Dozorov. This might account to some extent for the twilight nature of 'Lines on Harbin.' In fact, Russian Harbin has recently experienced a revival, including care of its cemeteries.

Figures

1 This map accompanies the article published in 1895 by John Ross that forms the basis of the Introduction in Chapter One. There is no indication of the construction of a railroad or of the city of Harbin. The Argun, Amur and Ussuri Rivers stand out as the frontier of Manchuria from west to east. (Photo: Aberdeen University)   5
2 The frontispiece from *Nord en Ost Tartarye ...* published in 1692 by Nicolas Witsen, a prosperous director of the Dutch East India Company. The book ran to 660 pages, giving many details of the peoples inhabiting the vast region of North and East Tartary, including the Manchus. (Bruno Naarden)   14
3 The Map of Eastern Tartary published by Pieter de Hondt in 1751 was taken from maps drawn up for the Jesuits. Note Nerchinsk ('Nerchinskoy') on the River Shilka to the northwest, the location of the negotiations with Russia conducted by the Jesuits acting for China leading to the Treaty of Nerchinsk of 1689. (Wikimaps)   20
4 Nikolai Muravyov-Amurskii was created a Count in 1858 with the suffix taken from the River that he had done much to acquire for the Russian Empire. He resigned in 1861 after the accusation that he was attempting to become the 'Siberian tsar' and other innuendos and moved to Paris. His portrait was painted by Konstantin Makovskii in 1863. (Wikipedia)   23
5 This railway construction gang shows Chinese gangmasters at the front and 'coolies' at the back, with European, mostly Finnish, managers in between. The photo may be viewed either as an example of the 'yellow peril' threatening white civilisation or as a pointer towards 'yellow Russia' involving harmony between the races. (Leena Dukes)   43
6 A French cartoon depicting the carve-up of China entitled 'The Chinese cake.' From left to right, Queen Victoria, Kaiser Wilhelm II, Tsar Nicholas II of Russia, French Marianne, Japanese samurai. Qing official behind them. (Wikimedia Commons)   53
7 Army officer Vladimir Arsenev was captivated by the primordial nature of Manchuria and the surrounding area as he went about his official task of surveying the land. He was assisted by a number of

	native guides represented by Dersu Uzala in the eponymous film by the Japanese director Akira Kurosawa. (Wikipedia)	58
8	General Dmitry Khorvat, military engineer and manager of the Far Eastern Railway, in the company of fellow officers from interventionist forces in Vladivostok in 1918. (Wikipedia)	81
9	The *Russkii Klub* at the All-Russian Fascist Union branch headquarters in Manchouli, north-western Manchukuo in 1940. As John Stephan says: 'A brilliantly lit swastika tauntingly faces the Soviet frontier, just two miles away.' (John Stephan)	108
10	Manchuria (subtitled Manchukuo) from the map of China published in the 1930s in the series *Philips' Authentic Imperial Maps*, as it was still in 1945 on the eve of the Soviet invasion. (George Philip & Son, Ltd.)	120
11	*Damansky Island: The Border Conflict of March 1969: A Military Affair*, to give a translation of the front cover of the book by D. S. Riabushkin. The disputed island in the River Ussuri near its confluence with the River Amur forms a background for the watchful Soviet soldier. (Russkie Vitiazi)	139
12	St Sophia Cathedral, first built in 1907 in wood, then reconstructed from 1923 to 1932 in stone, has become a feature of the scenery and a museum in Chinese Harbin today. (Wikipedia)	148
13	The last old Russians in Harbin in the year 2000: photograph from the journal of the Russian Society in Ekaterinburg published in collaboration with State Archive of Sverdlovsk province. The final survivor Efrosiniia Andreevna Nikiforova died in 2006. (Nikolai Kuznetsov)	149
14	Children of the new Russians in Harbin celebrate Golden Autumn in October 2017 and Reading Day in 2015 as events in the calendar of the Russian Club. (VGBOU VO, VGUES, Vladivostok)	150
15	*Beloved Kharbin: A Town of Friendship between Russia and China: Materials of an International Academic Conference devoted to the 120th Anniversary of the City of Kharbin, the Past and Present of the Russian Diaspora in China, Harbin 16–18 June 2018*, translation of the front cover complete with a photo of Kitaiskaia Ulitsa (China Street) from the interwar period and crossed flags. (FGBOU VO, VGUES, Vladivostok)	151

Online

There are many interesting items which may be viewed free online. Among them are two silent films on Harbin in the 1920s as well as recent publicity videos, several on Manchukuo including a Japanese documentary from the 1930s, and accounts of August Storm 1945.

Preface

There are many problems of empire, a concept still in daily use. Russia in Manchuria is a particular problem, and this book is an attempt to describe by way of an analytical narrative its historical evolution in the context of global imperial developments. In this way, it seeks to demonstrate that the Russian Empire was different in some respects and similar in others to its rivals. Thus, the title and the subtitle are so closely linked as to be almost inseparable.

'Empire' encourages the waving of one's own flag and the striking of the flag of others, and both tendencies have been especially noticeable in the case of 'Manchuria,' a foreign designation for China's three north-eastern provinces – Dongbei. And so, throughout the book, I have made particular use of the perceptions of contemporary commentators, mostly from the English-speaking world that has produced two of the world's greatest powers, aiming to show their myopia as well as their insights.

A central part is played by Harbin, a Russian railway city on Chinese soil. Individual human characters are introduced, but as much to show how they were bound by circumstances as able to exert their own influence. We shall see how this observation plays out in the wide expanses of the Russian Far East over the course of several centuries, reserving much of the analysis to the Conclusion in order to keep the story moving.

I have tried to keep in mind how remote Manchuria must still seem to many readers, even though we all know how much the world has 'shrunk.' In 1938, the British Prime Minister Neville Chamberlain talked of Czechoslovakia as remote. Eighty or so years on, North Korea adjacent to Dongbei has seemed all too close.

From the vast literature on the subject, I have attempted to concentrate on books and articles that advance the major theme. Since this book covers such a wide chronological span, I have considered it more appropriate for readers to look for references in the notes to each chapter rather than providing an overall bibliography. The illustrations and maps along with suggestions for online viewing aim at providing a supplement to the analytical narrative.

Whatever merits the book may possess owe much to generous readers of successive drafts. Two doyens of Far Eastern Studies, Ian Nish and John Stephan, both gave an encouraging positive appraisal at an early stage. Two friends have subjected the revised work to searching scrutiny: Janet Hartley, author of *Siberia:*

A History of the People; and Alan Wood, pioneer in Siberian studies and author of *Russia's Frozen Frontier*. In Aberdeen, as ever, I have derived much benefit from my continued association with the History Department, in particular on this occasion from Tony Heywood. Three colleagues from Anthropology, David Anderson, Tanya Argunova-Low and Dmitry Arzyutov, have been especially helpful. In a brief but busy visit to Vladivostok in 2017, I received most useful advice and guidance from two associates of the Far Eastern University, Kirill Kolesnikov and Vladimir Sokolov; the bookseller and publisher of the journal *Rubezh* Alexander Kolesov; and the independent scholar Andrei Sidorov, who also made helpful comments on the first version and gave me his copy of an indispensable book, G. V. Melikhov: *Man'chzhuriia: dalekaia i blizkaia* (*Manchuria: Afar and Near*). The little I know and understand of Chinese history has been mostly supplied by Wang Li of Jilin University and Zhiang Naihe of Nankai University. Associates of the libraries at the Universities of Aberdeen, Edinburgh and Oxford could not have been of greater assistance. I thank Peter Sowden and other members of the Routledge team for seeing the book through its various stages of production in an efficient and considerate manner. The dedication is to my wife Cathryn, who first drew my attention to Russia's Far East, and has provided much guidance and support since. Neither she nor any of those mentioned above is to be held responsible for the book's errors and misunderstandings, which are all my own work.

King's College, Old Aberdeen
1 February 2021

Acknowledgement

Paul Dukes died on 25 August 2021, aged 87, after a short illness. Until only weeks before his death, he had enjoyed very good health. This volume, one of two he was in the process of completing, was already at the copyediting stage. Having followed in our father's footsteps, we are both academics, and know something of what it takes to see a manuscript through to publication. Keen to do so in this case, we very soon realized that we would require expert help from historians. We will forever be grateful to Paul's dear colleagues and friends, Tony Heywood, Murray Frame, and Janet Hartley, for their generous offers of help and for the great lengths to which they then went to complete references and respond to other queries raised by the publishing team. While the author remains solely responsible for the text, we would like to emphasize that he never got to see the final version.

Ruth and Daniel Dukes

A note on names

Personal and place names have posed many problems, especially of transliteration. Abandoning fruitless attempts at complete consistency, I have tried to ensure that readers will be able to recognise them.

Changes in place names are listed here mostly in chronological order.

Towns
Beijung post-1949
Changchun: Hsinking
Dairen: Dalny: Dalian
Mukden: Shenyang
Newchang: YoSin: Niu-Chwang: Niux-huang: Yingkou?
Peking pre-1949
Port Arthur: Lushun
Tientsin: Tianjin
Tsitsikar: Qiqihar

Provinces (south to north)
Fungtien: Shen-king: Mukden: Shenyang; Liaoning
Kirin: Jilin
Tsitsikar: Heilongjiang

River
Sungari: Songhua Jiang

1 Introduction to Manchuria
Early empire

Introduction to Manchuria

'The name Manchuria is a purely geographical term, and is unknown to both Chinese and Manchus,' a Scottish missionary John Ross wrote in an article of 1895. However, he added: 'There was a kingdom of Manchu established three centuries ago ..., which gradually extended its sway over its smaller neighbours ... [and] also included what is now known as the Russian Maritime Province to the north of Korea.'[1] Born in Gaelic-speaking Northern Scotland in 1842, but learning English as well, Ross completed his theological education in Glasgow and Edinburgh before travelling to China to pursue his vocation 30 years later. As part of his calling, he translated the New Testament into Korean, among other publications including his article of 1895.

In 1891, John Ross brought out a book with the title *The Manchus: The Reigning Dynasty of China: Their Rule and Progress*. In the Preface, he declared:

> We have long inferred that China must from her nature, assume an attitude of suspicion and defiance towards Russia; and she has long succumbed under the humiliation of taxes levied on opium at the dictation, and under the compulsion of the British Government.[2]

But China was stirring from inertness, and in her own manner.

In a 'Preliminary Dissertation on the Political Principles of China' which followed, Ross observed: 'It is to the commanding influence of thought that China owes her continuous history. It is because mental power is, and always has been more highly esteemed than physical force.' He declared: 'China will not, therefore, merely append Western forms of civilization, but is sure to gradually assimilate them to her own constitution.' China was modernising her army, but 'Chinese opposition to the laying of railways [...] is like that to Christian missions, wholly and only political.' Thus, he continued, 'Until the Chinese government is convinced that western nations have no serious designs upon her freedom, we do not expect to see railways and other western mechanical and steam-power appliances largely employed.' Ross suggested:

DOI: 10.4324/9781003161769-1

> We ourselves are subjected to by designing or timid men to a periodical Russian scare, and surely the Chinese have much more reason to believe in the ability and the desire of western powers to injure her than we in that of Russia to maim us.[3]

It should not be forgotten, Ross averred, that

> the Chinese were a cultured people more than twenty centuries before Scott opened our eyes to the grand moods and the gentle soothing voice of nature, and before the lake poets sang its praises to an all but sullen audience.

Moreover, they had developed printing, gunpowder (if only for fireworks) and the compass or 'needle-fix-the-south,' as well as spectacles and playing cards. They had taken embroidery with silk and the carving of ivory to a high level. Their agriculture was advanced, as well as their codification of laws. Their government was '*absolute only for the wellbeing of the people*,' Ross emphasised, adding later that '*absolute government, founded on and governed by democratical principles*' made 'the Chinese people one of the most democratic in the world' even if the government was based on divine right.[4]

Therefore, Ross considered,

> We do not believe that Russia will now be ever able to conquer China, and we are certain that the Chinese people would suffer in most things and benefit in nothing by transference to the Russian rule.

The Chinese peasants, in his view, were happier and more cultured than their Russian counterparts. Nevertheless, Chinese dynasties became corrupt and rebels based their action on justice: 'better the storm of revolution than quietude under the blighting cancer.' The Chinese were more Whig than conservative in other words.[5]

Ross concluded his 'Preliminary Dissertation on the Political Principles of China' with the assertion: 'Whether we will or no, China is rapidly becoming a great and powerful nation; but the reception of Christianity alone can make the Chinese a moral people, who will benefit the whole world.'[6]

The Rev. Ross next begins the Introduction to his monumental work with the observation:

> As soon might we expect the water oozing from a mossy rock to become a mighty river, bearing on its bosom the peaceful fleets of all nations as the few ignorant descendants of the Tartar Aisin Gioro to become, by their own despicably insignificant resources, the legislators of a fourth of mankind, and the rulers of a fourth of mankind, and the rulers of the most populous empire under the sun.
>
> If it was necessary that the movements of the Manchus should have been regulated by wise bravery, it was even more essential that reckless folly should misguide their no less brave opponents.[7]

(Ross rejected the comparison of the Manchu conquest of China with the British conquest of India because British troops in India were conscious of their own superiority, in weaponry in particular, and their opponents 'equally conscious of their own inferiority.')

The Manchus were also inspired by their sacred bird, the magpie, who makes a critical intervention in the story of the origins of Manchuria. Several centuries ago, Ross tells us, three heaven-descended maidens were bathing in a lake below the White Mountains when a magpie dropped a fruit on the skirt of the youngest who ate it before dressing and, as a consequence, bore a son who could speak from birth and was remarkable in a number of other ways. When he was full-grown, his mother told him that 'he was born of Heaven, to set to rights the troubled nations,' and having given him the name Aisin Gioro, which means Gold Dynasty, she ascended into Heaven.[8]

The remarkable nature of the young man was recognised by three local contending peoples, who elected him their joint ruler, whereupon he gave them the name 'Manchu' which means 'pure.'

The myth was accompanied by history from the middle of the sixteenth century when an obscure chieftain named Nurhaci extended his power over most of what was to become known as Manchuria. Giving himself the title Ying-ming, which means 'Brave and Illustrious,' he turned his attention from 1618 to the conquest of China. Nurhaci died in 1626, but is usually credited with the founding of the Qing or 'Pure' dynasty (as in Manchu so in Mandarin according to Ross), even if his son actually established it in 1644.

After a survey of several versions of the consequences of eating the red fruit recorded from 1635 to 1739, the historian Lin Sun has commented:

> Through analysis of the Manchu origin myth, the history of the Manchus can be traced as they moved from being conquerors to rulers of a vast empire. The myth that had originally served to underpin the unity of the ruling elite and to legitimate a dominant clan in order to prevent future divisions from the 1640s, disseminated among the wider group of Manchu, Mongol, and Han bannermen [Chinese clansmen], all of whom were invited to claim a Manchu identity based on the original myth.[9]

As he moved to begin the conquest of China, Nurhaci did not leave his native land completely behind him. Both he and his successors made formal visits for reasons varying from the mystical to the practical and maintained much of Manchuria (although they did not call it that) as a frontier region of their empire beyond the Great Wall. For several centuries, this included the Wild East, bandit country, a refuge for runaways, known in the West as Tartary. To protect their agricultural lands, from the middle of the seventeenth century onwards, the Manchu rulers had been building the Willow Palisades stretching for hundreds of miles, protected by a deep ditch and intermittent garrisons.

The myth of the birth of 'Manchuria' was not unlike that of many other societies throughout the world. Some would say that all humankind originated in the story of another young woman eating fruit, that we are all the children of Eve. But the Rev. Ross was almost certainly not among those who considered the Garden of Eden to be mythical. To take another outstanding example, Rome was said to have originated with Romulus and Remus being suckled by a she-wolf. Rome, of course, went on to become a great empire that was the model for the Western world, Russia in this case included. As Mary Beard points out,

> since the Renaissance at least, many of our most fundamental assumptions about power, citizenship, responsibility, political violence, empire, luxury and beauty have been formed, and tested, in dialogue with the Romans and their writing.[10]

Great Britain and Russia both made use of the classical heritage as they expanded. A British player in the Great Game is said to have succinctly reported 'peccavi' which would be widely understood as 'I have Sindh,' while Russians at the highest level drew on their Greek heritage via the Second Rome, Byzantium, as they named emperors Alexander and Nicholas.

The body of Ross's book on the Manchus need not detain us. It is a detailed narrative running to some seven hundred pages describing the manner in which their dynasty extended its hold throughout China. Suffice it to say that a major role is played by a series of individual leaders exhibiting what Ross had called 'wise bravery.'

In his article on Manchuria, which, in the estimate of a leading authority, he saw 'as playing a historically pivotal role in the geopolitics of Northeast Asia,'[11] Ross described the geography of what was known to the Chinese as the 'Three Eastern Provinces' (from south to north Fungtien, Kirin and Heilungkiang) just before they were transformed by the arrival of the railway. He attached a helpful map (Figure 1).

From the port of Newchang by the adjoining Liaotung Peninsula, Ross observed, a magnificent, virtually unbroken plain stretched north-east to the Amur River with just an occasional hill. Higher ground could be found towards Mongolia to the west and adjacent to Korea to the east, where the Changbai Shan or Ever White Mountain, which appeared to be continually covered in snow because of the colour of its stone, rose to about 8000 feet. This height had been calculated by two recent travellers, Messrs James and Younghusband (whom we shall meet again at the end of the next chapter). The double range south of the town of Liaoyang called the Chienshan or the Thousand Peaks contained many Buddhist and even more Taoist monasteries.

The Ever White Mountain was a watershed for the Ussuri River which flowed directly north to form the boundary between Manchuria and the Russian Maritime Province and for the Sungari River which was a tributary of the mighty Amur River, which formed another boundary between Manchuria and China. The Russians had excluded the Chinese from the Amur, but for some years, a small Russian steamer had some years plied the Sungari as far as Kirin, the middle of the three provinces. The Yalu River separated Manchuria from Korea, while the

Figure 1 This map accompanies the article published in 1895 by John Ross that forms the basis of the Introduction in Chapter One. There is no indication of the construction of a railroad or of the city of Harbin. The Argun, Amur and Ussuri Rivers stand out as the frontier of Manchuria from west to east. (Photo: Aberdeen University)

Liao River flowed through the great plain of Manchuria to enter the sea about 20 miles from Newchang.[12]

April could be said to be the only spring month, for May quickly became summer. 'So rapid is the growth under the bright sunshine and the penetrating power of the daily increasing heat,' Ross remarked, 'that wheat sown in the beginning of April is cut down in the end of June or the beginning of July.' Up to the end of July, rain was rare and light, so clouds were regarded with special favour 'not only as containing the promise of needed rain, but as a feature of beauty in the usually cloudless sky.'[13] Towards the beginning of August, when the heat was greatest, the heaviest rains came. Floods could cause great havoc, with farmers sinking to their knees as they tried in vain to save some of their crops.

September was the normal harvest month, and then, a finer month than October in Manchuria would be difficult to find anywhere. But frost crept in at night towards the end of October and then applied its iron grip from November till March. Thus, after one month of spring, there were four and a half months of summer, one and a half of autumn and five of winter. At least ten months of the year were very dry.

The main crop was sorghum, a variety of millet. It resembled barley, and, boiled whole to be eaten often with beans or other vegetables, was far more nutritious than rice. Sorghum could be used for making spirit, as was almost all the barley grown. Wheat was widely cultivated. There were many kinds of beans, one of which (this was soy, although Ross does not name it) was valuable as the main item of export. Beans could also be crushed under a great wheel of granite weighing several tonnes to produce oil used in cooking or for light. Maize or Indian corn was also extensively grown. Tobacco and opium were largely exported, as was indigo. Vegetables, in particular a large cabbage and a bitter turnip, were consumed locally, often soaked in brine, for the Chinese never used salt in its pure state. Garlic was highly valued, while shallots could be both cultivated and wild. Cucumbers, marrows, eggplant and chilli were common, as were melons. Grapes, plums, apricots and peaches were grown according to prevailing conditions, while mushrooms could be found in the mountains. Root crops consisted of potatoes, sweet potatoes, carrots, turnips, kohlrabi and groundnuts. They were never fed to cattle. There was plentiful game, too, deer, wild boar, goats and hare, while fish from the rivers and the sea were also readily available. The Scotsman Ross was no doubt surprised to learn that the Chinese did not appreciate the flavour of salmon.

There was gold in the Manchurian hills running from the Sungari River to the sea. However, with the exception of a famous mine in Kirin, 'where the miners have for generations made a little kingdom of their own and defied the Government,' the present dynasty had forbidden the extraction of the precious metal, and for two reasons. One was superstitious, 'based on the belief that it is unlucky to interfere with the configuration of the earth.' The other was to do with law and order since, when the supply of gold ran short, unsuccessful miners 'went with their matchlocks to the nearest highway and helped themselves to the goods of travellers.' Silver and copper abounded in many localities but were bound by the same laws as gold. Manchuria was 'particularly rich in good coal and excellent iron,' but the working of them was barely tolerated: 'In many places coal crops out above the ground, but the people dare not touch it.'[14] Manchurian iron attained a price higher than European, and a German officer had declared that swords made in Mukden were as good as any. However, Ross noted, the smelting processes were so crude and primitive that it cost more to put this iron on the local market than to introduce the metal from Scotland or Belgium.

The most noteworthy tradesmen were furriers and tanners. Mukden, the city at the centre of the most southerly of the three eastern provinces comprising 'Manchuria,' Fungtien, was among world leaders in quantities of furs cured, while tanners produced vast numbers of skins from horses, mules, donkeys, deer and sheep.

The size of the population was difficult to calculate in such a great territory. Of the three provinces, Fungtien (also known as Mukden) had accommodated over the previous 20 years hundreds of thousands of diligent farmers and produced new cities. Kirin was already possessed by the ploughman, but Tsitsikar or Heilungkiang to the north was still waiting for husbandmen to exploit its huge resources. Overall, Ross calculated that the population could not be less than 25,000,000, and could be as much as that of England.[15]

Although the country was named after the Manchus, many of them had emigrated as soldiers to China when the new dynasty was established, while there had been a great influx of Chinese, who formed at least three-quarters of the population. Only in Mukden were the Manchus still able to assert their personality, although their language held out in some remote valleys against the Peking dialect of Chinese. Ross declared: 'Competent judges have pronounced the inhabitants of Manchuria to be possessed of an amount of comfort greater than that of any other Asiatic people,' with light taxation and abundant if coarse food, fuel and clothing.[16]

In his article, the Rev. Ross moved on to note: 'In the voluminous history of China the affairs of other nations are noted only when these nations come into friendly relations or hostile conflict with the Celestial Empire.' He proceeds to give a survey of successive dynasties before concluding: 'The lessons of the numerous changes in Manchuria throughout the past two thousand years are an emphatic protest against much of the sentimental teaching of the present day.' For Ross, 'the amelioration of the savage is due to the individual, not to the race.' Thus, 'the most valuable product of this earth is ... the man who can dare and who can do, the man who can be the leader of men into a life nobler than they have hitherto led.'[17] No doubt the Scottish missionary would have agreed with his fellow-countryman Thomas Carlyle that the history of the world was but the biography of great men. He probably had in mind empire-builders among others although he gave no examples. And he must have had at least an inkling that the greatest change in the history of Manchuria was about to occur with the coming of the railway. But Harbin, soon to be a considerable city as a railway junction, does not appear on the map that he attached to his article because it as well as the railway were yet to be constructed, and Manchuria as a whole was evidently awaiting modernisation.

Early empire

So, 'Manchuria' was born of empire, and not the Chinese empire: 'foreign devils' gave it the name, and then exploited it, especially from the nineteenth century until the middle of the twentieth. The first foreigners to come were the Russians, who were also the last to leave. Then came the British, the French, the Germans and the Americans. These were the main intruders, but they were joined by others from smaller European empires. And, of course, to varying extents, the Japanese and Koreans had always been there.

Russia was involved in Manchuria from the seventeenth century onwards before Northeast China was given that name. However, even before then, there had been significant expansion across the vast steppe in the other direction from what was generally known as Tartary.

The Tartar or Mongol invasion of Europe in the early thirteenth century spread terror far and wide. Under their renowned leader Chinggis Khan, who had already raided China, and then under his successors, the horse-borne horde swept across the vast Asian steppe to invade the land of the Russes and beyond. The Russian chronicle gives a harrowing description of the fall of one of many cities:

> The prince, with his mother, wife, sons, the boyars and inhabitants, without regard to age or sex, were slaughtered with the savage cruelty of Mongol revenge; some were impaled, or had nails or splinters of wood driven under their fingernails. Priests were roasted alive, and nuns and maidens ravished in the churches before their relatives. No eye remained open to weep for the dead.[18]

For many years, Chinggis Khan was a name to terrify the Russians, who were obliged to pay tribute to his successors while some of the princes from Russian cities collaborated with the invaders. Readers who have seen the film *Alexander Nevsky* will no doubt recall how the hero appeases the Mongols as he gives his primary attention to the defeat of the Teutonic Knights. Chinggis had been a skilful politician as well as a fearsome warrior and remains a great hero for his own people today, with great statues in Ulan Bator, the capital of Mongolia, Manchuria's neighbour. Thus, already, a difference of Asian and European viewpoints basic to this book is apparent, in the short run leading to further atrocities on both sides as well as a certain amount of more collaboration.

But we need to be clear that, along with Mongolia, Manchuria was not seen in the West in earlier times as more than an amorphous and vague area. What became Manchuria was understood from the sixteenth century onwards to be a part of Tartary that was the northern outlier of Cathay or China.

A much-celebrated if inconclusive victory over the Tartar Mongols took place at Kulikovo by the Don River in 1380. Later, a major counterattack against them was launched in the sixteenth century by Ivan IV, whose title as tsar along with some of his ideology was taken from Rome, while he was also inspired by thoughts of a new Jerusalem. Ivan, best known as the Terrible, took Kazan on the Volga River in 1552 and Astrakhan at its mouth in 1556. The way was open for the conquest of Siberia, in which a leading part was played by the Cossacks. These bands of frontier freebooters bound together in an interdependent fraternity were the cutting edge of infiltration. Under their most famous leader Ermak, a worthy counterpart to the Elizabethan seadogs Francis Drake and John Hawkins and the Spanish conquistadors Hernando Cortes and Francisco Pizarro, they soon established a firm presence in Western Siberia with the encouragement of Ivan, who was keen to get his hands on furs and other natural riches, including, if possible, gold and silver.

Ivan's counterpart in England was also interested in commercial expansion in the same direction as he clearly demonstrated in 1553 in 'the letters missive, which the right noble Prince Edward the Sixt, sent to the Kings, Princes, and other Potentates, inhabiting the Northeast parts of the world, towards the mighty Empire of Cathay.' King Edward declared:

> For the God of heaven and earth, greatly providing for mankinde, would not that of all things should be founde in one region, to the ende that one shoulde have neede of another, that by this meanes friendshippe might be established among all men, and every one seeke to gratifie all, as well to seeke such things as we lacke, as also to cary unto them from our regions, such things as they lacke. So that hereby not onely commoditie may ensue both to them and us, but also an indissoluble and perpetuall league of friendship be established between us both, while they permit us to take of their things, such whereof they have abundance in their regions, and we againe grant them such things of ours, whereof they are destitute.[19]

The letter reached Ivan the Terrible, who replied in a friendly fashion, and encouraged English merchants, who duly found their overland way to Cathay via Tartary.

In 1589, during the reign of Queen Elizabeth, Richard Hakluyt published his great propagandist work, *The Principall Navigations, Voiages and Discoveries of the English nation, made by Sea or over Land.* The book was divided into three parts, considering in turn: Asia and Africa; Russia and the Middle East; and the Americas including regions 'further than any Christian has yet pierced.' The second part includes what was to become known as 'Manchuria,' placing it in a wider context:

> the worthy discoveries of the English towards the North and Northeast by sea, as of Lapland ... toward the great river Ob, with the mighty Empire of Russia, the Caspian Sea, Georgia, Armenia, Media, Persia, Boghar in Bactria, and diverse kingdoms of Tartaria.

Manchuria would of course come under this last heading: 'diverse kingdoms of Tartaria.' Hakluyt's inclusion of Russia in the great land mass of North Eurasia unwittingly anticipates some of the geopolitical ideas of later times. Much earlier, the British and Russian peoples had already been connected according to a publication of 1568:

> Arthur which was sometimes the most renowned king of the Britons, was a mighty, and valiant man, and a famous warrior. This kingdom was too little for him, and his mind was not contented with it. He therefore valiantly subdued all Scania, which is now called Norway ... and all the Islands beyond Norway ... and all the other lands and Islands of the East Sea even unto Russia.[20]

Looking in the other direction across the sea, Hakluyt again pointed towards more recent strategic concepts. He suggested that colonies in North America would 'yield to us all the commodities of Europe, Africa and Asia.' A Captain Christopher Carleill, who had previously sailed to Russia in or about 1582, argued similarly in 1583 that trade with North America was free of encumbrances, adding:

> I doubt not by God's grace, that for the ten ships that are now commonly employed once the year into Muscovia, there shall in this voyage twice ten be employed well, twice the year at the least.[21]

The trade with North America would take some time to become a cornucopia, but already there were signs that the 'Columbian exchange' as it was to be called could lead to great mutual advantage.

'Columbian exchange,' of course, takes its name from the famous 'discovery' of America by Columbus in 1492, at a time when the colonial world was dominated by Spain and, to a lesser extent, Portugal, both operating mostly by sea. By the seventeenth century, these two empires were being overtaken by the Dutch expanding overland as well as by sea before the great struggle for global predominance between the French and the British in the eighteenth century. In the shorter run, in Britain in 1603, from beyond a wall named after the Roman Emperor Hadrian, and from a country often seen as wild by its neighbour to the south, James VI of Scotland moved by invitation rather than conquest to become James I of England and to introduce a new Stuart dynasty in place of the Tudors expiring with Elizabeth. In 1613, after a turbulent Time of Troubles, Mikhail Romanov was elected tsar by the Russian establishment.

British and Russian dynasties, whose early histories are about to become part of our narrative, were both influenced by classical imperial tradition but developing their own exclusive heritage, too. Geoffrey Elton wrote succinctly of successive views of divine right in the island kingdom: 'The Tudors appealed to fact – God spoke through the arbitrament of war. The Stuarts believed in an indefeasible right which no amount of adverse circumstances could lessen or destroy.' According to their *Primary Chronicle*, the warring peoples of what was to become Russia said to each other in 862: 'Let us seek a prince who may rule over us, and judge us according to the Law.' Then, the account continues: 'They accordingly went overseas to the Varangian Russes ... just as some are called Swedes, and others Normans, English and Gottlanders.' Thus, the Russians were distantly related to the invaders of England in 1066.[22]

Throughout the early seventeenth century, under Mikhail and his successors, Cossacks and others continued infiltration into Siberia, while the Stuarts expanded the British Empire across the seas.[23] A significant moment arrived in mid-century with a worldwide crisis shaking Britain, Russia and China alike.

From crisis to advance

In a letter of June 1646, James Howell, later Historiographer Royal to Charles II, wrote to the Earl of Dorset, Lord Chamberlain of Charles I:

to take all Nations in a lump, I think God Almighty hath a quarrel with all Mankind, and given the reins to the ill Spirit to compass the whole earth, for within these twelve years there have been the strangest Revolutions and horridest Things happen'd not only in *Europe*, but all the World over, that have befallen mankind, I dare boldly say, since *Adam* fell, in so short a revolution of time.

Howell continued:

I will begin with the hottest parts, with Africa, where the Emperor of *Ethiopia* ... was encounter'd and kill'd... . In Asia, the *Tartar* broke o'er the four-hundred-mil'd Wall, and rushed into the heart of *China, as far as Quinzay* [*Hangchow*] and beleaguer'd the very Palace of the Emperor. who rather than become Captive to the base *Tartar* burnt his Castle, and did make away himself, his Thirty Wives and Children. The great *Turk* hath been lately strangled in the *Seraglio*, his own house. The Emperor of *Muscovia* going in a simple procession upon the Sabbath-day, the Rabble broke in, knocked down and cut to pieces divers of his chiefest Counsellors, Favourites, and Officers before his face; and dragging their bodies to the Market-place, their heads were chopp'd off, thrown into Vessels of hot Water, and so set upon Poles to burn more bright before the Court-gate. In *Naples*, a common fruiterer hath raised such an insurrection ... *Catalonia* and *Portugal* hath quite revolted from *Spain* ... knocks have been 'twixt the Pope and *Parma*: the *Pole* and the *Cossack* are hard at it, *Venice* wrestleth with the *Turk* ... . And touching these three Kingdoms, there's none more capable than you Lordship to judge what monstrous Things have happen'd; so that it seems the whole Earth is off the hinges.[24]

The greatest of the 'revolutions' was in January 1649 with the execution after a formal trial of the King of England, Scotland and Ireland, Charles I. For Howell, this was a 'black Tragedy ..., the more I ruminate upon it, the more it astonisheth my imagination, and shaketh all the cells of my Brain.'[25] For many of us today, the execution of Charles I was an event fully deserving of the more comprehensive meaning given to the term 'revolution' in later years.

The King's republican successor, Oliver Cromwell, intended that his Commonwealth would be a new Rome and a new Jerusalem leading to the conversion of all humanity (aims coincidentally reminiscent of Muscovite Orthodox ideology). Cromwell devised a Western Design to wrest control from the Spanish in the Caribbean, involving the first deployment of British military power for transoceanic colonial purposes. The Western Design met with little success but aroused public awareness of the economic as well as moral purpose of overseas empire more successfully than had Hakluyt in the previous century while persuading the Protestant Dutch to collaborate with the Catholic Spanish in what was seen as a threat to both of them.[26] The restored Stuart King Charles II developed his own plan for colonial expansion under central control.[27]

Introduction to Manchuria

Meanwhile, having established itself in the northern capital of Peking in 1644, the Manchu Qing dynasty continued the struggle to consolidate its power throughout China. Beyond the Great Wall, it soon began to plant a wide Willow Palisade to separate a settled agricultural region from the nomadic pastoral frontier. In Russia, the Romanov dynasty survived the crisis of the middle of the seventeenth century to consolidate its position and encourage imperial expansion as far as the Pacific.

In the spring of 1649, most famously, E. I. Khabarov set off on a campaign to the East, then returned to the Siberian town of Iakutsk a year later with the news that he had found a good route to the Amur River. The *voevoda* or military governor of Iakutsk, D. A. Frantsbekov, gave permission on his own initiative to Khabarov to proceed on a second expedition in accordance with the tsar's ukaz, and with letters of introduction from the tsar. In August 1652, Khabarov submitted a long report to Frantsbekov telling of many violent encounters with Manchus, Daurs and other native peoples along the Amur but putting forward 'the possibility of establishing a settlement on the upper reaches of the river.'[28]

The Cossacks conducted further exploratory expeditions in the Far East, slaughtering many of the local inhabitants and extracting tribute from them. But they also helped to found settlements such as Albazin and Nerchinsk, and were by no means ignorant ruffians since, for example, they were ruled in a *krug* or circle by a rough democracy and their literacy rate was higher than that of the population at large.[29]

From 1654 to 1656, the first diplomatic mission to China from Russia was led through Mongolia by Fedor Isakevich Baikov. Later embassies proceeded via Manchuria, the first of them in 1670 by Ignatii Mikhailovich Milovanov, who recorded the route but briefly, the next in 1675 by Nikolai Gavrilovich Spafarii, who described more fully the places he stayed in, complete with the all-important stove known as a *kan*, while somewhat unsure about geographical location in general.

The transition 'from space to place' was under way not only for the Russians but also for the Chinese. The idea of a special region was nurtured by the Manchu Qing dynasty as it consolidated its power further south.[30] It extended its Willow Palisades beyond the Great Wall marking the boundary of Manchuria, comparable perhaps to the Antonine wall constructed by the Romans beyond Hadrian's. In the spring of 1682, Emperor Kang Xi visited Manchuria for a second time, to inspect the new shipbuilding works set up in Jilin in preparation for an offensive against Russia, but also to honour the Changbai Mountains, to which he had instituted a ritual sacrifice in 1677. He was moved to write poetry, too, as well as attending to administrative matters. Kang Xi sent further offerings in the years following, as acts of reverence and in the reinforcement of the Qing dynasty.

Kang Xi made considerable use of the Jesuits in various capacities. They delved deep into Chinese history, searching through the mists of the centuries for the old kingdom, the *tsarstvo Tenduk* or *Nikanskoe tsarstvo* as it was variously called, and discovering possible links with early Christianity and the legendary Prester John. More practically, they used their mathematical skills in surveying and map-making.[31]

A certain amount of Russian progress in the direction of map-making was made towards the end of the seventeenth century by the Siberian-born Semen Ulianovich Remezov, who believed that he had a 'spiritual talent given by God' and was in favour of 'all sorts of clever sciences.' He produced a number of maps of Siberia adorned with rivers, trees and other natural phenomena but without precise boundaries, especially to the Far East. Valerie Kivelson judiciously comments:

> Remezov's work, with all its idiosyncracies, provides insight into the way that Muscovite ideologies of legitimacy and expansion played out in the distant reaches of the realm at this moment of transition before the Petrine reforms. Through his unique vision, we can see how the Muscovite imperial Orthodox mission took shape in the peripheries, how a local agent on the front line saw his role and his purpose.

However, as she also points out:

> Remezov and his fellow imperial agents did not see 'empire' as a single political entity with coherent shape, definition and boundaries … . Remezov could plausibly distinguish lands belonging to other 'great powers,' as he did by drawing in the Great Wall, but within the patchwork … of tribes and peoples of Siberia, such a boundary would make no sense.

Remezov and his fellows, according to Kivelson, all shared 'a pictorial vision rather than a geometric one' and tried to keep their maps from foreign prying eyes in the secretive Muscovite manner. In contrast, West European maps were boldly showing at least some thick imperial boundary lines.[32]

Nancy Shields Kollmann tells us that, among visitors to China, 'Ambassadors Nikolai Spafarii (1674) and Isbrandt Ides (1692–5), for example, penned reports and created maps that were widely circulated in manuscript (Spafarii) and print (Ides) across Europe.' Most famously, in 1687, Nicolas Witsen, a prosperous director of the Amsterdam Chamber of the Dutch East India Company, completed a large map of the Russian territory in Europe and Asia reaching over to 'Chinese Tartary' and the ocean beyond. The map astonished the Royal Society in London in 1691, the President Robert Southwell writing that it marked the discovery of a new world similar to that made by Columbus. Then, in 1692, Witsen first published *Nord en Oost Tartarye*, a book of 660 pages that served as a companion to the map by providing detailed descriptions of the peoples inhabiting the area (Figure 2).[33]

However, there was still a long way to go before adequate maps were produced when a great need for them arose.

From expansion to withdrawal

Reacting against the intruding 'man-devouring demons,' and having established themselves throughout mainland China and Taiwan, Manchu forces pushed the Russian newcomers back in 1685, a 5,000-strong army equipped with 40 cannons

14 *Introduction to Manchuria*

investing Albazin and soon forcing the garrison to evacuate to Nerchinsk while taking 40 Cossack prisoners. Inexplicably, the Manchus soon left Albazin, allowing the Russians to return and strengthen the fortress. A second siege was carried on without success for nearly a year. The government back in Moscow sent Count Fedor Golovin with plenipotentiary powers to negotiate with the Jesuits acting on behalf of the Emperor. Golovin camped a short distance from Nerchinsk in a tent covered in rugs with a golden inkwell and clock inside. His Chinese counterparts including the Jesuits were encamped nearby, so close indeed that each side could see and hear the other. Golovin went to the negotiations dressed in green brocade trimmed with sables while the Chinese dignitaries wore silk decorated

Figure 2 The frontispiece from *Nord en Ost Tartarye* ... published in 1692 by Nicolas Witsen, a prosperous director of the Dutch East India Company. The book ran to 660 pages, giving many details of the peoples inhabiting the vast region of North and East Tartary, including the Manchus. (Bruno Naarden)

with dragons. The negotiations were carried on in Latin. Emphasis was given to the Chinese preponderance of power by the presence of troops who could easily have accounted for Golovin's bodyguard. The resulting Treaty of Nerchinsk of 1689 was inevitably imprecise in some respects, with the lower Amur and seaside Primor'e officially declared territory without borders. While the Russians were expelled from the mainstream Amur Valley and Albazin was destroyed, the Chinese agreed not to occupy the lands given up by the Russians and kept their promise not to infiltrate the resulting buffer zone up to the nineteenth century. Moreover, the Russians were allowed to continue their profitable caravan trade. In return for furs and small amounts of manufactures, tea, silk goods and other textiles could be brought back, as well as rhubarb, widely believed to be essential for good health and a profitable state monopoly until towards the end of the eighteenth century.[34]

Cossacks in the settlements along the Selenga River flowing into Lake Baikal attempted to benefit from trade (both legally and illegally) at the same time as developing agriculture. Local Mongol Buryats complained about the infiltration of their pastures while raids from Mongolia itself were a source of further discomfort. The administration in Irkutsk, the outpost of the Moscow government, appeared less than accommodating to such an extent that the Selenga Cossacks revolted against it at the end of the seventeenth century as well as bickering among themselves. At this time, living in the Russian Far East was far from easy, for this was a wild frontier country, separated from Moscow by a distance greater than that from London to the trans-Atlantic colonies in North America, with maps providing only limited guidance. Laws were difficult to enforce. Moreover, movement and transportation were much more arduous by land than by sea until the arrival of the railway at the end of the nineteenth century.

Nevertheless, Cossacks were not alone in their search for freedom away from the control of the central government. Merchants were quick to seek out opportunities for trade. Old Believers, intent on preserving their old-time religion after the modernising reforms of the Patriarch Nikon looked towards Tartary where they thought they would find the sanctuary of Belovod'e or White Water. At least a few peasants who were unhappy at the burdens placed upon them realised that there were vast lands for them to run to. Then, the future Peter the Great, who overthrew the Regent, his half-sister Sophia, in the same year as the Treaty of Nerchinsk, was to develop a considerable interest in China.

Conclusion

In 1895, two years before the arrival of the railway that was to produce a great transformation, a Scottish missionary John Ross published a comprehensive article on the geography of 'Manchuria,' the name given by foreigners to the three north-eastern provinces of China. Turning to history, Ross concentrated on the founders of Manchuria while expressing a belief in the importance of the role of the individual in general at the same time as showing his deep appreciation of Chinese civilisation. He noted that Russia and Great Britain were among the first foreign powers to interest themselves in the amorphous region known as Tartary from which Manchuria was to evolve.

Medieval Russia had made the first contact with the Far East in the shape of the invading Mongol hordes most famously associated with the name of Chinggis Khan. By the sixteenth century, Ivan the Terrible made a successful counterattack, and Edward VI wrote to him proposing a collaboration in the search for the riches of Cathay or China via Tartary. With Ivan's encouragement, the Cossacks made deep inroads into Siberia.

In 1589, Richard Hakluyt published a comprehensive view of world developments including the establishment of links between England and Russia and the beginning of what was to become known as the 'Columbian exchange' across the Atlantic Ocean.

The arrival of the Stuart dynasty in Great Britain in 1603 and of the Romanov dynasty in Russia in 1613 was to have a wide-ranging impact. Recovering from a worldwide crisis in the middle of the century, Great Britain during the Interregnum of Oliver Cromwell and the Restoration of the Stuarts on the one hand and Russia under Alexei Romanov on the other continued imperial expansion across the Atlantic Ocean and the Eurasian continent. In 1689, however, Alexei's son, the future Peter the Great, came to power as Russia was halted in its tracks by China.

Notes

1 The Rev. John Ross, 'Manchuria', *The Scottish Geographical Magazine*, Vol. 11, No. 5 (1895), p. 217.
2 John Ross, *The Manchus or the Reigning Dynasty of China: Their Rise and Progress* (London: Houlston and Sons, 1891), p. 8.
3 Ibid., pp. xii, xv, xvi.
4 Ibid., pp. xvii, xix, xxiii.
5 Ibid., pp. xxiv–xxvii.
6 Ibid., p. xxxii.
7 Ibid., p. 1
8 Ibid., p. 4.
9 Lin Sun, 'Writing an Empire: An Analysis of the Manchu Origin Myth and the Dynamics of Manchu Identity', *Journal of Chinese History*, Vol. 1, No. 1 (2017), p. 25. There were versions of the myth in Japanese and Korean, too.
10 Mary Beard, *SPQR: A History of Ancient Rome* (London: Profile Books, 2016), p. 535.
11 James H. Grayson, 'The Legacy of John Ross', *International Bulletin of Missionary Research*, Vol. 23 (1999), p. 169.
12 Ross, 'Manchuria', pp. 218–22.
13 Ibid., pp. 222–3.
14 Ibid., p. 224.
15 Ian Nish, *The History of Manchuria, 1840–1948: A Sino-Russo-Japanese Triangle*, Vol. 1, *Historical Narrative* (Folkestone: Renaissance Books, 2016), p. 4, writes that the population is estimated as 15 million in 1900, 18 million in 1911 and 30 million, of which 28 million were Chinese, in 1931. The further north, the sparser the population.
16 Ross, 'Manchuria', p. 227.
17 Ibid., pp. 230–1.
18 S. A. Zenkovsky, *Medieval Russia's Epics, Chronicles and Tales* (New York: Dutton, 1963), p. 18.

19 For Edward VI's letter, see Richard Hakluyt, *The Principall Navigations, Voiages and Discoveries of the English Nation, Made by Sea or Over Land, to the Most Remote and Farthest Distant Quarters of the Earth in Any Time within the Compasse of These 1500 Yeeres*, photo-lithographic facsimile with an introduction by David Beers Quinn and Raleigh Ashlin Skelton and a new index by Alison Quinn, Three Parts in Two Volumes, published for the Hakluyt Society and the Peabody Museum of Salem at the University Press, 1965 (henceforth Hakluyt with modernised spelling), pp. 264–5.
20 William Lambard, *Archiomenia, sive de priscis anglorum legibus libri*, published in Hakluyt, p. 249.
21 Hakluyt, pp. 637, 720.
22 G. R. Elton, *England under the Tudors* (London: Putnam, 1956), p. 9; Samuel H. Cross, ed. and trans., *The Russian Primary Chronicle* (Cambridge, MA: Harvard University Press, 2003), p. 59.
23 See in general Paul Dukes, Graeme P. Herd and Jarmo Kotilaine, *Stuarts and Romanovs: The Rise and Fall of a Special Relationship* (Dundee: Dundee UP, 2009).
24 James Howell, *The Familiar Letters*, ed. Joseph Jacobs (London: David Nutt, 1890), pp. 512–3. For a comprehensive recent analysis, see Geoffrey Parker's great book, *Global Crisis: War, Climate Change and Catastrophe in the Seventeenth Century* (New Haven and London: Yale University Press, 2013).
25 Ibid., p. 552.
26 Nicholas Canny, *The Origins of Empire: British Overseas Enterprise to the Close of the Seventeenth Century*, volume 1 of *The Oxford History of the British Empire* (Oxford and New York: Oxford University Press, 1998), pp. 20, 35, 167.
27 Ibid., p. 448.
28 Basil Dmytryshyn, E. A. P. Crownhart-Vaughan and Thomas Vaughan and others, ed. and trans., *Russia's Conquest of Siberia: To Siberia and Russian America: Three Centuries of Russian Eastward Expansion*, volume 1, *A Documentary Record, 1558–1700* (Portland: Western Imprints, 1985), pp. 237, 278.
29 See Christoph Witzenrath, *Cossacks and the Russian Empire, 1598–1725: Manipulation, Rebellion, and Expansion into Siberia* (London: Routledge, 2007), pp. 95, 119, 187–8.
30 See Mark C. Elliott, 'The Limits of Tartary: Manchuria in Imperial and National Geographies', *The Journal of Asian Studies*, Vol. 59, No. 3 (2000), p. 603; Valerie Kivelson, *Cartographies of Tsardom: The Land and Its Meanings in Seventeenth-Century Russia* (Ithaca and London: Cornell UP, 2006), pp. 198–200. See also Peter C. Perdue, 'Boundaries, Maps, and Movement: Chinese, Russian, and Mongolian Empires in Early Modern Central Asia', *The International History Review*, Vol. 20, No. 2 (1998), pp. 263–286.
31 Elliott, 'The Limits', pp. 608–12.
32 Kivelson, *Cartographies*, pp. 133–9, 189; Valerie Kivelson, 'Early Mapping: The Tsardom in Manuscript', in Simon Franklin and Katherine Bowers, eds., *Information and Empire: Mechanisms of Communication in Russia, 1600–1850* (Cambridge: Open Book, 2017), p. 31.
33 Nancy Shields Kollmann, *The Russian Empire, 1450–1801* (Oxford: Oxford University Press, 2017), p. 178; Bruno Naarden, 'Nikolaas Vitsen i Tartaria', in N. P. Kopaneva and B. Naarden, eds., Nikolaas Vitsen, *Severnaia i Vostochnaia Tartariia*, 3 vols. (Amsterdam: Pegasus, 2010), Vol. 2, p. 998; Vol. 3, pp. 63–4. Taken from the edition of 1705.
34 G. V. Melikhov, *Man'chzhuriia: dalekaia i blizkaia* (Moscow: Nauka, 1991), pp. 12–8; Mark Mancall, *Russia and China* (Cambridge, MA: Harvard UP, 1971), pp. 141–62.

2   Empire before the railway, 1689–1892

Russia and China

The year 1689 was significant for both Stuarts and Romanovs. James VII and II was ejected from his throne to be replaced by his sister Mary and her Dutch husband, who became William III, while Peter I removed his half-sister Sophia from her Regency to assume supreme power for himself in fact (if constitutionally sharing it with his half-brother Ivan V until the latter's death in 1696).

Like their predecessors, William and his subjects pursued a vigorous commercial policy, concentrating on the Atlantic to keep control of the colonies but also reaching out into Asia, in particular, India. In China from 1699, English operations centred on the southern city of Canton, trading in silk, porcelain and tea. Canton, P. J. Marshall tells us, 'was to become the sole European point of access to China' in the eighteenth century.[1] Thus, until nearly the middle of the nineteenth century, Russia had northern China to itself, so to speak, without any substantial interference from its imperial rivals.

In September 1697, in Utrecht, William III met the future Peter the Great during the young tsar's Great Embassy to the Netherlands and England. In December, Gilbert Burnet, Bishop of Salisbury, gave a sermon describing how 'a mighty Northern Emperor, covered with Laurels, and us'd to victories, resolving to raise his Nation, and enlarge his Empire comes to learn the best methods of doing it.'[2]

On his return to Russia, Peter suffered a defeat by Sweden in 1700 but then strove for a resounding victory in the Great Northern War for control of the Baltic Sea which he completed by 1721, when he also formally announced the creation of the Russian Empire.

This was a significant moment in Russian history.

In particular, Peter tried to keep control over the East from his 'Window on the West,' the new capital St Petersburg. For example, in 1706, he issued a special decree ordering his people to observe the boundary set up by the Treaty of Nerchinsk, but this did not stop him from a search for gold nearby, an initiative that nearly brought him to war with China. Throughout the early modern period, Russia had vainly hoped to find precious metals in Siberia and beyond. There had been talk of a 'silver mountain' as well as gold, and the renowned innovator Peter was following here in the footsteps of his predecessors. 'Money is the artery of

DOI: 10.4324/9781003161769-2

war,' he himself famously said, and he did all he could to get it by commerce, too, maintaining state control over trade with China.[3]

In order to achieve his imperial aims, Peter employed spiritual in addition to temporal means, extending the authority of the Church to Irkutsk on Lake Baikal and beyond. Decrees of 1706 and 1710 announced the enforced conversion of all native peoples to Orthodoxy, with the death penalty for those who resisted. In 1715, one of the most important events in the history of Russo-Chinese relations occurred, the establishment of a permanent Orthodox mission to Peking. This did much to smooth relations between the two neighbours in general. A few years earlier, the first Russian emigrants made their way to the Chinese capital in the shape of the prisoners taken at Albazin. A hundred or so Cossacks brought their own priest, icons and Holy books along with them, and soon built a chapel. They entered the Chinese military service while other Russians came along later to study the Mongolian, Manchurian and Chinese languages.

In 1718, another Chinese map was drawn, making use of developments in Western cartography. Already, the division of Manchuria (by whatever name) into three provinces was apparent. According to Jesuit sources, 'The FIRST is that of Shin Yang called by the Manchus Mugden'; 'The SECOND GREAT GOVERNMENT is Kirin ula Batum'; 'The THIRD GOVERNMENT that of Tsitsikar, a new city built by the Emperor to secure the Frontier against the Russians,' with the garrison consisting of Manchu Tartars and the inhabitants mainly Chinese. But they added:

> So that to obtain an exact knowledge of these vast Countries, we must wait till the Russians give us maps drawn by Mathematicians sent on purpose to settle the Geography thereof; for those which have hitherto appeared were regulated solely by Journals or uncertain Reports as is evident from the Confusion and Mistakes with which they abound in adjusting the Limits of that Empire and the neighbouring Countries.'[4]

Although somewhat ambiguous, this observation might well refer to the work carried out by Jesuits. Certainly, Vladimir Sokolov writes of the map of 1718: 'In the opinion of specialists, this atlas was not only the best of those of Asia then in existence, but also better and more accurate than any European atlas of the time'[5] (Figure 3).

All the while, a top priority was to keep open the caravan trade with China via Kiakhta on the Selenga River. Towards the end of his reign, Peter tried to settle outstanding questions especially concerning commerce with the Chinese government. Three years after his death in 1725, possibly making use of the map of 1718, the Treaty of Kiakhta was signed in the summer of 1728, delineating new borders and allowing for a Russian caravan to be sent to Beijing once every three years, primarily to exchange furs for tea, while trade along the borders could be carried on continuously.[6]

In the later eighteenth century, as the industrial revolution was beginning, Russia made a considerable contribution through the export of iron as well as

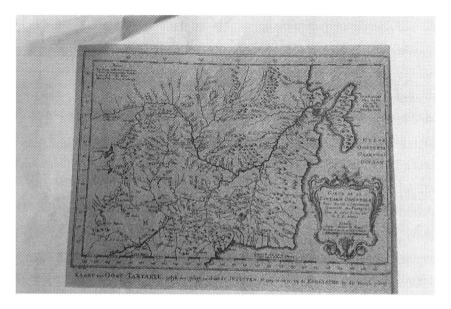

Figure 3 The Map of Eastern Tartary published by Pieter de Hondt in 1751 was taken from maps drawn up for the Jesuits. Note Nerchinsk ('Nerchinskoy') on the River Shilka to the northwest, the location of the negotiations with Russia conducted by the Jesuits acting for China leading to the Treaty of Nerchinsk of 1689. (Wikimaps)

timber and naval stores as the newly independent USA also played an increasingly important part in the Atlantic commerce and the Pacific fur trade.[7] Interested in expansion in general, Catherine the Great gave emphasis to the development of Russian America without neglecting China. Indeed, she began her reign in July 1762 by abolishing most of the Crown's monopolies and opening up the Chinese caravan trade to all merchants. However, ongoing tensions with China led to commercial and diplomatic relations being cut off from 1764, and even the calling of a conference in October of that year to discuss preparations for war. But soon, negotiations were begun at Kiakhta in July 1768 and a protocol was signed in October of that year revising the Treaty of Kiakhta of 1728 with Russia agreeing to lift customs barriers at the frontier. Hans Jakob Fries, a Swiss doctor in Russian state service visiting Kiakhta in the summer of 1776, met both Chinese and Russians as well as Herr Brand, ordered by the Imperial Russian Medical Council to supervise the trade in rhubarb, which was widely believed to be essential for good health. Trade developed more generally, if not without further tensions.[8]

Catherine, from a small German principality by birth but a passionate Russian patriot by adoption, was keen on a 'Greek project' to take over southern Russia as far as the Black Sea. She also encouraged the extension of the empire into the Caucasus, where the fortress of Vladikavkaz [Rule over the Caucasus] was constructed by 1784. She instituted a Siberian kingdom (*tsarstvo*) which would be less of a dependency of Russia than a self-reliant dominion with its own currency. While this and subsequent attempts at more centralised reform were less than successful, the Empress might well have made a greater impact through her Edict of Toleration in 1773, which discouraged forcible conversion to Orthodoxy. Her motives were not completely in the rationalist spirit of the Enlightenment, however, since the edict might have promoted loyalty to the Crown as it discouraged Muslims from focusing on Mecca and Buddhists from looking to Tibet.[9] Moreover, as the French Revolution took a more radical turn, Catherine and her noble establishment turned more conservative.

In 1793, during the first British embassy to China, Lord George Macartney visited the Great Wall. He surmised that besides a defence against the enemies of China: 'She might intend to shut out from the fertile provinces of China the numerous and ferocious beasts of the wilds of Tartary, to ascertain and fix her boundary, and to prevent emigration.' But, now the wall's use for defence seemed almost at an end: 'For the Emperor now reigning has extended his territory so far beyond it that I doubt whether his dominions without the wall are inferior to those within it.' En route, Macartney stayed at palaces built for the Emperor 'on his annual visit to Tartary.' However, his journey onwards was largely in vain as the Emperor's response to George III's request for a permanent embassy was negative, concluding: 'You, O King, should simply act in conformity with our wishes by strengthening your loyalty and swearing perpetual obedience so as to ensure that your country may share the blessings of peace.'[10]

In the early nineteenth century, returning from a spell of exile imposed on him by Alexander I for overstepping the mark in a reform of Russia as a whole, the bureaucrat Mikhail Speransky was encouraged by the tsar to make another attempt at imposing administrative order on Siberia in particular. The reform of 1822 included the designation of the Buryats among others as 'wanderers' who would not escape paying tribute to the central government. To control these and the other inhabitants, an East Siberia Governor-General was installed in Irkutsk.[11]

Dedicating to Speransky his book on his travels through Siberia on foot and horseback from 1820–3, the Scot Captain John Dundas Cochrane described himself as 'a rough pioneer' but ventured his surprise regarding the benefits that could be gained by the exploitation of the Amur River 'that the Russians have not attempted to open a treaty even for the privilege of navigating the river.'[12]

Cochrane perhaps gave the impression that Russia was no longer interested in expansion. In fact, Alexander I encouraged infiltration beyond Alaska into California while attempting to restrict the American fur trade with China.

The Great Game of empire

A couple of decades later, the situation changed as other imperial powers, especially Britain, also became interested in China. In the eloquent words of C. A. Bayly: 'The assault on the legitimacy of the Manchu Mandate of Heaven only really got into full swing after 1842, with the increasing devastating defeats of the regime by the Western powers and, later, Japan.'[13] The Opium War of 1839–42 came to an end with the unequal Treaty of Nanking opening up other ports to Britain while leasing Hong Kong for a hundred and fifty years. Not surprisingly, the Chinese response to foreign incursion was negative. One group of 'Patriotic People' from the southern Canton province in 1841 compared the 'English barbarians' to predatory wolves, asking: 'Except for your ships being solid, your gunfire fierce, and your rockets powerful, what other abilities have you?'[14]

Indeed, for better or worse, a lead in Far Eastern expansion was given by the major industrial power Britain, whose share of Chinese foreign trade was soon to be over 60%. Russia's was under 20%, while the USA in third commercial place led France, Germany and other European states put together.[15] Most of the Western infiltration into China was to the south via the sea, with Japan sailing in from the East while Russia was to the fore in Manchuria overland. No doubt, Russia's contribution would have been greater if there had been better means of transport. But Count E. F. Kankrin, Nicholas I's Minister of Finance, told the Scottish geologist, Sir Roderick Murchison:

> Railroads can never answer here for the next century, because there are no great commercial or manufacturing *entrepôts*, and especially because they would, in charging the country with enormous cost, throw out of employment thousands of peasants, whose sole subsistence in winter is derived from transporting commodities from Moscow and the south to the north.[16]

In 1847, Nicholas I appointed Nikolai Muravyov to the post of Governor-General of East Siberia, who had fought against Turkey and in the Caucasus before serving as governor of the province of Tula near Moscow (Figure 4). For John Stephan, Muravyov was

> a convinced expansionist, yet his imperial convictions were leavened by a progressive credo that included liberation and land for serfs, a public judiciary and jury system, and freedom of the press. Autocratic by nature, he recognized and rewarded talent without regard to antecedents.

In 1851, Muravyov ordered the formation of the Trans-Baikal Cossack host and soon sent a detachment to secure the mouth of the Amur River. The tsar gave his permission, but with the caveat that there should be 'no smell of gunpowder.'[17] While in Central Asia the counterparts of Muravyov came up against mountains and the British with whom they engaged in the 'Great Game,' the way was more open for him and his men in the Far East.

Empire before the railway, 1689–1892 23

Figure 4 Nikolai Muravyov-Amurskii was created a Count in 1858 with the suffix taken from the River that he had done much to acquire for the Russian Empire. He resigned in 1861 after the accusation that he was attempting to become the 'Siberian tsar' and other innuendos and moved to Paris. His portrait was painted by Konstantin Makovskii in 1863. (Wikipedia)

If most renowned in Central Asia, the 'Great Game' was in a real enough sense global, pitting Russia, Britain and other imperial powers against each other for control over peoples who often resisted submission. A signal moment was the arrival on 14 July 1853 in Tokyo Bay of four US Navy ships under Commodore Matthew C. Perry, who, as historian Walter LaFeber puts it, 'forced Japan open because Washington officials wanted it as a strategic way station to the potentially rich Chinese markets.'[18] Just a few weeks later, on 22 August, the Russian frigate *Pallada* commanded by Vice-Admiral Yefimy Putiatin arrived in Nagasaki with the official aim of a stopover en route for an inspection of Russia's North American possessions but the unofficial purpose of opening up Japan to trade. Putiatin's secretary was a bureaucrat Ivan Goncharov, later to write the novel *Oblomov* about a man who finds it difficult to rise from his sofa, now himself to travel around the world as the expedition's self-styled Homer.

Goncharov's odyssey took him to London, where the Duke of Wellington's funeral left him cold, but his first meeting with the ubiquitous merchant impressed him. 'Everywhere,' he was to write, 'this image of the English merchant floats over the elements and over the labour of man, and triumphs over nature.'[19] In Cape Town, Goncharov observed how the British combined head-spinning progress and cultural influence with brute force. He was revolted by the manner in which the British, and Americans too, sold opium in Shanghai which he dubbed 'the warehouse of the poison.' He asks: 'I don't know who should civilize whom: couldn't the Chinese, with their politeness, meekness, and, yes, their knowledge of trade, civilize the English?' But, as Edyta Bojanowska rightly comments, the Russian, French and American treatment of indigenous communities in Siberia, North Africa and North America was hardly any better while 'just about everyone accused everyone else of hypocrisy.'[20] In Japan, the American and Russian expeditions combined the threat of force with the offer of mutually beneficial treaties.

The clash of empires in the Near East, the Crimean War from 1854 to 1856 with Britain and France ranged with Turkey against Russia, was the noisiest in the West but had echoes in the Far East. Muravyov was able to enhance his reputation with a defence of Petropavlovsk when the 'smell of gunpowder' was sensed in an Anglo-French bombardment.

There was suspicion but also polite fraternisation among the belligerents. Captain Bernard Whittingham of the Royal Engineers noted in the Preface from London of 6 January 1856 to his book on the expedition against the Russian settlements in Eastern Siberia:

> The dominions of Russia have been silently and securely extended in Central and Eastern Asia, and it is impossible to converse with an intelligent Russian officer without perceiving the immense advantages that these conquests are acquiring for that Power.

Whittingham asserted later in his book that it should be the British purpose 'to unravel the ties with which Russia is slowly and surely binding both the Japanese and Tartars.' He referred to 'Mantchou Tartars' but not to Manchuria.[21] A naval officer, John M. Tronson in the Preface from the Clyde dated July 1859 to his book on a voyage to the Far East on the HMS *Barracouta* with a paddle wheel and six guns thanked among others a fellow officer F. H. May for charts and sketches of the little-known coast of Tartary. He went on to describe his friendly conversations with Russian officers, and his observations of the 'Mantchou Tartars,' wearing deerskin coats and birch-bark moccasins while smoking incessantly. Both the Manchu and Mongol Tartars were being forced to learn Chinese, Tronson averred, as even much beset upon China was involved in the business of imperial expansion.[22]

However, confronted from 1850 by the internal problem of the Taiping Rebellion and subsequent intervention from Britain and France in particular, the Chinese government was obliged to make huge concessions to Russia in the Treaty of Aigun of 1858, in particular ceding the left bank of the Amur River. Muravyov took advantage of some loose wording in the Treaty of Tianjin concluded a month later to occupy the coastal region as far as Korea. He ordered a military post named Khabarovsk in honour of the seventeenth-century explorer to be constructed at the confluence of the Amur with the Ussuri while renaming an up-river settlement Blagoveshchensk (Good Tidings) in celebration of the agreement with the Chinese. To the south, an even more assertive name was to be given by Muravyov to the port on the Sea of Japan previously dubbed Port May by the British. Changing Victoria Bay to Peter the Great Bay and giving Prince Albert Peninsula his own name, Muravyov officially christened the anchorage Vladivostok (Rule over the East) in 1860.

In 1860, too, a British naval lieutenant, William C. Arthur, gave his name to what was to become an important port on the Liaotung Peninsula. The fact that a junior officer could give his name to a British 'discovery' probably reflected its lowly importance at the time. If it had been considered of greater significance, Queen Victoria, who had a son called Arthur among other children, would not have been amused. Certainly, China was in no position to counter foreign incursions into their empire while their capital was occupied by the British and French. The nature of the destruction of the Summer Palace was conveyed in a letter home by 'Chinese' Charles Gordon (later killed at Khartoum in Sudan). 'The French have smashed everything in the most wanton way,' he wrote, adding 'There were carts after carts of silks taken away.' Then, after hearing of four Englishmen being tortured to death, the British ambassador Lord Elgin ordered further destruction, Gordon observing:

> We accordingly went out and, after pillaging it, burnt the whole place, destroying in a vandal-like manner most valuable property which could not be replaced for four millions … . although I have not as much as many, I have done well.[23]

In exchange for foreign withdrawal, the Chinese were obliged to ratify the terms of Aigun and Tientsin in the Treaty of Peking of 1860.

Made a Count with the suffix to his name of Amurskii in 1858, Muravyov was sufficiently annoyed by the accusation that he was attempting to become the 'Siberian tsar' and other innuendos to resign his post in 1861 and move to Paris, where he died in exile in 1881.[24] Muravyov-Amurskii was the counterpart of empire-builders elsewhere, like Sam Houston in Texas before him and Cecil Rhodes in Africa after him, for example. He co-founded the Amur Company in 1858, helped to form new bands of Cossacks on the Amur in 1859 and on the Ussuri in 1860 and encouraged settlers.

And his enthusiasm for the Russian Far East was widely shared. For example, the exiled patriot Alexander Herzen wrote to the Italian nationalist Giuseppe Mazzini that the Russian takeover of the Amur amounted to 'one of civilization's most important steps forward' to the Pacific. He went on to observe:

> The United States sweeps everything from its path, like an avalanche. Every inch which the United States seizes is taken away from the natives forever. Russia surrounds adjoining territories like an expanding body of water, pulls them in and covers them with an even, uniformly covered layer of autocratic ice.

Consequently:

> The North American States and Russia represent two solutions which are opposite but incomplete, and which therefore complement rather than exclude each other. A contradiction which is full life and development, which is open-ended, without finality, without physiological discord – that is not a challenge to enmity and combat, not a basis for unsympathetic indifference, but a basis for efforts to remove the formal contradiction with the help of something broader – if only through mutual understanding.

Herzen was among those who saw the Amur as a counterpart to the Mississippi. Together, Russia and America could outstrip Europe and make the Pacific Ocean the new Mediterranean. They would each have a vision of a 'manifest destiny.'[25]

In 1860, dedicating his book by special permission to Queen Victoria, 'Sovereign of the Vast Indian Empire,' Thomas Witlam Atkinson promised in his Preface to look closely at the approaches of Russia to that subcontinental empire as well as Russian relations with China. Certainly, those relations were developing, Atkinson noting that in the Far East:

> Ten years hence the aspect of this region will be materially changed; flourishing towns will be seen on the banks of the Amoor; the vessels moored on the shore will show that the people are actively engaged in commerce and other industrial pursuits, while the white churches with their numerous turrets and green domes will prove that religion and civilization have taken the place of idolatry and superstition. A country like this, where ... all the necessities of life can be easily produced ... is destined to have a great future.

Atkinson's vision was somewhat marred by the basic fact that John Massey Stewart has established concerning Atkinson: 'the awful truth is that he never got to the Amur at all.'[26]

Meanwhile, often through the agency of the Russian Geographical Society founded in 1845 with the patronage of Nicholas I and encouragement of Sir Roderick Murchison, the Scottish geologist, a considerable amount of exploration was being conducted into 'Man'chzhuriia,' a term with a Japanese origin soon coming into common use. From the time of the Treaty of Tianjin in 1858, there was a permanent embassy in Peking at the centre of a considerable Russian community including church officials.

In January 1861, Henry Arthur Tilley wrote a Preface in Alexandretta, Syria, claiming inaccurately to be the first Englishman in Russian settlements north of the Amur but nevertheless unique enough in his participation in a round-the-world voyage from 1858 to 1860 in a Russian ship. Tilley gives an interesting description of Muravyov:

> about forty-five years of age, short in stature, with rather red yet agreeable features, and a great suavity of manners. He is said to be a man of few words, but of great promptness of action, and to have a manner peculiar to himself in making treaties with Oriental powers.

Always on the move, Muravyov travelled with a large suite including an Orthodox bishop who had spent ten years in Peking.[27] Tilley was given only two days' notice of his inclusion in the voyage of the *Rynda* (named after a member of Ivan IV's entourage), but, he asked somewhat quizzically, 'what is not possible in our land of railways, telegraphs, and sewing machines?' He enjoyed good relations with the Russian officers and crew throughout the voyage, and was certainly given a privileged insight into Russian operations on the Amur and beyond. For example, he saw the paddle steamboat *Amerika* built in Boston for the Russian government and discovering Vladimir Bay on the 'Gulf of Tartary' in 1857 while accompanying Admiral Putiatin on a mission to China. But Tilley believed that there was no chance of immediate colonisation to any great extent. He noted:

> Special correspondents from St. Petersburg wrote home that railways were in contemplation from Moscow to Nicolaivsk [Nikolaevsk on the Amur], and that public subscriptions were on foot throughout all Russia for that purpose. So much amusement did this intelligence create on board, that the extract was forwarded to St. Petersburg to be laughed at there.

Tilley believed that it would be years before such an attempt would be possible.[28]

In 1861, too, Ernest George Ravenstein, FRGS, published *The Russians on the Amur: Its Discovery, Conquest, and Colonisation*, beginning his Preface of October with

> The progress of Russia in Asia, her rapid strides in the direction of India. And the acquisition from China of provinces far exceeding the British Islands in extent, cannot fail of being important to a nation with such vast interests at stake in China and the East as England has.

Ravenstein described several of the Russian Geographical Society's expeditions, and much else.[29]

On 21 November/3 December 1864, Russia's Foreign Minister Prince Alexander M. Gorchakov sent a circular despatch to Russian Representatives abroad. He declared: 'The position of Russia in Central Asia is that of all civilised States which are brought into contact with half-savage, nomad populations, possessing no fixed social organisation.' Fortified posts were necessary against 'permanent disorder,' but the 'civilised States' found it necessary to extend their frontier ever further. 'Such has been the fate of every country which has found itself in a similar position,' Gorchakov continued, adding:

> The United States in America, France in Algeria, Holland in her Colonies, England in India – all have been irresistibly forced, less by ambition than by imperious necessity, into this onward march, where the greatest difficulty is to know when to stop.

Russia, in particular, should have two fortified lines, one in Central Asia from the Aral Sea along the River Syr-Daria, the other from China to the Lake Issyk-Kyl (both lines terminating to the north of one of the main bones of contention with Britain, Afghanistan.) The strong implication was that the eastern line would continue along the valley of the River Amur, particularly since Gorchakov wanted the lines to be fixed, stressing 'the interest that Russia evidently has not to increase her territory, and, above all, to avoid raising complications on her frontiers, which can but delay and paralyse her domestic development.' Nevertheless, Gorchakov considered: 'Very frequently of late years the civilisation of these countries, which are her neighbours on the continent of Asia, has been assigned to Russia as her special mission.'[30]

In 1864, another country with a 'special mission' or 'manifest destiny,' the USA was preoccupied with Civil War, although poised for great expansion soon afterwards. In 1867, albeit against considerable internal opposition, Secretary of State William H. Seward negotiated the purchase of Alaska from Russia. At the same time as Russia drew back from North America, its caravan trade with China went into steep decline, according to Vice-Admiral Sir H. Keppel in a report on 'Russian Tartary' to the Secretary of the Admiralty in 1868:

> I was struck with the utter absence of trade and enterprise. The whole country is simply in military occupation. Private enterprise cannot flourish owing to the high export duty on native produce. The soil does not support its inhabitants, all the corn being imported. It is frequently necessary during the winter to issue rations even to those who are not Government servants.[31]

But transport by rail would create new dreams for the Far East as a whole at the end of the century, and before then, this was by no means a closed region. Other means of communication improved: by 1870, Russian post offices were established in Peking and other Chinese cities; in 1871, the Siberian telegraphic line was extended to Shanghai and Nagasaki by underwater cable. Moreover, the government encouraged centres of free trade, attracting foreigners as well as Russians to Blagoveshchensk and Khabarovsk as well as Vladivostok, all of which became thriving commercial centres. Vice-Admiral Keppel's gloomy estimate of the economy of the Russian Far East was becoming less accurate as Manchurian grain was supplied to both the army and gold companies. Russians played a significant part in the tea trade with China mainly carried on by British merchants, who also figured largely in the opium trade.[32]

The new imperialism

At the beginning of 1871, the Prussian-led German Empire was proclaimed at Versailles just after France had been defeated conclusively in a short war. In the summer of 1878, a Congress was held in Berlin aimed at achieving stability in Europe, in particular by reducing Russia's influence in the Balkans. In the winter of 1884–5, a Berlin Conference attended by Russia and all the major European powers aimed at the establishment of wider 'spheres of influence' in what an article in *The Times* of London called 'The Scramble for Africa.' Soon, the scramble could be located elsewhere, including China, with Japan and the USA among those joining in. A new driving force was the second industrial revolution of steel, oil and electricity, involving the need for new markets and raw materials. Railways expanded rapidly while steam-powered, ironclad navies depended on bases and coaling stations.

In 1875, Captain Bonham Ward Bax published a book about the 'Eastern Seas' including the 'Coast of Russian Tartary,' which he considered to possess many splendid harbours including Vladivostok, 'about to become the head-quarters of the naval forces in Eastern Siberia.' Bax noted that telegraph was now possible to Europe via China and Japan or across Siberia. Mail took 60 days to reach St Petersburg.[33] As the new phase in the struggle for empire was beginning, in 1878 a Russian Volunteer Fleet was organised to counter British incursions during the Russo-Turkish War of 1877–78. The Ili crisis during which Russia advanced into Sinkiang was brought to an end under the international pressure by the Treaty of St Petersburg in 1881.

In the Far East in 1875, Japan let Russia have the whole of the island of Sakhalin in exchange for its own guaranteed ownership of the Kuril Islands. In dealings with Korea, a gateway to Manchuria, Japan was the first to make a treaty in 1876 followed, with China's encouragement, by the USA and European powers in the 1880s. In 1882, the United States began this process, establishing diplomatic relations with the secluded kingdom of Korea which opened itself up to the Western world but also to the imperial rivalry. In 1883, at the invitation of China, a German official was made adviser to Korea and immediately assumed wide powers in foreign policy, supporting Russia in particular as a counterweight to Japan. But Japan could not be kept out of Korea while the USA joined Britain and others in unhappiness at the growing Russian influence, exacerbated in the Russo-Korean agreement of 1884 by which Russian officers were to help train the Korean armed forces in exchange for the use of the ice-free port of Port Lazarev (Wonsan).

In 1883, the clergyman and prison reformer Henry Lansdell crossed Siberia to Vladivostok, where he was hospitably received by the governor. En route, he formed the opinion that the treaties extending Russian rights in the Far East were unwelcome to 'John Chinaman.'[34] However, from 1883 to 1886, the Chinese joined the Russians and others in a gold rush leading to the rough democracy of the so-called 'Zheluga Republic' or California on the Amur, including elected leaders and strict laws.[35]

Meanwhile, there was no shortage of Russians pressing for 'forward policies' in Central Asia and the Far East. An outstanding example was Nikolai M. Przhevalskii, best known in the West for his identification of a species of wild horse on the Mongolian steppe, but also stating that he was 'convinced of the rotten state of China,' and finding that: 'The Chinese people are a nation long past its prime.' For Chekhov: 'People like Przhevalskii I loved without end.' The great writer compared him to the 'discoverer' David Livingstone, declaring: 'One Przhevalskii or one Stanley is worth ten institutes or a hundred good books.'[36]

Suspicions about Russian intentions were being aroused among imperial rivals, in particular, the British also playing the 'Great Game.' Major-General Sir Charles MacGregor was among those writing on the subject.[37] In 1885, a young army officer Francis Younghusband who had read a number of books on Manchuria, Mongolia and North China and compiled itineraries from them succeeded in convincing his superiors, including Sir Charles MacGregor, that 'if the Indian Empire were to be saved, I must at once be sent on duty to Manchuria' under the leadership of a member of the Indian Civil Service, H. E. M. James.[38] Younghusband wrote later of Manchuria's many interests as 'the cradle of the present ruling dynasty of China' and 'its lovely scenery.' Moreover, Younghusband observed, 'as its proximity to Russian territory on the one hand and Japan on the other gave it military and political interests also, we felt that time spent in such a country would not be wasted.'[39] After a few months of military exercises in India, Younghusband and his companions set off for Manchuria in March 1886. In Newchang, the main treaty port, the party was lucky enough to recruit Henry Fulford of the Chinese consular service as interpreter and adviser. As they moved on together towards Mukden, the capital of Manchuria, Younghusband was not happy with the dirty wayside inns in which they stayed, nor with the long low platforms on which they usually had to sleep next to other travellers. And in Mukden itself, they were continually followed by 'a hooting, yelling crowd,' some of whom poked holes in the paper windows of their rooms and watched them closely even at their ablutions.[40]

Out in the country, leaving the masses behind them, the expedition was able to scrutinise 'John Chinaman' at leisure. Younghusband considered that the Chinese immigrants, who had largely replaced the original Manchus, 'were, in fact, doing here exactly what our colonists have been doing for so many years in Canada.'[41] Crossing the Yalu River, short of supplies and bothered by midges, the British travellers went on to climb 'The Long White Mountain,' where the intrepid Younghusband braved the treacherous rocks and bitter cold to make scientific, especially topographical, observations.

After several weeks of further arduous travel, the expedition reached the central Manchurian town of Kirin, where Younghusband did what he could to find out about the local production of field guns and rifles. He and his companions were given warm hospitality by local gentlemen, who were extremely polite and good in conversation, if not with Europeans: 'they are lamentably ignorant of geography, for instance, and they generally annoy the stranger by asking if his country is tributary to China.' But Younghusband also realised that from 'such a lofty standpoint' as he occupied, the Chinaman was 'not all simple self-conceit' since 'he had in him the pride of belonging to an empire which has stood intact for thousands of years, and which was approaching civilisation when we ourselves were steeped in barbarism.'[42] Later, en route for the frontier, he observed that villages were of considerable size and that small hamlets or separate farmhouses were rare 'probably on account of the brigandage, which was very rife all over North Manchuria.'[43] He and his companions dropped by a French Roman Catholic mission where they received 'that warm, heartfelt greeting which one European will give to another, of whatever nationality.'[44] Younghusband was able to inspect a fort at Sansung on the Sungari River equipped with Krupp guns transported there with enormous difficulty but allowed to go to rust and ruin.

The British party crossed the frontier with Russia without difficulty via the town of Hunchun and soon encountered a band of Cossacks, 'hard, strong-looking men, fair in complexion, with cheery good-natured faces.' Although in barracks inferior to the Chinese at Hunchun if rough and clean, the Cossacks were careless in dress, simply fed and poorly paid, but apparently 'ready to buckle to and fight there and then.'[45] After the lavish local entertainment, Younghusband and his colleagues proceeded to the Russian port of Novokievsk, south of Vladivostok. As well as dispensing more generous hospitality, the commandant said that his government was anxious to colonise Eastern Siberia with Russians. Younghusband imagined that 'with a railway to aid in its development, all those regions about the Amur and its tributaries ought to equal the most thriving parts of Canada.'[46] More of the overland railway soon, for the moment, a remark about a development on the sea: a British fleet had recently appeared in the nearby bay and aroused the apprehension that it was about to seize the port as Port Hamilton consisting of a group of small islands about ten miles to the south of Korea had just been taken. In his own account of the expedition, Mr James recorded the comments of the commandant, Colonel Sokolowski:

> Ma foi, said he, what is it that you'd get if you did take the place? A few old mud and log barracks, some ponies and harness, and these barren hills. I wish you joy of them.[47]

The long, difficult winter journey back to Peking was relieved in Mukden by a tea party including cakes, scones and muffins provided by the ladies of the Scottish Mission, according to Younghusband, compared with other trials experienced, 'in our disreputable condition ... the hardest of them all.' There was also a conversation with John Ross, whose description of Manchuria opened this book, and other clergymen.[48] At Newchang, Mr James left for Port Arthur, where, he considered, Englishmen would soon be followed by Americans and Russians. James commented with some evident irony:

> It is, indeed, impossible not to admire the imperturbable calmness with which the Chinese, looking – and I do not want to blame them – absolutely and entirely to their own interests, play off against one another the disinterested European nations who only want to benefit the poor dear Chinese.

Giving up Port Hamilton to the Chinese, James considered, could help to make them friendly to the British.[49] Indeed, Britain soon gave up Port Hamilton, partly owing to international pressure.

Crossing the Great Wall, the Younghusband and Fulford encountered two English navvies walking along the road, one enquiring of the other about them 'I wonder who the – that is, Bill?' They themselves were miners in a colliery owned by Chinese but managed by an Englishman, a Mr Kinder. At first afraid of a steam engine imported from Hong Kong by a 'foreign devil,' the Chinese were now accepting the beginning of a railway towards Tientsin, with an extension to the east and another projected into Manchuria.[50]

More hospitality ensued in Tientsin, where the British consul introduced Younghusband to his Russian counterpart and Russian merchants, and in Peking at the British Legation, where he met Europeans of every nationality, remarking that 'it is only in the last thirty of the three thousand years during which the Chinese Empire has existed that such a thing has been possible.'[51] Mr James, who had played such an important part in the expedition, having left for Japan, Younghusband now met up with Colonel M. S. Bell, V. C., of the Royal Engineers, whom he had previously encountered in the Intelligence Department in India. He managed to arrange to travel back with Bell to India overland, setting off in spring 1887, about a year after arriving in Manchuria.

At this point, we are to take our leave of Younghusband for now, but not before summarising some of his conclusions about his travels. While recognising that all religions 'shared the feeling that there was some Great Spirit or Influence guiding and ruling all things,' he also believed that there was 'something in the Christian religion vastly superior to others.' And, while he indicated that Christianity had been a huge influence on European civilisation in general, he also believed in the special qualities of the English people.[52] More particularly, in his official report on the Manchurian expedition compiled in Peking with the help of the British envoy, Sir John Walsham, Younghusband came to the conclusion that there was no sign of immediate Russian threat to Manchuria.[53]

The situation was about to change radically with the coming of the railway. The distinguished American historian G. A. Lensen wrote that by the end of the nineteenth century:

> the flood of allegations ascribing aggressive designs to the tsarist government continued unabated, even though it was privately conceded that Russia

was too weak in the Far East to expand by force. The reason was the lack of trust in what the Russians said, another was the usefulness of the Russian 'menace.' Repeatedly the Russian bear was used as a bugbear by the various powers to intimidate and contain their rivals or to justify their own moves in the international balance of intrigue.[54]

The phenomenon of Russophobia persisted into the twentieth century, alternating with periods of rapprochement, as we will see below.

Conclusion

Pushed back from the frontiers of Tartary at the end of the seventeenth century, Russia resumed interest in them and beyond throughout the eighteenth and nineteenth centuries. There was considerable excitement about the potential of the Amur Valley, even thoughts of a counterpart to California.

The conflict between Great Britain and Russia in Central Asia led to the Great Game of Empire. Russophobia reached a new height in the Crimean War by the Black Sea which had distant repercussions near the shores of the Far East. Generally speaking, however, although Great Britain and Russia were both becoming more interested in the Far East as the global competition for empire intensified, there was no serious clash before the coming of the railway in what was now widely known as Manchuria.

Notes

1 P. J. Marshall, 'The English in Asia to 1700', in Nicholas Canny, ed., *The Origins of Empire: British Overseas Enterprise to the Close of the Seventeenth Century* (Oxford: OUP, 1998), p. 461.
2 Paul Dukes, Graeme P. Herd, and Jarmo Kotilaine, *Stuarts and Romanovs: The Rise and Fall of a Special Relationship* (Dundee: Dundee UP, 2009), pp. 194–5.
3 Chechech Kundachinova, 'The Muscovite Silver Crusade: Power, Space, and Imagination in Early Modern Eurasia', *Ab Imperio*, No. 4 (2019), pp. 49–72; Lindsey Hughes, *Russia in the Age of Peter the Great* (London: Yale UP, 2003), p. 353.
4 Jean-Baptiste Du Hald, *A Description of the Empire and Chinese-Tartary.... from the French of P. J. B. Du Halde, Jesuit*, Third Edition, Vol. 2 (London: J. Watts, 1741), pp. 236, 245, 248, 249. First published in French in 1735.
5 Vladimir Sokolov, 'Pervaia nauchnaia ekspeditsiia na krainii iugo-vostok Tartarii v 1709-1710gg.', *Rubezh*, No. 10 (2010), p. 350.
6 The foregoing account of Peter the Great's policies and their immediate sequel from James Forsyth, *A History of the Peoples of Siberia: Russia's North Asian Colony, 1581–1990* (Cambridge: Cambridge University Press, 1992), pp. 8–9, 84–108, 154; John J. Stephan, *The Russian Far East: A History* (Stanford: Stanford University Press, 1994), pp. 26–32; Christoph Witzenrath, *Cossacks and The Russian Empire, 1598–1725: Manipulation, Rebellion and Expansion into Siberia* (London: Routledge, 2007), pp. 5–7, 24–5, 31–3; G. V. Melikhov, *Man'chzhuriia: dalekaia i blizkaia* (Moskva: Nauka, 1991), pp. 6–14. Vladimir Sokolov, 'Pervaia nauchnaia ekspeditsiia', pp. 349–53.
7 Paul Dukes, *October and the World: Perspectives on the Russian Revolution* (London: Macmillan, 1979), pp. 26–8; G. E. Aylmer, 'Navy, State, Trade and Empire', in Canny, *The Origins*, p. 475.

34 *Empire before the railway, 1689–1892*

8 Isabel de Madariaga, *Russia in the Age of Catherine the Great* (London: Weidenfeld and Nicholson), pp. 470, 474; Walter Kirchner, trans. and ed., *A Siberian Journey: The Journal of Hans Jakob Fries, 1774–1776* (London: Frank Cass, 1774), p. 133. And see Clifford M. Foust, *Rhubarb; The Wonder Drug* (Princeton: Princeton UP, 2016), originally published 1992; *Muscovite and Mandarin: Russia's Trade with Russia and Its Setting* (Chapel Hill: University of North Carolina Press, 1969).
9 Forsyth, *A History*, pp. 169–70, 199.
10 *An Embassy to China: Being the Journal Kept by Lord Macartney during His Embassy to the Emperor Chi'en-lung 1793–1794*, ed. and intro. J. L. Cranmer-Byng (London: Longman, 1960), pp. 116, 340.
11 Forsyth, *A History*, pp. 156–7. John LeDonne. 'Building an Infrastructure of Empire in Russia's Eastern Theater, 1650s–1840s', *Cahiers du Monde russe*, Vol. 47, No. 3 (2006), p. 603.
12 Captain John Dundas Cochrane, *Narrative of a Pedestrian Journey through Russia and Siberian Tartary from the Frontiers of China to the Frozen Sea and Kamchatka*, Fourth Edition (London: Charles Knight, 1825), pp. ix, 419.
13 C. A. Bayly, *The Birth of the Modern World, 1780–1914* (Oxford: Blackwell, 2004), p. 143.
14 'Placard of the Patriotic People of Kwantung Denouncing the English Barbarians, 1841', Szu-yu Teng and J. L. Fairbank, *China's Response to the West – A Documentary Survey* (Cambridge, MA: Harvard UP, 1954), p. 36.
15 B. A. Romanov, *Russia in Manchuria, 1892–1906*, trans. Susan Wilbur Jones (Ann Arbor: J. W. Edwards, 1952), p. 3. The work was originally published as *Rossiia v Man'chzhurii* by the E. S. Enukidze Oriental Institute of Leningrad in 1928.
16 Michael Collie and John Diemer, eds., *Murchison's Wanderings in Russia: His Geological Exploration of Russia in Europe and the Ural Mountains, 1840 and 1841*, British Geological Survey Occasional Publication no. 2 (London, 2004), p. 154–5.
17 Stephan, *The Russian Far East*, pp. 44, 46.
18 Walter LaFeber, *The Clash: U.S.-Japanese Relations throughout History* (New York: Norton, 1998), p. xviii.
19 Edyta M. Bojanowska, *A World of Empires: The Russian Voyage of the Frigate Pallada* (Cambridge, MA: Harvard University Press, 2018), pp. 2, 28, 34.
20 Ibid., pp. 41, 90, 103.
21 Captain Bernard Whittingham, *Notes of the Late Expedition against the Russian Settlements in Eastern Siberia; And of a Visit to Japan and to the Shores of Tartary and the Sea of Okhostk* (London: Longman, Brown, Green and Longmans, 1856), pp. vi, 243, 299.
22 John M. Tronson, *A Voyage to Japan, Kamschatka, Siberia, Tartary and Various Parts of the Coast of China in HMS Barracouta* (London: Smith, Elder, 1859), pp. vi, 283, 331, 337.
23 Lord Elton, *General Gordon* (London: Collins, 1954), pp. 44–5. Lord Elgin's father took the Elgin Marbles from the Parthenon in Athens.
24 Stephan, *The Russian Far East*, pp. 48–50, 53.
25 Paul Dukes, *The Superpowers: A Short History* (London: Routledge, 2000), pp. 22–3; Mark Bassin, *Imperial Visions: Nationalist Imagination and Geographical Expansion in the Russian Far East, 1840–1865* (Cambridge: Cambridge University Press, 1999), pp. 2, 166–7.
26 Thomas Witlam Atkinson, *Travels in the Region of the Upper and Lower Amoor and the Russian Acquisitions on the Confines of India and China*, Second Edition (London: Hurst and Blackett, 1861), p. 453; John Massey Stewart, *Thomas, Lucy and Alatau* (London: Unicorn, 2018), p. 260.
27 Henry Arthur Tilley, *Japan, the Amoor, and the Pacific; with Notices of Other Places Comprised in a Voyage of Circumnavigation in the Imperial Russian Corvette 'Rynda' in 1858–1860* (London: Smith, Elder and Co., 1861), pp. 190–2.

28 Ibid., pp. 208, 240, 242, 244–5.
29 E. G. Ravenstein, *The Russians on the Amur: Its Discovery, Conquest. And Colonisation with a Description of the Country, Its Inhabitants, Productions, and Commercial Capabilities and Personal Accounts of Russian Travellers* (London: Trubner and Co., 1861), p. vii.
30 Quoted in *Correspondence Respecting Central Asia*, C 704, 1873, pp. 72–5, as in R. C. Bridges, Paul Dukes, J. D. Hargreaves, and William Scott, *Nations and Empires: Documents on the History of Europe and on Its Relations with the World since 1648* (London: Macmillan, 1969), pp. 168–70.
31 Ian Nish, *The History of Manchuria, 1840–1948: A Sino-Russo-Japanese Triangle* (Folkestone: Renaissance Books, 2016), Vol. 2, *Select Primary Sources*, p. 18.
32 A. I. Krushanov and others, *Istoriia Severo-Vostochnogo Kitaia, XVII-XXvv.*, kniga 1 (Vladivostok: Dal'ne vostochnoe izdatel'stvo, 1987), pp. 256–9.
33 Captain B.[Bonham] W. [Ward] Bax, *The Eastern Seas: Being a Narrative of the Voyage of HMS 'Dwarf' in China, Japan, and Formosa, with a Description of the Coast of Russian Tartary and Eastern Siberia, from the Corea to the River Amur* (London: John Murray, 1875), pp. v–vi, 162, 164, 176.
34 Henry Lamsdell, *Through Siberia* (London: Sampson Low, Marsden, Searle and Rivington, 1893), p. 542, Chapter LII, 'Vladivostok'.
35 Mark Gamsa, 'California on the Amur, or the 'Zheluga Republic' in Manchuria (1883–1886)', *Slavonic and East European Review*, Vol. 81, No. 2 (2003), pp. 236–66.
36 David Schimmelpenninck van de Oye, *Towards the Rising Sun: Russian Ideologies of Empire and the Path to War with Japan* (Dekalb: Northern Illinois University Press, 2001), pp. 35–6, 39–40.
37 In particular in Major-General Sir C. M. MacGregor, *The Defence of India: A Strategical Study* (Simla: Government Central British Press, 1884), a work full of military statistics, marked 'Confidential' on the title page.
38 George Seaver, *Francis Younghusband: Explorer and Mystic* (London: John Murray, 1952), p. 8.
39 Captain Frank E. Younghusband, C. I. E., Indian Staff Corps, Gold Medallist, Royal Geographical Society, *The Heart of a Continent: A Narrative of Travels in Manchuria, across the Gobi Desert, through the Himalayas, the Pamirs, and Chitral, 1884–1894*, Fourth Edition (London: John Murray, 1904), pp. 3–5.
40 Ibid., p. 7.
41 Ibid., p. 10.
42 Ibid., pp. 19, 20.
43 Ibid., p. 22.
44 Ibid., p. 24.
45 Ibid., p. 33.
46 Ibid., p. 38.
47 H. E. M. James, of Her Majesty's Bombay Civil Service, *The Long White Mountain or A Journey in Manchuria: With Some Account of the History, People, Administration, and Religion of that Country* (London and New York, Longman, Green, and Co., 1888), p. 356.
48 Younghusband, *The Heart of a Continent*, p. 44.
49 James, *The Long White Mountain*, p. 407.
50 Younghusband, *The Heart of a Continent*, pp. 50–1.
51 Ibid., p. 54.
52 Ibid., pp. 304–10.
53 Patrick French, *Younghusband: The Last Great Imperial Adventurer* (London: HarperCollins, 1955), p. 42.
54 G. A. Lensen, *Balance of Intrigue: International Rivalry in Korea and Manchuria*, 2 vols (Tallahassee: University Presses of Florida, 1982), Vol. 2, pp. 853–4.

3 The arrival of the railway and war with Japan, 1892–1906

The Trans-Siberian railway: Nicholas II and his bureaucracy

Generally speaking, according to Younghusband's careful observations, there had been little foreign interest in Manchuria by the end of his visit in 1887. However, the situation was about to change, since the appointment of Sergei Iulevich Witte as Minister of Finance in August 1892 was to lead to the construction of the Trans-Siberian Railway, already a gleam in the eye of several earlier Russian statesmen. The son of a bureaucrat from the Baltic provinces (a circumstance that allowed his enemies to call him a 'German'), S. Iu. Witte was educated in Odessa before entering state service as a railway administrator, claiming with some justification that he worked his way up from the ticket office to head of a Railway Department in the Ministry of Finance in 1889. He developed ideas of patriotic protectionism and peaceful penetration which he was to apply as Minister of Finance.

In August 1892, too, the Franco-Russian Military Convention, together with the Franco-Russian Agreement of the previous year, 'virtually eliminated all financial risk earlier associated with the enterprise.'[1] In a full report submitted to Tsar Alexander III in November 1892, Witte emphasised that the great project of the Trans-Siberian Railway 'ranks it as one of those *world events* that usher in *new epochs in the history of nations* and not infrequently bring about the radical upheaval of established economic relations between states.' He hoped that it might prove to be a rival in world communication comparable to the Suez Canal while constituting a weapon that would enable the Russian navy to exert 'control over the entire movement of international commerce in Pacific waters.'[2] Comparing the commercial possibilities with those already being realised by the railway in Canada, Witte suggested that Russia could become a rival with Great Britain, in the tea industry in particular, and with all the imperialist powers in general. Attracted by the grandiose schemes of the Buryat Slavophile and entrepreneur P. A. Badmaev, he went so far as to suggest 'from the shores of the Pacific and the heights of the Himalayas Russia would dominate not only the affairs of Asia but those of Europe as well.'[3]

The tsarevich, the future Nicholas II, was charged by his father with the task of laying the foundation stone for the railway in Vladivostok towards the end of a round-the-world tour in 1891, Alexander expressing his sincere desire to facilitate communications between Siberia and the other parts of the Empire and thus [I] will demonstrate to this region, which is so dear to My heart, My very keen interest in its peaceful prosperity.[4]

One of the tsarevich's companions was Prince E. E. Ukhtomskii, who managed to convey some of his enthusiasm for the Orient. Ukhtomskii wrote: 'Russia, more powerful in Asia than the Europeans, casts its gaze to the East, which presents remarkable possibilities for the creative energies of the Russian people.'[5] Even though Nicholas had been wounded in an attempt on his life in Japan, his love of the Far East was undimmed, and he no doubt welcomed his appointment in 1893 as chairman of the committee concerned with the construction of the Trans-Siberian Railway.

In the spring and summer of 1893, just before the railway was built, Charles Wenyon MD travelled across Siberia by the Great Post Road. On the way, he encountered many delays and difficulties. He also met many Russian officers and officials, whom he found for the most part as well educated as their brothers elsewhere and possessed a certain openness indicating their 'freedom from bondage to the absurd conventionalisms of caste.' Wenyon was told that if Britain ruled the waves, Russia ruled the land, a sentiment he welcomed since

> The civilization of Russia may be less developed than our own, but it is very far ahead of the civilization of the Chinese; and what is spoken of as Russian encroachment in Eastern Asia may be not only the best thing for the welfare of our race, but, in the nature of things, inevitable. ... that Christian civilization was destined to regenerate China and overspread the earth.[6]

Here, Wenyon tacitly agreed with Younghusband. Was it the case, as the nineteenth century was coming to an end, that the Great Game of Empire between Britain and Russia in the Far East was about to be replaced by a new rivalry between the Western world as a whole and the Eastern? But suspicion of Russian motives among the powers increased as plans for the Trans-Siberian Railway unfolded.

And not only on land, for Witte had talked of the railway as a means of promoting the dominance of the Pacific Ocean by the Russian navy. Possibly, he was aware of the book published in 1890 by the American naval officer Alfred T. Mahan, *The Influence of Sea Power upon History, 1660–1891*, describing the manner in which Britain had achieved great power status because of its maritime activity. As the American frontier was closing, and the American economy was booming, the USA was indeed looking outward, and the lesson was not lost on Germany and Japan. Was Russia to follow in their wake?

B. A. Romanov asserted in 1928:

> The Manchurian question reached its full growth in the history of the international relations of the Russian Empire in 1895, assumed priority status and combat rank and became, without interruption, the basic problem of Russian foreign policy for the next ten years ... . At the point of a railway line Russia

was forcing an entry into the sphere of international economic and political competition in the Pacific.[7]

B. A. Romanov wrote the most scholarly work on Russia in Manchuria from 1892 to 1906, but, while respecting his choice of these terminal dates, I recognise that there is a case not only for 1895 as the point at which the Manchurian question came to maturity, but also that 'full growth' is a relative concept and chronological division can often be a matter for discussion. There is indeed an argument that 1894, the date of the accession of a pre-revolutionary ruler with the same family name as the historian, should receive some emphasis.

The Romanov Tsar Alexander III died towards the end of October 1894, to be succeeded by his son, the last tsar. Nicholas II was a failure. Weak and stubborn, careful and reckless in turn, he made the task faced by his ministers extremely difficult. Nevertheless, as far as the expanding empire was concerned, a degree of continuity can be detected in what we might call 'bureaucratic encroachment.' As an example of this process, let us turn to an individual and his work. After graduation from Moscow University in 1858, A. N. Kulomzin embarked on a tour of England, Scotland and Western Europe to examine in particular systems of banking and finance. The ongoing industrial revolution made a great impact on him as did arrangements for education and government, especially in Britain. He returned a 'liberal,' working as a Peace Arbitrator during the implementation of the Great Reform of 1861. After further administrative experience, he was elevated to the position of Secretary to the Council of Ministers in 1882 and held that office for more than 20 years. From 1891 to 1902, he was also Secretary to the Siberian Committee after becoming Secretary to the Siberian Railway Committee. In 1896, he went on a six-month tour of Siberia which confirmed him in his belief that the attachment of the borderlands to the centre was a task too great to be left to incompetent provincial officials, the improvement of whom could be achieved only by a reformed system of education.[8]

In the last years of the nineteenth century, with the arrival of the railway, peasant emigration to the Far East grew considerably, encouraged by the Ministry of the Interior's Resettlement Administration set up after Kulomzin's return from Siberia. A High Commission under his Chairmanship was created to investigate landholding and land use in the region beyond Lake Baikal. Among its other publications was one devoted to materials on lease and rent, composed by V. Treiden and published in St Petersburg in 1898. This work clearly demonstrated how difficult it was to impose definitions first developed in European Russia on lands where peasants, both new arrivals and long established, Cossacks, who had been the first foreigners to arrive, and 'natives,' who had been there from time immemorial, were all attempting to develop farming, arable, pastoral and/or nomadic and/or to concern themselves with forestry. This difficulty was especially the case in the Manchurian and Mongolian borderlands, where rivalries were often violent. Nevertheless, a vast amount of statistics was gathered, some no doubt rough calculation, guesswork or even invention, all helping to stake Russian imperial claims. Treiden argued that the situation became more peaceful and regular after Russia gave its support to China in the war against Japan, to which we now turn.[9]

War between Japan and China: the Chinese Eastern Railway

On 1 August 1894, Japan declared war on China after much bickering about the influence in Korea and other questions, and won a speedy victory. The other powers were alarmed at the unpreparedness of the Chinese army and the efficiency of the Japanese. Furthermore, the government in Tokyo was seen to harbour ambitious plans for expansion, partly in response to those of Russia. The Japanese leaders contemplated control over Korea as it established independence from China; the institution of a military base on the Chinese coast between Shanghai and Canton as the protector of economic expansion and the occupation of the South Manchurian coast including the Liaotung Peninsula. Alarmed at the harsh terms of Peace of Shimonoseki imposed on China in the spring of 1895, especially their threat to Russian interests in Manchuria, Witte managed to gain the support of France and Germany to oblige Japan to leave the Liaotung Peninsula. He also managed to secure a loan from the French banks allowing the Chinese government to pay a large indemnity. To counterbalance the French influence, Germany offered the support of its navy to Russia. After some hesitation, Great Britain supported Japan, while the USA supported peace and stability at the same time as defending its own interests in its policy that came to be known soon as the 'Open Door.'

In the spring of 1896, visiting Moscow for the tsar's coronation, the Chinese statesman Li Hung-Chang conducted negotiations between his country and Russia on the basis of the initiatives already taken by the Chinese emperor. Some of the agreements were kept secret until 1910. In the event of the outbreak of further hostilities with Japan, China would open all its ports to Russian warships, while lines of communication would be made easier by the construction of a Chinese Eastern Railway (CER) bypassing the Amur route direct through Manchuria to Vladivostok. The territory taken up by the CER would constitute a special zone under the Russian control in a concession to last 80 years, with China given the option to buy the railway after 36 years. The administration of local justice was to be decided by the local Russian and Chinese residents themselves. (In fact, by the due date of the option to buy, 1932, the Japanese puppet state Manchukuo had just been created.) In the immediate future, the CER would be financed by a Russo-Chinese bank, in which French banks would again play a major part. Moreover, a beginning was made to a line from Harbin south to Dalny in the Liaotung Peninsula. Russia also concluded a secret agreement with Li Hung-Chang giving Russia a monopoly of the exploitation of the natural resources of Manchuria while securing the departure of Chinese troops and the right to build a railway to Peking. General P. N. Simanskii aptly noted that the CER began the peaceful conquest of Manchuria, adding: 'Instead of Siberian infantry rifles here the engineer's compass and the pickaxe did their work, commanded not by an army general but by a finance minister.'[10]

In November 1897, Germany seized Kiaochow on the Shantung Peninsula after the murder of two German missionaries. Other governments used this pretext for their own seizures, Britain taking nearby Wei Hai Wei also on the Shantung peninsula and France Kwang Chow Wan nearby Indo-China. But Russia took most, obliging China in March 1898 to hand over Kwantung, the southern part of the Liaotung Peninsula, including Dairen [Dal'ny] and Port Arthur for 25 years, and to grant a concession for a South Manchurian Railway to be built from Harbin to Port Arthur while agreeing to keep Chinese forces out of the territory concerned. Soon, declared the newspaper *Novoe Vremia*, it would be possible to travel by rail from Lisbon to the Pacific Ocean, and by 1903 the link had indeed been established via the South Manchurian Railway with the Chinese Eastern Railway. Some Russians wanted more, including a port in Korea that would enable ice-free Port Arthur to link up with Vladivostok, but their government agreed to accept Korean independence with its Japanese counterpart, which allowed a Russian sick bay to be maintained in Nagasaki from 1886 to 1908.[11] Russia also sought, if with limited success, to allay British alarm in April 1898 with an agreement separating spheres of interest: Russia would not seek railway concessions in the valley of the River Yangtze while Britain, busy in any case in Africa, would not seek any such north of the Great Wall. Japan and China entered a new rapprochement.

In the summer of 1897, the CER was inaugurated. In the summer of 1898, a signal moment occurred in the history of a settlement already begun by Chinese fishermen: in Manchu, 'Haerbin' means 'a place for drying fishing nets.' The 'company town' of Harbin was 'found and founded,' as David Wolff puts it, as the administration of the CER under its general manager D. L. Khorvat moved there from Vladivostok for four main reasons: (1) building from the centre as well as the extremities would accelerate construction; (2) construction would proceed faster also because of the lack of distractions; (3) the esprit de corps of both managers and workers would be fostered; (4) dealings with both Chinese officials and local inhabitants would be facilitated.[12] Indeed, Harbin continued to be officially administered by the Chinese authorities, while the bulk of the labour force was Chinese.

Encroachment by foreign powers fuelled Chinese resentment in the 'Wild East' of Manchuria, and a number of secret societies flourished. The least ideological of these presented the greatest threat. They were the *hunhutsy* (or redbeards), who had already been active for many years. Far from being *robingudy* (Robin Hoods), they robbed the poor as well as the rich, and were among the worst oppressors of the peasants, some of whom, realising that they could not beat them, joined them. Other recruits were deserters from the army, failed prospectors and vagrants. The *hunhutsy* could be well armed with the most up-to-date rifles (sometimes acquired by way of military gambling debts) as well as with primitive pikes, and some of their bands were powerful enough to extort protection money from large companies. Like other thieves, they could steal away in the night and were not easily detected by day, since they were able to merge with the general populace.

Perhaps the *hunhutsy* could be compared with the Cossacks of old, but the more recent Cossacks were hired as guards, for the railway in particular. They wore a uniform consisting of a black jacket and light-blue breeches with yellow stripes, a peak cap with yellow around it and on top. To distinguish them from regular soldiers, who were not allowed in Manchuria, they had no shoulder tabs.

The officers displayed a dragon on their buttons and cockades: the rank and file resisted this badge, considering the dragon to be the seal of the Antichrist, but they were reconciled by permission to wear it at the back rather than the front of their caps. Service with the Manchurian guards was considered unbecoming to the officers, but they and their men were well rewarded. Allegedly, when Witte asked a Cossack about his standard of living during his visit of 1902, he received the reply: '*Sverkhestestvenno khorosho, vashe vysokoprevoskhoditel'stvo!*' (Supernaturally good, Your Excellency!)'[13]

The Boxer challenge and response

On 3 June 1899, the French representative in Peking, Pichon sent a comprehensive view of the situation in China to Foreign Minister Delcassé. 'There is no gainsaying that the partition of China is being accomplished,' Pichon observed. This was not a violent partition as in the case of Poland in the late eighteenth century, but 'a methodical, scientific partition without armed resistance on the part of those who suffer it, who seem reconciled by centuries of degradation to the impossibility of preventing it.' Dismemberment could lead to strife among the powers, but relations between Britain and France had improved, while Russia, predominant in most of the northern provinces, had recognised British predominance in the Yang-tse basin. Germany was established in Shantung and Japan in Fukien, while France and the USA were striving to confirm their presence, too.[14]

But just as Pichon said that there would be no resistance to foreign partition, an anti-foreign movement known as 'The Society of Harmonious Fists' or the Boxers erupted. The Dowager Empress issued a decree in June 1898 in support of the Boxers declaring a national war against the imperialist powers, who banded together to defeat the Chinese Army and occupy the capital Peking in August. Some partition was indeed the aim of most of the imperialist powers, although the USA was keen to establish the Open Door as opposed to concessions made to individual states, leading in fact as its power grew to the extension of its own sphere of influence.

Chinese forces approached Blagoveshchensk on the Amur in the summer of 1899 and bombarded it across the river but were driven back with heavy losses, while Harbin was evacuated and under siege for a month before the Russian army disguised as a Railway Protection Unit penetrated as far as Mukden. There was some suspicion of Russia on the part of the other great powers: for example, the ambassador in St Petersburg of France, a friendly power, found the explanation of the War Minister General Kuropatkin of his military campaign in Manchuria unconvincing enough to exclaim:

> The Russian government, whose principal objective is to sustain its position in Manchuria and, if need be, to voluntarily disinterest itself from the rest of China would maintain until the end the fiction that it is not at war with China, and it is only against the rebels that it has to fight to re-establish order and

to help the Chinese government respect the conventions it has reached with Russia.[15]

Coming from a military background, and having seen service in Central Asia, Aleksei Kuropatkin had been appointed War Minister in 1898, and would no doubt have taken a most patriotic line of explanation. In any case, France, Russia and the other powers were able to agree to impose a large indemnity on the Chinese government after suppressing the Boxer Rebellion.

In a 'Lecture on the Great Siberian Railway' at the end of 1900, the British railway engineer Arthur John Baring suggested that 'How far the Siberian railway will have the effect of strengthening Russia's military position in the Far East is an open question,' calculating that 'If Russia were engaged in a serious war (with Japan for instance) she would have to put 10,000 men in the field exclusive of those required to guard the railway through Manchuria.' A *Guide to the Great Siberian Railway* also published in 1900 more idealistically asserted:

> The civilizing policy of Russia in the East, which may be regarded as an exception to that of other countries, was guided by other principles and was directed to the mutual welfare of nations by the maintenance of peace throughout the immense extent of her dominions. The honour of having planted the flag of Christianity and civilization in Asia is due to Russia. The near future will show the results of the activity of our Government and of our civilizing enterprises, which will add to the glory and power of Russia and her Sovereign Chief.[16]

Immediately after the suppression of the Boxer Rebellion, Harbin was extended by land purchase and by 1901 a line of ditches was dug that doubled its area. In an agreement of 1902, the Chinese accepted the purchased extension while the Russians limited the city to what was called 'Harbin-Central Station.' A government official with much railway experience in Central Asia as well as the Far East, Colonel (from 1904 General) Dmitrii Leonidovich Khorvat, was appointed manager of the CER in 1902 and remained in post until 1918. One of the engineers involved in the subsequent development noted:

> Railroad building in Russia during the last half-century has produced a special category of construction specialists, living their own peculiar way of life and usually bound to each other and their leaders by internal soldiering.

Incentives to such specialists included the 'rights of actual state service,' rank and pensions. Recruitment could also be informal, as noted by a second railroad builder:

> One or another engineer with whom we were acquainted would invite us. We trusted and followed him. As sections were completed, the builders, headed by their engineers, would move to new construction sites. We lived like migrating

Arrival of the railway and war with Japan 43

birds and were little interested in regulations. We loved our work. Of course, somewhere in St. Petersburg at the Board there were staff lists and budgets, but we received our pay from the section heads and asked no further.[17]

Manual labour was performed mostly by Chinese workers, who were much cheaper and less demanding than their Russian counterparts, and supplied by Chinese gangmasters (Figure 5). But these workers could cause alarm. I. Levitov, an overseer at the Harbin workshops, argued in 1901 in his book *Zheltaia Rossiia* (*Yellow Russia*) that a wave of Chinese immigrants could engulf Russia if they were not held back at the natural frontier of Lake Baikal. Starving Chinese, Levitov asserted, were not allowed to leave their province except to Manchuria, which he called 'the Chinese Siberia,' although there was plenty of space elsewhere. 'Coolies,' as he called them, using the word originating from Hindi, worked like animals in Europe, and, given the chance, would spread from Manchuria to take it over. Similarly, he added, W. H. Dixon had written in his book *White Conquest*: 'If a seventh part of the Chinese people came ever to America, they would swamp the ballot-boxes, and under a Republican Constitution they might assume the ruling power.' However, said Levitov, as far as Siberia was concerned, 'I do not see the slightest danger from the Chinese, provided that not one of them was allowed beyond Baikal.' In this case, he argued, the use of cheap Chinese 'coolies' would allow Russians to establish manufacturing industries in China as permitted by the

Figure 5 This railway construction gang shows Chinese gangmasters at the front and 'coolies' at the back, with European, mostly Finnish, managers in between. The photo may be viewed either as an example of the 'yellow peril' threatening white civilisation or as a pointer towards 'yellow Russia' involving harmony between the races. (Leena Dukes)

Treaty of Shimonoseki of 1895 and a 'Yellow Russia' of a more agreeable kind would take shape.[18]

The Russian government placed all Manchuria under occupation with the excuse of protecting the railway. The treaty of 1896 allowed for 'lands actually necessary for the construction, exploitation and defence of the line,' and General Grodekov, commander of the Amur military district, argued that the Boxer rising had made defence difficult and that *soldatskie slobody* or soldier settlements should be manned by Zabaikal Cossacks in a manner that would make for the more harmonious 'Yellow Russia.' In 1903, the Ministry of Finance contemplated appropriate action in response, but nothing came of it.[19]

Towards war between Russia and Japan

Suspicion of Chinese and Russian collaboration had much to do with the Anglo-Japanese Alliance of January 1902. The USA's opposition to Russian pretensions in Manchuria was expressed by Secretary of State John Hay, who feared that the American hand stretched out to China 'would be less persuasive to the poor Chinese than the club that [Russia] held over them' but also asserted that Americans must do 'all we can with the means at our disposal,' including working hand in hand with Japan and China, to open the ports in Manchuria.[20] Mounting international pressure was an influence on a Russo-Chinese treaty of March committing Russia to complete evacuation of Manchuria by September 1903. Back in European Russia, the situation was not helped by peasant and worker unrest from 1901 to 1903.

Japan was building up its forces for war continually since 1895, putting more troops into the field in 1900 than any other power. It attempted in vain to secure Russian recognition of its hold over Korea. Meanwhile, it grew increasingly alarmed at the operation of the Chinese Eastern Railway since 1903, as well as Russian procrastination in negotiations beginning in July of that year, with the British and American support, on the questions of both Korea and Manchuria.

Meanwhile, however, Germany disavowed interest in Manchuria while seeing Russian preoccupation with it as a distraction from affairs in the Balkans. Indeed, Kaiser Wilhelm II encouraged Tsar Nicholas II to develop Russia as a Far Eastern Great Power, holding back the tide of the Yellow Peril composed of millions of Chinese soldiers led by Japanese officers, while taking power in Korea to forestall an adversary's creation of 'a new sort of Dardanelles.'[21] Such talk was music to the ears of many Russians who believed in holding back the floodtide from the East.

Some Russians even wanted to take the fight to their Asiatic inferiors as they believed them to be. Witte was not among them, declaring:

> Military struggle with Japan in the near future would be a major calamity for us. I do not doubt that we would vanquish the foe, but our victory would come at the cost of many casualties as well as heavy economic losses. Besides, and most important … it would arouse the strong hostility of public opinion.

But he admitted that his expansionist policy was partly responsible for the more aggressive views of others, writing:

> Imagine that I invited some friends to The Aquarium [a nightclub in St. Petersburg], and they all proceeded to get drunk. Then, going on to a brothel, they ended up starting a fight there. Would I be responsible? I only took them to the Aquarium. They did the rest.[22]

One of the most notorious profligates was a retired Guards Officer, Captain A. M. Bezobrazov, who managed to involve the tsar himself in a project for the exploitation of the timber in the valley of the River Yalu in North Korea. His influence was considerable after the retirement of Witte in the summer of 1903. The machinations of Bezobrazov and his cronies may have been partly responsible for the dropping of the railway constructor, but, perhaps more significantly, Witte's financial policies were blamed for an economic depression. Bezobrazov probably also influenced the decision of Nicholas II to appoint Admiral E. I. Alekseev based in Port Arthur to a Far Eastern viceroyalty directly responsible to himself. Furthermore, a naval Captain A. M. Abaza, appointed secretary-general of a newly formed Far Eastern committee in St Petersburg, was Bezobrazov's cousin.[23]

The Russians were slow to complete the evacuation of their troops from Manchuria as agreed in 1902 while attempting to exclude all other powers. Indeed, the Bezobrazov group advocated a series of military operations leading in the direction of the annexation of Manchuria by Russia and the intensification of economic exploitation along with foreign collaborators to such an extent that the new province would pay for itself. They also manipulated in their favour the management of the CER. While Witte had advised withdrawal from Korea and moderation in Manchuria, the Bezobrazov group was in favour of defence of Manchuria along the Korean border. There was general agreement that it would be impossible to fulfil the terms of the treaty with China of March 1902.

The Minister of War General Kuropatkin visited Japan in June 1903 and then participated in a high-level discussion of Manchuria in Port Arthur in July. Immediately afterwards, the appointment of Admiral Akekseev as Viceroy of the Far East was a decision highly unlikely to please the Japanese government. Bezobrazov appeared to be at the height of his powers, but the outbreak of the war with Japan was to lead to the precipitate collapse of his various, already overextended enterprises.

In the autumn of 1903, the writer and traveller B. L. Putnam Weale, who had spent many years in the Far East, wrote a series of letters from Manchuria published in 1907 as a book entitled *Manchu and Muscovite*. The book was dedicated to 'the Gallant Japanese Nation,' while the publishers added a note pointing out that it was a 'very timely and instructive work written before the outbreak of war between Russia and Japan.' The author made no secret of his disdain for Russia observing that it was not much good at trade in beans and wheat, the mining of coal or the felling of timber, although somewhat better in the extraction of gold. Apart from trade, there were several sources of business in Manchuria: the railway; the navy and naval works; the army and army commissariat. To carry on business, and indeed for the purpose of day-to-day existence, say to secure a government contract or hotel room: 'The first thing you must be armed with in Manchuria is a big pocket book of rouble notes.'[24]

On the railway, second class was as good as first in Putnam Weale's estimation, but one often needed a little extra money to secure it. In general,

> The iron horse, with its hideous screech has frightened all that [the past] away now, and the unromantic but frugal Shantung coolie is completing the destruction of Nuhachu's [the founder of 'Manchuria] descendants and their old-world ways.

Riding the rails, 'You see nothing except a railway track and a few dozen stations.' The stations, 'these little blobs,' were ludicrously overmanned, with up to 5,000 staff for 1,500 miles of track, as opposed to the hundreds of employees that would be necessary in Britain. Some of the express trains were 'as nearly perfect as you can get anything in the world,' but in general 'Manchuria is the home of slow trains.' Moreover, the Russian Empire of the iron track could well be destroyed by 'the Vandals of the twentieth century,' the Russians themselves.[25]

Putnam Weale described the three Chinese eastern provinces that constituted Manchuria thus:

> the southern, Fengtien [or Mukden], populous, contented, containing large towns and just like the Northern provinces of China proper; the central, Kirin, settled in the great rich valleys and plains through which the railway runs to Harbin – wild in the north and east which were once controlled by the so-called Chinese military; and finally the northern province, Heilung [or Tsitsihar], practically uninhabited.

Since the Boxer Rebellion in 1900, the Chinese administration had been disrupted somewhat, but nevertheless, its machinery had been mostly undamaged 'in spite of Commissair bullying, in spite of threats, outrages and many other things.' This was partly because the Russian Consuls-General in Mukden, Kirin and Tsitsihar in fact interfered but little, to some extent because the Chinese were smarter than the Russians, bleeding them financially. The Russo-Chinese Bank that had been set up by an imperial decree in December 1895 had political as well as financial aims, ultimately seeking to emulate 'Anglo-Saxon methods, and ideas' and to assimilate China, but there was a long way to go.[26]

In Harbin, which he called 'the very centre of China,' there were about 30,000 Russians and 250,000 Chinese. Putnam Weale closely observed the Russians at their leisure, noting that they had to be amused or would die of boredom. The nightlife became more spectacular the later it became. The Russians liked to compare their city with its counterparts in the American West, although none of their newspapers was a daily and news was censored without the benefit of

Reuters news agency, while the American West had no problem comparable to that of the 'yellow man.' Moreover, 'Harbin had got a bad attack of the nerves,' with bribes expected by the *hunhutsy* bandits led by Chinese officers. Left to themselves, the bandits were not normally dangerous as long as they were paid off, Putnam Weale suggested. But when the expected war came, the large Russian army of 'unknown quality' might not be able to give a good account of itself. He concluded:

> Until the British Government decides that England's only policy is to insist that her interests extend right up to the actual frontier-stones of the Russian Empire, and promptly retaliates, should a Cossack be moved past these frontier-stones, we will continue to present the ridiculous and unmanly figure we do to-day in the Far East. Japan is fighting England's battle almost as much as she is fighting her own.[27]

Putnam Weale was to change his mind after the Russo-Japanese War, as we shall see in the next chapter.

The Russo-Japanese War, 1904–5, and after

On the very day, 8 October 1903, by which Russia had agreed to evacuate Manchuria, both China and the USA signed treaties with Japan opening up to foreigners the ports of Antung and Tatungkow at the mouth of the Yalu as well as the city of Mukden. So, Chinese resistance to Russia was supported by the USA as well as Japan and Britain, in alliance since 1902. Although France was to extend a loan of 350 million roubles to Russia in April 1904, it adhered to its agreement with Britain. Germany also lent money but held aloof diplomatically. While Japan was preparing its fleet for action, in B. A. Romanov's evocative assessment, the floundering by Nicholas II and his advisers testified

> to a complete helplessness to comprehend the rigid international conjuncture in which Russia's military weakness left her baffled by the immediate problems of the day, and to the hopelessness of the domestic situation, battering at the supreme government like some sort of fevered dream recurring intermittently with paralytic symptoms.[28]

Among the problems was the Trans-Siberian Railway, still incomplete at the outbreak of war. The crossing of Lake Baikal was a particular problem, especially in winter, when a sledge route carried mostly officers and a temporary rail line gave way when the ice cracked and many soldiers were drowned.

However, the line around Baikal was completed in 1904, and, given the many problems that huge distances involved, the construction of the railway into Manchuria was a great technical feat. On the other side, the Japanese were improving their railway system to the extent that they were poised in the event of their victory to reach St Petersburg via Siberia.[29]

The war was ignited by Japan's concern about Russian military expansion and Russian ambitions for naval supremacy in the Korean Straits. On 5 February 1904, Japan broke off relations with Russia before a surprise attack on Port Arthur on the night of 8–9. Russian fleet retaliated, but, as is well known, the ensuing war was a disaster at sea while far from a success on land for the tsar's armed forces. The Baltic Fleet was virtually annihilated in the straits of Tsushima after a circumnavigation of the globe beginning with the Dogger Bank incident in which British fishing boats were mistaken for Japanese ships and some of them were sunk. On land, Russian strategy was divided between the 'Kuropatkin school' which wanted to concentrate on the defence of the north, and the 'Alekseev school' which wanted to hold on to both north and south.[30] The choice was made not so much on the drawing board as the battlefield since, while the engagement at Mukden in Southern Manchuria, if far from complete defeat for the army, inflicted heavy losses on it.

Kuropatkin was relieved of his post after Mukden, but had his own ideas about the reasons for the Russian reverses, dividing them into three main groups: independent of the War Ministry; dependent on the War Ministry; and dependent on the officers in the field. First, the absence of diplomatic arrangements allowing the army to move freely; the subordinate part played by the fleet; the inferiority of the railways; and the internal disorders in Russia affecting the spirit of the army. Secondly, the delay in the mobilisation of reinforcements for the Far East; the transfer into the reserve of well-trained soldiers while untrained elderly reservists were being sent to the front; the belated despatch of drafts to the front (a responsibility shared with the railways); the delay in the promotion of those who had distinguished themselves in the field; the deficiencies in the technical equipment; the faults of the organisation including lack of protection for communications, dearth of transport and unwieldy organisation; and deficiencies in personnel of both officers and men. Thirdly, the absence of a true military esprit de corps among the troops; the poor spirit of many of them in action; the lack of determination on the part of commanders at all levels to perform the tasks allotted to them; and the breakdown of the organisation under the stress of war. Kuropatkin considered that the Russian army was inferior to its enemy in technical troops and equipment, unsatisfactorily commanded and insufficiently trained, and unable to make full use of superiority of numbers. However, Kuropatkin argued that most of the army in the field would have agreed with him that victory would have ensued if peace had not been concluded so hastily. He asserted that the numbers were increasing and morale was rising while the enemy was weakening in both these respects.[31]

But the government back in St Petersburg did not believe that Russia was in a potentially strong position when it accepted US President Theodore Roosevelt's offer to convene a peace conference at Portsmouth, New Hampshire in August 1905. Roosevelt had written enthusiastically to an old Japanese acquaintance immediately after Tsushima that 'Even the Battle of Trafalgar could not match this,'[32] but he did not now want Russia to be humiliated, and sought the restoration of a balance of power. Moreover, the veteran negotiator Sergei Witte made a good impression and played his hand skilfully. He accepted the loss of the Liaotung

Peninsula and the South Manchurian Railway to Japan, and recognised Japanese supremacy in Korea. However, Japan agreed to Russian predominance in North Manchuria including continued control of the Chinese Eastern Railway. Witte managed to resist the Japanese demand for an indemnity and for Japanese exclusive hold on the island of Sakhalin, which was divided between the two powers. The Treaty of Portsmouth was signed on 5 September 1905.

On 22 December 1905, the Treaty of Peking was concluded between Japan and China accepting the major provisions of the Treaty of Portsmouth and opening up Manchuria to Japanese encroachment.

The war gave a huge boost to the self-esteem and world-wide reputation of Japan. In Russia, it sparked a revolution which would also make a global impact, especially beyond the West, leading Lenin to declare in an article at the beginning of January 1905 on 'The Fall of Port Arthur' that 'A progressive and advanced Asia has inflicted an irreparable blow on a backward and reactionary Europe'[33] The Russian people, who could be as patriotic as any in times of victory, were incensed by what they saw as crushing defeat. Of course, there were social and economic causes for the revolution as well, more than enough reasons for insurgency in both towns and countryside.

In May 1905, A. N. Kulomzin joined with other senior officials in a memorandum to Nicholas II arguing that educational and agricultural policies had been neglected. Moreover, 'The fastening of our borderlands to the centre is a never-ending condition.' Of the mass of the peasantry, the memorandum averred:

> Lacking any culture, knowing no feeling of respect for private property, educated on the communistic principles of the *obshchina* [commune] and not trained in any strict fulfilment of the law, [the peasantry] is becoming an obedient weapon in the hands of the enemies of order ... . we deeply believe that the evil criticism and condemnation of all governmental activity and of its best intentions which reigns in our educated and semi-educated society and which goes as far as hysterical hallucinations coupled with total ignorance of the nature and difficulties of legislative work, all this, together with the lower classes' instinctive striving to overthrow private property, which expresses itself in riots and mass pogroms, is eating away the roots of our state order. All the forces of political reason and will must be directed into the struggle against the calamity.[34]

The wider empire experienced turmoil, too, including the Far East. In 1904, V. I. Nemirovich-Danchenko, co-founder and co-director of the Moscow Arts Theatre, noted that a breakdown in law and order was already occurring in Harbin. The officers and men charged with the distribution of supplies to hundreds of thousands of soldiers and horses found ample opportunity for graft and corruption. And fortunes could be made in 'entertainment,' too. Avoiding both the tedium of long periods of waiting and the danger of sudden action, those who could escape the front sought oblivion that was temporary before it became permanent. One memoirist noted that, with rumours of another engagement,

Harbin was filled with mad debauch. The champagne flowed in rivers, the courtesans were doing a splendid business. The percentage of officers fallen in battle was so great that all expected certain death, and so bade good-bye to life in wild orgies.

The casualties of war were brought to Harbin. Another eyewitness was struck by the long rows of white tents flying the Red Cross

which had come as ghosts during the night when such a mass of wounded had been brought in that the hospitals, numerous as they were, could no longer hold them. It was from these tents that the wail of the wounded rolled out to crush the soul.[35]

In such circumstances, the CER General Manager Khorvat found it necessary to set up food committees to fight inflation, while a Railway Club was formed to cater for off-duty relaxation away from Harbin's fleshpots. In spite of the fact that their line was under martial law, Horvat and his associates fought to hold their own against what they considered to be unreasonable demands made upon them by the military. Viceroy Alekseev, soon to depart, wrote in July to Finance Minister Kokovtsov in St Petersburg of Horvat's 'energy, knowledge, experience and devotion' deserving promotion to the rank of major-general, but this gesture did not help to heal the breach between the army and railway. Kuropatkin, now in sole charge after the departure of Alekseev, decreed in October 1905 that Harbin should be administered as an 'armed camp.'[36]

Instead of unalloyed joy, the Peace of Portsmouth in August 1905 brought further demoralisation to the army as well as extreme homesickness. In David Wolff's evocative description: 'Vengeful brooding joined drinking, gaming, and whoring as favourite pastimes in Harbin.' There can be no doubt that railway–military tensions contributed to violence breaking out in November 1905, as the patience of servicemen ran out after they had waited more than two months for trains to take them home. In the same month, meetings were held at the Railway Club in the wake of the Tsar's October Manifesto conceding constitutional reform. Red flags could be seen and the Marseillaise was sung on the streets. A CER official V. P. Lepeshinskii was later arrested and sent to prison for his revolutionary activities, which appear in fact to have been quite moderate. Khorvat accepted that Harbin should become a 'self-administering town' in order to maintain good order. But dissent continued as a nationwide postal-telegraph strike cut and then restricted contact with the rest of Russia. Strikes broke out on Central Asian railways.

At the end of January 1906, a Cossack General Pavel Mishchenko from Manchuria, appointed 'Special Governor-General of the Vladivostok Fortified Zone' by the tsar, used promises and threats to overcome local insurgents and political leaders, executing more than 50 of them and imprisoning over 300. Meanwhile, in Transbaikalia, strikes and agitation led to the proclamation in December 1905 of a 'Chita Republic.' In January 1906, the Trans-Siberian Railway that passed through Chita was put under martial law, and armoured trains converged from both directions to restore order. Some 400 railway workers and soldiers were put on trial. Nine were shot and seven were hanged out of the 147 found guilty. One of the leaders, an exiled Social Democrat named Viktor Kurnatovsky managed to escape to Australia where he worked as a dishwasher until Lenin summoned him to Paris in 1910 to report on the Chita Republic. The local Governor-General Kholshchevnikov was released from house arrest only to be court-martialled for dereliction of duty.[37]

The repercussions of the turbulent events of 1904–6 were to be felt throughout the Russian Empire, including the Far East, in the following years.

On 16 August 1905, in the Preface to his book on *Great Japan*, Alfred Stead wrote:

> I confess frankly to an intense admiration and a feeling almost of awe at the sight of this magnificent national force moving in nearly perfect harmony towards the definite end of the nation's welfare. To my mind it is difficult to place any limit upon the future of such a thinking and educated power.

In his Foreword, the Earl of Rosebery, former Liberal Prime Minister, observed: 'Three things may move us: obvious decline, sudden catastrophe, or some stimulating example. The last of these is furnished by Japan.' Party had caused dissension in Britain, but in Japan: 'It appears to be a rivalry of faction for the goal and prize of efficiency.'[38] Stead averred that nothing had opened the eyes of the world to the progress of Japan than the fall of Port Arthur, adding 'Japan, a brown race, a nation of Asia, has demonstrated her right to sit above, and, as she has done so by the force of arms, Western civilization has acknowledged her claim.' The outstanding traits of the Japanese army were 'sobriety, cleanliness, self-reliance, and intelligence.' In the Manchurian campaign, the Russian army had been defeated because of their inferiority not in courage 'but in intelligence, education, and enthusiasm.' Moreover, the Russians were much more cruel in their behaviour than their Japanese opponents, and had tried to make the Chinese army into 'a native army similar to the native army in India,' possibly making a reality of the 'Yellow Peril,' although the limit of Japanese endeavours in this direction 'might be to enable the northern viceroys to protect their territories from foreign aggression.' The prospect of world peace would be much enhanced by a new triple alliance of Japan, Great Britain and the United States.[39]

A British military attaché with the Russian army during the war against Japan, Major J. Howe, reported that some of his hosts often showed hostility towards Britain. Howe wrote: 'Many officers talked openly of an invasion of India as being an easy operation which would recompense them for their losses in Manchuria.' Meanwhile, as far as British statesmen such as Lord Curzon and generals such as Kitchener were concerned, the Russian threat to India remained a worry. In 1904, Curzon had sent an expedition under Colonel Francis Younghusband, whom we have previously met as a lieutenant visiting Manchuria, to Tibet. Younghusband exceeded his original instructions in persuading the Tibetans to admit no agents of another power and to give no concessions on their territory. In 1905, the British gave the Emir of Afghanistan a subsidy and a commitment to defend him against any other power, in return for which the Emir promised to deal with any other power solely via the British government, The most likely identity of 'any other power' was clear enough, and the Great Game was far from over, although there were pointers towards old enemies agreeing to bury the hatchet as negotiations began in St Petersburg in the summer of 1906. From the Russian point of view, the threat in the Far East was looming along with that from Europe even though Japan was also to become an ally.[40]

Conclusion

Japan's victory over Russia demonstrated to other peoples dominated by the European empires that they too could begin to challenge the right of the West to rule the world, implicitly questioning an entry in *The Modern Encyclopedia* of 1904 that concluded: 'The sovereigns of China, Japan, and Morocco are often, although with little propriety, called *emperors*.'[41]

In the same year, Halford Mackinder, an Oxford graduate whose career was to involve travel and politics as well as education, gave a lecture to the Royal Geographical Society with the title 'The Geographical Pivot of History' that was to achieve wide renown. Mackinder gave great emphasis to the great continent of Eurasia and its European 'heartland,' supplementing Captain Mahan's argument on the influence of sea power.

In 1866, just after the end of the American Civil War, an American telegraph official could already declare: 'We hold the ball of the earth in our hand, and wind upon it a network of living and thinking wire, till the whole is held together and bound with the same wishes, projects, and interests.' Mr. O. H. Palmer continued:

> Thus the commerce of the world will find its path ... for the telegraph is to precede all, rapidly and cheaply we press it forward as the swift-running courier...then the stately ship soon to make way for the more rapid steamer, finally the iron way joins the circle, and girds the world with steam and electricity.[42]

Thirty years passed before the 'iron way' reached Manchuria at a time when international rivalry was intensifying (Figure 6). Both China and Japan were concerned with the impact that the Trans-Siberian and Chinese Eastern railways might have, not to mention the Western powers. Unrest in China at the beginning of the twentieth century in the shape of the Boxers was followed by the Russo-Japanese War making a great impact not only in the Far East but throughout the world, contributing in particular to the first Russian Revolution.

Meanwhile, the remarkable railway city of Harbin populated by Chinese and Russians grew amid a hinterland frequented by bandits. From the very beginning, there was a distinctive quality about Harbin, much accentuated with the arrival of the war as it provided shelter for the wounded and entertainment for officers and men awaiting the call from the front or recovering after a stint in the frontline.

Arrival of the railway and war with Japan 53

Figure 6 A French cartoon depicting the carve-up of China entitled 'The Chinese cake.' From left to right, Queen Victoria, Kaiser Wilhelm II, Tsar Nicholas II of Russia, French Marianne, Japanese samurai. Qing official behind them. (Wikimedia Commons)

Notes

1 B. A. Romanov, *Russia in Manchuria, 1892–1906*, trans. Susan Wilbur Jones (Ann Arbor: J. W. Edwards, 1952), p. 41. The work was originally published in Leningrad in 1928.
2 Ibid., pp. 2, 42. Witte's italics. On Witte and earlier enthusiasts, see Steven G. Marks, *Road to Power: The Trans-Siberian Railroad and the Colonization of Asian Russia, 1850–1917* (London: Tauris, 1991).
3 Romanov, *Russia*, p. 47.
4 Ian Nish, *The History of Manchuria, 1840–1948: A Sino-Russo-Japanese Triangle*, 2 vols. (Folkestone: Renaissance Books, 2016), Vol. 2, *Select Primary Sources*, p. 23. A

triumphal arch was built to commemorate the tsarevich's visit in 1891. It was destroyed in 1930 and rebuilt in 2003.
5 David Schimmelpenninck van der Oye, *Towards the Rising Sun: Russian Ideologies of Empire and the Path to War with Japan* (Dekalb: Northern Illinois University Press, 2001), p. 51.
6 Charles Wenyon, *Across Siberia: On the Great Post Road* (London: Charles H. Kelly, 1896), pp. 16, 90–1, 101.
7 Romanov, *Russia in Manchuria*, p. 1.
8 D. C. B. Lieven, 'Bureaucratic Liberalism in Late Imperial Russia: The Personality, Career and Opinions of A. N. Kulomzin', *Slavonic and East European Review*, Vol. 60, No. 3 (1982), pp. 413–32.
9 V. Treiden, *Vysochaishe uchrezhdennaia pod predsedatel'stvom stats-sekretari Kulomzina kommisiia dlia izsledovaniia zemlevladeniia i zemlepol'zovaniia v Zabaikal'skoi oblasti: materialy, vypusk 9: arenda* (St Petersburg: Gosudarstvennaia tipografiia, 1898), pp. 1–6.
10 Schimmelpenninck van der Oye, *Toward the Rising Sun* (Dekalb: Northern Illinois University Press, 2001), p. 145.
11 Dmitrii Pavlov, 'Kitaiskii kvantun pod rossiiskoi arendoi (1898–1905): pretsedent modernizatsionnogo kolonializma?', *Rossiiskaia istoriia*, Vol. 1 (2018), pp. 85–6. The Russian administration in Kwantung is more broadly covered in V. P. Kazantsev, and E. A. Popravko, *'Idëm na Vostok!': Dokumental'ne ocherki rossisskoi politiki na Dal'nem Vostoke v kontse XIX-nachale XXvv* (Sankt-Peterburg: Petropolis, 2019), especially *Ocherki XIII–XX*.
12 David Wolff, *To the Harbin Station: The Liberal Alternative in Russian Manchuria, 1898–1914* (Stanford: Stanford University Press, 1999), pp. 25, 27.
13 On *hunhutsy* and Cossacks, see G. V. Melikhov, *Man'chzhuriia dalekaia i blizkaia* (Moscow: Nauka, 1991), pp. 101–3. The Cossack guard was disbanded in 1920. Ibid., p. 107.
14 *Documents Diplomatiques Français, 1871–1914*, First series, XV, pp. 333–7, as quoted in R. C. Bridges, Paul Dukes, J. D. Hargreaves, and William Scott, *Nations and Empires: Documents on the History of Europe and on Its Relations with the World* (London: Macmillan, 1969), pp. 180–3.
15 Ian Nish, *The History of Manchuria*, Vol. 2; p. 41.
16 Arthur John Berry, *Lecture on the Great Siberian Railway*, delivered at the Military School of Engineering, Chatham (London: Waterlow and Sons, 1900), pp. 3, 22; *A Guide to the Great Siberian Railway* quoted by Ian Nish, *The Origins of the Russo-Japanese War* (London: Longman, 1985), p. 17.
17 This paragraph from Wolff, *To the Harbin Station*, pp. 29–31.
18 *Doklad I. Levitova, Zheltaia Rossiia* (SPb, 1901), pp. 36, 38, 40, 50. The quotation is from William Hepworth Dixon, *White Conquest*, in two volumes, Vol. II (London: Chatto and Windus, 1878), p. 282; Wolff, *To the Harbin Station*, pp. 43–4.
19 F. B. Skvirskii, 'Soldatskie slobodki v Zheltorossii: tsarskii plan voennoi kolonizatsii Man'chzhurii', *Vestnik Man'chzhurii*, No. 4 (1930), pp. 14–6.
20 Romanov, *Russia in Manchuria*, p. 13
21 Hugh Seton-Watson, *The Russian Empire, 1801–1917* (Oxford: Clarendon Press, 1967), p. 386.
22 Witte to the foreign minister Count Lamsdorf in 1901 and then to General Kuropatkin in 1903, David Schimmelpenninck van der Oye, *Toward the Rising Sun*, pp. 80–1.
23 Ibid., pp. 188–90; Seton-Watson, *The Russian Empire*, pp. 588–91.
24 B. L. Putnam Weale, *Manchu and Muscovite* (London: Macmillan, 1907), pp. 99–100, 150–1, 156–9. The author's real name was Bertram Lenox.
25 Ibid., pp. 112, 119, 372, 376, 396–7, 516.
26 Ibid., pp. 123–7, 288, 299–300, 318.
27 Ibid., pp. 148, 164, 313, 469, 531.

28 Romanov, *Russia in Manchuria*, p. 16.
29 Felix Patrikeeff and Harold Shukman, *Railways and the Russo-Japanese War: Transporting War* (London: Routledge, 2007), pp. 50, 93.
30 Nish, *The Origins*, p. 254.
31 General Kuropatkin, *The Russian Army and the Japanese War ...* (London: John Murray, 1909), pp. 177–80.
32 Quoted in David Wells and Sandra Wilson, eds., *The Russo-Japanese War in Cultural Perspective, 1904–05* (London: Palgrave Macmillan, 1999), p. 23.
33 Lenin quoted by Ivar Spector, *The First Russian Revolution: Its Impact on Russia* (Englewood Cliffs: Prentice Hall, 1962), p. 123.
34 Lieven, 'Bureaucratic Liberalism', pp. 427–8.
35 This paragraph from Wolff, *To the Harbin Station*, pp. 121–3.
36 Ibid., pp. 123–5.
37 John Stephan, *The Russian Far East: A History* (Stanford: Stanford UP, 1994), pp. 101–5.
38 Alfred Stead, *Great Japan: A Study of National Efficiency* (London: John Lane, 1906), pp. ii, iii, vi, ix. 'Dedicated with Much Admiration to the Japanese Nation.'
39 Ibid., pp. 16. 277, 315, 464–5, 473.
40 Philip Towle, 'The Russo-Japanese War and the Defence of India', *Military Affairs*, Vol. 44, No. 3 (1980), pp. 113, 115–6.
41 Charles Annandale, ed., *The Modern Encyclopedia of Universal Information*, Vol. 3 (London: Gresham, 1904), p. 376.
42 O. H. Palmer, *Statement of the Origin, Organization and Progress of the Russian-American Telegraph Western Union Extension ...* (Rochester: Western Union, 1866), pp. 33, 165.

4 To the First World War and Russian Revolution, 1906–18

Relations between Russia, Japan and China

On the Hills of Manchuria was a lament for the Russian losses in the war of 1904–5 against Japan concluding:

> Around us, it's calm,
> The fog blown away by the wind,
> warriors are asleep on the hills of Manchuria,
> and Russian weeping cannot be heard.

In Japan, there was a popular song entitled 'Comrade' including the lines:

> Here. Many hundreds of leagues from home.
> The red setting sun of Manchuria
> Shines down on a stone at the edge of a field,
> Beneath which my friend lies.[1]

The former enemies mourned their dead, sometimes together, and were chary of engaging in any further conflict in the Far East. Nevertheless, some analysts have seen the Russo-Japanese War as a prelude to the First World War. The outcome of the war of 1904–5 encouraged both France and Britain to continue large loans to Russia as the three powers joined in the Triple Entente of 1907, a fateful rival to the Dual Alliance of Germany and Austria-Hungary. In the same year, Britain and Russia agreed to call the Great Game of empire a draw in Central Asia (although there were replays throughout the twentieth century): the Anglo-Russian convention created zones of influence for the two powers in Persia or Iran, with perhaps half an eye on the pretensions of Germany in Turkey and beyond. Russia accepted that Afghanistan was outside its sphere of interests; it recognised the special interest of Britain in Tibet because of its proximity to India, while agreeing that both powers should negotiate with Tibet exclusively via China. However, in July 1914, an Anglo-Tibetan agreement provided for military instructors and mining engineers to go to Tibet, which the British looked upon as a state separate from China. Needless to say, the Chinese did not agree and refused to recognise the agreement,[2] but the Great Powers were preoccupied in July 1914 by a crisis in Europe leading soon to the outbreak of the First World War. Willy-nilly (or Willy-Nicky), right up to 1914, Russia gave its future enemy, Germany, the advantage of a favourable customs tariff, while Kaiser Wilhelm tried to persuade Tsar Nicholas to concentrate on Asia while he busied himself with Europe, and the Emperor cousins protested their friendship up to the eve of hostilities.[3]

Certainly, the Russo-Japanese War of 1904–5 brought a fresh focus to the Far East, as explorers, businessmen and commentators as well as statesmen thought about it anew. Nikolai Baikov plunged into the Manchuria taiga from the Chinese Eastern Railway (CER) while, more famously, Vladimir Arsenev was captivated by the Ussuri taiga, which, in John Stephan's evocative words, 'came to symbolize for him primordial Nature, mysterious, ineffably beautiful, elusive, threatening, and threatened.' Arsenev made use of his encounter with Dersu Uzala from the Nanai people to create a composite figure representative of the inhabitants of the Far East including his chief guide who was Chinese.[4] His journals were used as a basis for the film *Dersu Uzala* directed by the Japanese director Kurosawa, an impressive account of the encounter between rationalism and animism. Yet, we must not be carried away by the appeal of the compelling story to neglect Arsenev's activity in archaeology, for example near Harbin, nor the overall scientific significance of his work, which, as Vladimir Sokolov points out, should be viewed in the tradition of Russian military Far Eastern studies; his voluminous researches in historical anthropology were linked with the interests of the imperial government.[5] Similarly, the growing amount of anthropological work being carried out from Africa to the Pacific could not be divorced from the concerns of other empires (Figure 7).

Meanwhile, Harbin and the CER were attracting more commercial attention, too. The American financier E. H. Harriman attempted to make use of the 'Open Door' soon after the conclusion of the Portsmouth Treaty by acquiring control of the railway from Port Arthur to Changchun just ceded by Russia to Japan. Already known at home as 'the railroad king' and the director of an American trans-Pacific shipping company, Harriman now hoped to set up a round-the-world freight and passenger service which would include purchase of the CER and use of the Trans-Siberian Railway, with a trans-Atlantic steamship line to complete the global circuit. The cash-strapped Japanese government was attracted to the idea and came to a preliminary if unsigned agreement in Tokyo with Harriman who sailed for home believing that his great idea was on course for realisation. However, riots against the Portsmouth Treaty for its perceived leniency to Russia persuaded the Japanese government to delay rather than cancel the project.[6] Harriman died soon afterwards, but his dream was continued by Wall Street bankers and in Washington. Most notable, perhaps, was the scheme put forward by Secretary of State Philander Knox, who launched a project in 1909 for the 'neutralisation' of the Manchurian railways both Russian and Japanese via their transfer to a consortium of four New York banks. The State Department approached the British Foreign Office which considered the project to be inappropriately timed as well as

Figure 7 Army officer Vladimir Arsenev was captivated by the primordial nature of Manchuria and the surrounding area as he went about his official task of surveying the land. He was assisted by a number of native guides represented by Dersu Uzala in the eponymous film by the Japanese director Akira Kurosawa. (Wikipedia)

drafted, while the Russians and Japanese agreed to oppose it. The Chinese, eager for American support, alone supported the project.[7]

To turn to commentators, B. L. Putnam Weale, whom we have met in the previous chapter, had lost most of his enthusiasm for the land of the Rising Sun, writing after a tour in the Far East in the autumn of 1906 that: 'it is oligarchic Japan which constitutes the new problem in Eastern Asia … Japan which has taken Russia's place as the disturbing factor in the Far East'; 'the real menace to the Far East is the birth of a greater Japan.' In particular, there had been 'a general revolt in China against Japan's Manchurian policy.'[8]

Putnam Weale noticed great changes in Manchuria as he travelled about it. The government in St Petersburg had already shown an awareness of its significance to the Empire by making Admiral Alekseev Viceroy in 1902, but was keener now than before to exert its influence from afar. Thus, in Harbin it had spent a vast amount of money which it could ill afford on a grandiose building programme: for example, its main train station was said to have 'few compeers even in Europe' and to bear comparison with that in Cologne in particular. As before: 'The railway authorities are still practically supreme all over Manchuria; indeed that must be so, since some authority must replace that of the departed military.' Out in the country side, the '*hinghutsu*' [*hunhutsy*] bandits had increased in number by hundreds, even thousands and in ferociousness, too, 'educated by the battles of war.' In that war, the Russian side had shown itself to be an 'army of roysterers,' the converse of their efficient enemy, who had consolidated their presence in spite of the restraints imposed upon them by the Peace of Portsmouth.[9]

After the final evacuation date of that Treaty, April 1907, the Chinese government intended to introduce 'a model system of provincial administration.' Putnam Weale observed: 'With Russia in Northern Manchuria and Japan in southern Manchuria, such an experiment could be much more safely tried in Chinese Manchuria than in any province of China.' And so, it should be remembered that the President of the Chinese Eastern Railway was a Chinaman in Peking as a Chinese Viceroy was appointed for the three North-eastern provinces, with a governor in each of them.[10] Meanwhile, Great Britain had to be careful about the manner in which the Anglo-Japanese Alliance was continued. Indeed: 'While it might be possible, with honour, to remain outside an American-Japanese struggle, there could be no such holding back once Russia set her forces in motion.'[11]

In the Far East, a Russo-Japanese agreement on fisheries was followed by a political reconciliation of the recent belligerents in the summer of 1907, secretly drawing a line between their spheres of interest at the same time as paying lip service to the principle of the Open Door. However, neither side disarmed, so this was a truce rather than peace. In October 1907, the Russian government transferred the Trans-Amur Railway Battalion to the guard of the CER, which now amounted to a formidable total of 30,000 in clear contravention of the Portsmouth Treaty. Finance Minister V. N. Kokovtsov wanted to reduce this number in order to show that Russia had no aggressive intentions towards China, but consideration of his proposal was put off until the projected completion of the Amur Railway from Khabarovsk early in 1909.

Meanwhile, to counter what they perceived as a potential threat from Russia, the Japanese had consolidated their control of South Manchuria including the zone of the South Manchurian Railway (SMR) with their own considerable military force and formally incorporated Korea in their empire on 23 August 1910. For its part, the Chinese military force of older and newer units amounted to 75,000 by 1911. A. I. Denikin, later a White general in the Russian Civil War against the Reds, observed in 1908: 'We are facing the beginning of the revival of China and her army.' He went on to ask: 'Can we be indifferent and wait for the growing inequality of our military power to become obvious until we withdraw from not only occupied areas, but also the traditional Russian territory in wartime?'[12] There was a proposal to call up reservists for the CER guard in an emergency. When the question of the completion of the Amur Railway came up at the Third State Duma in March 1908, emphasis was given to the expansion of the Chinese army in Manchuria and there was talk of a Chinese military offensive against Russia as if already under way.

Because of the Russo-Japanese Treaty of summer 1907, there was less Russian concern about a clash with Japan, although some apprehension continued. For example, P. F. Unterberger, the Priamur Governor-General, warned the government in St Petersburg about the threat from Japan on several occasions between 1907 and 1909.

As far as China was concerned, the Russian expansionist spirit revived. At the beginning of 1909, while a new Manchurian Agreement was being negotiated in Peking affirming Chinese rights in the administration, the Russian community in Harbin sent a petition to St Petersburg expressing concern at the government's concessions to an empire increasingly incapable of self-defence, in Manchuria especially. The petition concluded:

> It will be far more profitable for Russia to join forces with Japan against China, than to support China against Japan. The only factor which determines the course of international politics is the factor of material force. At the present moment, force is all on the side of Japan, and it will therefore be a serious mistake if, instead of casting in our lot with the strong, we strive to make friends with the weak. As it is, the Chinese despise us for the feebleness implied by our vacillating and conciliatory policy.[13]

In 1910 and again in 1912, Russia and Japan agreed to collaborate against American intrusion into their spheres of influence.

The journalist J. O. P. Bland, who supplied much information concerning international affairs in 1912, made the comment that from the adventures of Khabarov in the seventeenth century to the exploits of Murav'ev-Amursky in the nineteenth century Russian bureaucrats and intellectuals alike had been possessed by the dream of a Far Eastern Empire. But the dream had been based on personal prejudices and sudden impulses rather than on a considered national movement with a rational foreign policy and integrated economic system Bland declared:

> There is, indeed, in Russia's foreign policy a Peter Pan quality of mercurial audacity, a keen zest for magnificent and unprovisioned excursions into the furthest Never-never Lands, a splendid contempt for logic and the results of experience, together with a Nelsonic eye for the dim outline of Nemesis in the distance. It is a policy which has been ever liable to sudden enthusiasms and equally sudden reactions of discouragement, frequently representing, even to the furthest frontiers of the Empire, nothing more than the whim of a court favourite, the greed of a Bezobrazoff, or the fatuous complacency of an Alexieff. Spasmodic, sentimental and unstable – yet reflecting also the indomitable courage and splendid virility of the Slav race.[14]

Bland's insights are brilliant, yet there is a case for saying that the Russian policy in Manchuria and the Far East was normally to avoid any renewal of hostilities. Partly as a peaceful consolidation of a Russian presence, the colonisation of Siberia and of the Far East, mainly in the area adjacent to the Trans-Siberian Railway, was encouraged by the government under Prime Minister P. A. Stolypin who, in 1908 as he attempted to get finance for the railway, observed (in a statement worthy of Dr Strangelove in the view of David Wolff): 'If we sleep our lethargic dreams, this [Far Eastern] territory will become saturated with foreign juices, and perhaps when we awake it will be Russian only in name.' During a tour of the Far East in 1910, Stolypin wrote to the tsar of 'an enormous, rudely democratic country, which soon will throttle European Russia.'[15] Like many previous government ministers, including Kulomzin, Stolypin was worried about losing central control over the vast area east of the Urals.

Developments in Harbin

Indeed, the Russian Far East was growing in significance as telephones, electric lights, trams and other appurtenances of industrialised civilisation began to appear in Vladivostok and other cities, as the railways extended. The first cinema joined a number of theatres in 1906. Recovering from a depression in the immediate postwar years, Harbin also grew rapidly at the junction of the CER and the SMRs to become the capital of Russian Manchuria. By the eve of the outbreak of the First World War, the population approached 70,000 including 34,000 Russians and 23,000 Chinese. There was indeed a separate Chinese city, suspected of harbouring bandits but also providing menial labour and a home for prosperous Chinese merchants. With an unofficial 'military' presence, the town was strategically placed to experience the vicissitudes of war and revolution.[16]

In 1908, a leading journalist wrote:

> Whatever the further fate ... of Manchuria, Harbin will always remain the commercial and administrative centre thanks to its brilliant position at the crossroads of various routes by water and over land, via the railway and commerce. Harbin is in truth a Russian town; more than 30,000,000 roubles have been spent on it; life here will always flow. Although in this capital of Manchuria not a single street along which you may safely walk or travel successfully since bridges and sidewalks are almost entirely absent, on the other hand the town possesses theatres, first-class restaurants and luxurious nightclubs, albeit be sure with incredible prices.[17]

Among the new buildings in Harbin was a merchants' hall built along the lines of the general store Muir and Mirrielees in Moscow. Representatives of many domestic and foreign firms were to be found there.[18]

In addition to Russians and Chinese, Japanese also gradually returned after the war while there were some Koreans in the city, too, and a handful of Europeans. Medical care improved, schools increased in number and variety, while Scout troops were among other new organisations. St Sophia Cathedral was completed in 1907. A synagogue and a mosque followed.[19]

Political parties born of industrialised civilisation also arrived, some of them determined to overthrow the tsarist regime as a whole. Strikes supported or even fomented by Social Democrats broke out from 1905 onwards.

In 1907, Harbin was made an international settlement and the problem of control was made more difficult, especially when local millers on 29 April declared a one-day strike for International Workers' Day, 1 May. The local CER guard commander responded by arranging for detachments to be posted at the station and on the waterfront from seven in the morning on that day. The police chief ordered his men to have their weapons fully charged. On May Day, Chinese boatmen ferried workers and other citizens across the River Sunguri. As a crowd numbering about a thousand which had assembled in the municipal park on May Day began to disperse, others remained to listen to political speeches, waving flags and singing. A telegram of support from the Social Democratic faction in the State Duma was received. In the evening, another crowd gathered in the town gardens back across the river, many of them with tickets for the theatre, others with their children. Suddenly, the cry rang out of 'Soldiers,' and shots were fired above the heads of the crowd, which dispersed in panic. The Russian consul-general V. F. Liuba who happened to be there persuaded the chief of police to call his men off, and they were hissed and whistled as they left. Subsequently, the chief of police accused Liuba of inciting the crowd. In his response, the consul-general suggested that the police chief was perhaps attempting to provoke an international incident.[20]

On 7 December 1907, the anniversary of the demonstration of 1905, another one-day strike was called. An additional reason was the imminent trial of the Social Democratic faction in the Duma in St Petersburg. The CER administration was caught unawares, its investigators asserting that, more than coincidence, the choice of the day for the stoppage 'proves the ease with which strikes take place on a signal from without.' Of course, internal dissidence was a probable further cause.

For May Day 1908, another mass demonstration and a one-day strike were planned. The CER gendarmes tried to forestall trouble by making some previous arrests, but could not prevent a crowd of about 10,000 gathering in a field across the Sungari. Proclamations were distributed, a group of young women marched with red flags and the Russian version of the Marseillaise was sung. The crowd was aroused by the announcement that among them listening to the speeches were two police informers, one of whom was beaten up while the other managed to escape.[21]

After reports of the incident reached St Petersburg, Prime Minister Stolypin asked Finance Minister Kokovtsov why the meeting in Harbin had not been dispersed. Kokovtsov replied that, since the CER ran through Chinese territory, General Manager Khorvat could not himself declare 'martial law' or other kinds of 'protection,' and could call on the frontier guard only if there were 'extreme necessity.' The possibility of injury to Chinese or other foreigners inhibited Khorvat's freedom of action further, while the administrative structure of the CER acted as a further restraint on its General Manager. In addition, there was a suspicion on the part of some bureaucrats that the CER was politically untrustworthy.[22]

At least some Far Eastern politicians in the Duma were also suspicious of the CER. For example, in 1908, the Social Democrat from the Amur Region F. N. Chilikhin regretted that peaceful relations with China had been endangered by the decision to build the railway through Manchuria. The Constitutional Democrat (Kadet) N. V. Volkov from the Transbaikal Region agreed, claiming that the building of the CER and the Russo-Japanese War were disasters for the economy and welfare of what he called 'our Far East.' Volkov also asserted that the enormous investments in Port Arthur and Dalny had been made at the expense of Vladivostok and the Far East.[23]

Peaceful politics were to be found in 1908 and 1910, in elections to the Assembly of the representative Harbin public administration, including Chinese participation. The Assembly's activity was somewhat restricted by the refusal of the USA and other states to recognise the municipal government in Harbin which led to some non-payment of local taxes. But the administration was able to remain solvent because of subsidies from the CER which also kept up a slaughterhouse, a hospital and a fire brigade. In other towns, the authorities banned access to foreign shops which quickly led the owners to change their minds about taxation.[24]

Academic activity was to be found in the development of linguistic and more general study of the culture of the Orient, as an aid to the promotion of trade but also as a means of developing understanding. Early in 1909, the Society of Russian Orientalists (ORO) was founded in Vladivostok, and helped to lead to the creation of a similar organisation in Harbin towards the end of the year. ORO limited membership to those who were actively interested in its aims. With a government subsidy, it obtained rooms in the Railway Assembly. (It was an independent organisation until 1927, when it merged with another academic organisation – the Society for the Study of the Manchurian Region.)[25] From 1909 to 1916, the ORO in Harbin published its own journal, *Vestnik Azii* (*Herald of Asia*), recording political and other developments in Manchuria.

At a non-academic level, many Russians knew at least a few words of Chinese, while rather more Chinese found it worth their while to learn some Russian in their shops, restaurants or laundries. The Chinese had their own newspaper and theatre, too. Of course, as well as those who sought close cultural acquaintance with Manchuria, there were some who wanted to add it to the Russian Empire.

In October 1909, the Minister of Finance Kokovtsov came to Harbin for a meeting with Prince Hirobumi Ito, a high-ranking official who had participated in the negotiations leading up to the Anglo-Japanese agreement of 1902 and played an important part in the preparations for the war against Russia in 1904 and then the movement towards the annexation of Korea that was to take place in 1910. On 13 October, Ito was given a full ceremonial welcome at the main Harbin station. During the following inspection of a guard of honour, a young, smartly dressed Korean broke through the ranks, shot Ito dead and wounded three members of his entourage. The assassin offered no resistance to arrest, but shouted out 'Long live Korea!' It emerged that he was a participant in a plot to kill Ito. Subsequently, the princely corpse was conveyed by train to Dairen, with a guard of honour at each station, and thence by boat to Japan. There were no serious immediate repercussions, although the Korean community in Harbin was increasingly concerned about the fate of their country. And the Priamur Governor Unterberger told Kokovtsov that 'as a result of the incident, Japan would soon attack Russia.' The rumour reached St Petersburg strongly enough for the tsar to send a minister to investigate. But he found nothing to worry about seriously.[26]

From 1910, Russian apprehension about international conflict continued. In May, War Minister V. A. Sukhomlinov ordered the commanders in the Priamur, Irkutsk and Omsk districts to consider their plans for mobilisation in case of a clash with China or Japan. Unsuccessful trade negotiations with China were followed by an ultimatum to China on 18 February 1911. On 6 April, the General Staff reported Chinese military preparation for an attack on Russia in Manchuria with a further warning from the staff section of the CER guard.[27] On the same day, the Finance Minister Kokovtsov who was also supervisor of the CER asked the Prime Minister Stolypin to allow the recall of CER guardsmen from Manchurian consulates and police stations. In addition, Russia sought collaboration with Japan to counter the threat from China. In May, N. A. Malevskii-Malevich, the Russian ambassador in Japan, proposed that the three powers arrange a rapprochement which would limit the Chinese military presence in the Manchurian railway zone. However, the Japanese Foreign Minister Komara pooh-poohed the suggestion as an exaggeration of the Chinese threat. Russian unease about Chinese intentions was not dispelled, however, and after Stolypin was assassinated on 1 September 1911, his replacement as Prime Minister Kokovtsov planned reinforcements for Manchuria. For its part, the Japanese government continued to worry more about an attack from Russia than any move by China. In July, Marshal Yamagata Aritomo wrote to governmental ministers that 'Russia is holding a grudge against us at all levels of society … . It is inevitable that Russia will try to revenge us early or late.'[28] On the other hand, the renewal of the Anglo-Japanese Agreement in 1911, which appeared to bring Japan closer to the Triple Entente, was accompanied by a series of Russo-Japanese agreements, for example bringing to an end claims held over from the War of 1904–5 and confirming the territorial rights of both sides.

The Mongolian question

Late in 1911, revolution in China overthrew centuries of imperial rule and established a republic. In order to preserve national unity, the first President Sun Yat-sen soon yielded power to a 'strong man' General Yuan Shih-kai who maintained his authority up to his death in 1916 soon after proclaiming himself Emperor in succession to the boy Emperor Pu Yi who had abdicated in 1912. Although the main action was to the south, there were some significant developments in Manchuria and adjacent regions, Mongolia in particular.

The Viceroy of the Three Provinces Zhao Erxun managed to hold on to power against the revolution at first while both Russia and Japan scented opportunities for takeover. General Khorvat, the manager of the CER in Harbin observed that 'the annexation of Manchuria is a question between Japan and Russia' while General E. I. Martynov, the commander of the local CER guard, suggested: 'The current storm in China presents immediate opportunities for Russia. So I hope this complication lingers. During this time, Russia should make collaborative efforts with Japan in winning territorial rights, and settle pending diplomatic issues with China.'[29] However, a Japanese plan for an incursion into Manchuria was opposed by Britain, Germany and the USA. Meanwhile, amid much talk of various railway extensions into Mongolia, Khorvat proposed that Russian troops be deployed in China to forestall Yuan Shih-kai's military intervention in Mongolia. But Foreign Minister S. D. Sazonov declared that the CER forces should remain neutral. Champing at the bit, local forces entered the Russo-Chinese border station at Manzhouli, but concentrated their efforts on Mongolia.

Russia consolidated its influence in Mongolia as Japan completed its 'amalgamation' of Korea after the agreement of July 1910. The Paris newspaper *Le Temps* reported that secretly Japan had assured Russia of a free hand in Mongolia as compensation for its takeover of Korea. In February and March 1911, the Russian Minister in Peking presented the Chinese government with a series of notes on trade culminating in a demand on 24 March that Russian terms be accepted in three days. *The Times* of London correspondent in Peking commented: 'The Chinese government was unable to understand the reason for the Russian Press campaign of intimidation, nor could foreigners at Peking reconcile the hostile *communiqués* issuing from St Petersburg with the pacific assurances given in Peking.' Nevertheless, China conceded all of Russia's demands with apologies.[30]

While Russia and Japan protested together against China's completion of a Manchurian Development and Currency loan with the syndicate of banks from the 'Four Nations' (Britain, France, Germany and the USA), the British Foreign Secretary Sir Edward Grey recognised that 'Russia and Japan had special interests in Mongolia and Manchuria' in a speech to the House of Commons on 11 June 1911. He accepted the Russian and Japanese declarations that the process of the partition of China had proceeded far enough for Japan's rights and special interests to be recognised 'in the regions of South Manchuria and the Eastern portion of Inner Mongolia adjacent to South Manchuria' along with those of Russia 'in the regions of Northern Manchuria, Mongolia and Western China.' Grey was not alone among European statesmen in accepting Russian and Japanese encroachment on Manchuria and Mongolia, the USA alone continuing to hope that the assurances of the Great Powers to China regarding its integrity and sovereignty could be maintained.[31]

An official of the Russian Ministry of Foreign Affairs, V. V. Grave, observed in 1912 following an expedition of 1910 that the situation regarding Chinese colonisation in Northern Manchuria was not dangerous, but it was 'threatening.' It would be better for Russian interests and security of possessions if the region were empty or populated by friendly colonists. The policy of the Chinese government after the Russo-Japanese War had been to send settlers. A total of two million was not likely to increase immediately after the Chinese Revolution of

1911, but could grow in ten to twenty years. Therefore, taking into consideration both the Russo-Japanese agreement of 1910 on the one hand and the continuing disorder in China on the other, Grave suggested:

> We are at the present time still masters of the situation in Northern Manchuria and on us depends the creation of circumstances favourable to our aims in the Far East in general and the Priamur District in particular, which unfortunately is economically dependent on the Chinese provinces bordering.[32]

The difficulty of adhering to international agreements made at the Hague Peace Conferences and elsewhere was illustrated by the mission to St Petersburg in July 1912 of the Japanese Prince Katsura. In June, the journal *Osaka Mainichi* had already announced that the object of the mission was

> to unite Japan, Great Britain and Russia in one agreement with regard to their Far Eastern policy. Japan and England being already combined for that purpose, it remained to bring Russia within the same orbit and thus to create a great political confederation which would exert a controlling influence over the doctrines of Eastern Asia.

The Pall Mall Gazette in London observed:

> The day may come when the principle which the Anglo-Japanese Alliance was framed to up hold – namely the maintenance of the territorial integrity of China – will have to be abandoned … . Even as matters now stand, neither Russia's recent action in Mongolia, nor British action in Tibet, nor Japan's special position in Manchuria, can be fully consonant with the upholding of that principle.

A special correspondent from *The Daily Telegraph* in London praised the statecraft of the Russian negotiator A. P. Izvolsky for reversing the previous policy of making common cause with China. He had been told by Katsura that, if Russia and Japan had understood each other more fully before 1904, 'history would have no sanguinary Russian campaign to record.' The correspondent pointed out that the results of the conversations were bold indeed:

> The destinies of the Far East will now be taken in hand by the Government of Japan and Russia, not indeed for the purpose of narrow, egoistic aims, but with a firm resolve to discharge what they regard as their cultural mission in that part of the globe, unhindered by the impulses of amateur outsiders, whose excellent intentions outrun their sense of political fitness.

The Americans were perhaps not alone in being considered 'amateur outsiders'; some Europeans might have been included too in this category, while J. O. P. Bland was to write of 'this cold-blooded and deliberate pact to dismember China.'[33]

First World War and Russian Revolution   67

The Russian position on the Far East was put by the Foreign Minister S. D. Sazonov in a speech of 26 April 1912:

> Northern Mongolia, or Khalka, has seceded from China, and entreated her Slav neighbour to espouse her cause. Some Russians have clamoured for the promulgation of a Protectorate, others have anathematised all forms of activity, whether intervention or mediation; but the Government has chosen the happy medium between these excesses. Inner Mongolia gravitates towards the South Manchurian Railway zone, Eastern Mongolia belongs to Manchuria; Northern Mongolia, which is sundered from China by the Gobi Desert, conserves a physiognomy of its own. The inhabitants of this province are nomads governed by princes. The Chinese element is independent.
>
> The secession was brought about by China persistently ignoring the institutions, customs and needs of the population, and attempting to quarter troops among them, to give them a Chinese Administration and to colonise the country. The Pontiff, or Kutukhtu, headed a successful Separatist movement. But Mongolia is unprepared for independence, lacking as she does leaders, money, and the army. Her separation from China would therefore compel Russia to occupy the country, or else permit the Chinese to re-enter it as conquerors. Anxious to escape from the embarrassing dilemma, the Russian Government agreed to mediate between China and Mongolia on three conditions: China must cease colonising the country, stationing troops there, and sending Chinese administrators thither.
>
> I myself fail to perceive grounds forcible enough to compel us to admit that the annexation of Northern Mongolia would be beneficial to us. Our interests require only that in conterminous Mongolia there should be no strong military State. Thanks to the neighbourhood of the Mongolians, our Siberian frontier is better protected than if we built fortresses along it, and stationed formidable garrisons there.[34]

Some semi-official newspapers in St Petersburg were pressing for Russian expansion into Sinkiang, which bordered on Tibet, giving testimony that the Great Game with Britain was not over and that the problems of empire as set out by Chancellor Gorchakov in 1864 persisted. Certainly, along with its neighbour Manchuria, Mongolia remained a constant in Russian geopolitical thinking.

The Mongols had indeed broken away from China after the revolution of 1911 and established an independent Outer Mongolia under a Buddhist religious leader, the Hutukhta (called the Kutukhtu by Bland), at the end of 1912. Far from being alarmed, the Russian government encouraged the formation of the new state and established a protectorate over it, the Russo-Mongolian Treaty signed just before independence giving Russians a preferred economic status and setting up a Russo-Mongolian Bank in the new capital, Urga. The Mongolian government agreed not to conclude any treaty with a foreign power without the Russian agreement. The Chinese government insisted on sovereignty in Mongolia, but recognised its autonomy. As for the Japanese, secure in Korea and South Manchuria, the extension of Russian influence was in harmony with previous agreements on spheres of influence, reinforced by a further secret agreement of 8 July 1912. Japan and Russia collaborated in resistance to American, British, French and German encroachments into Manchuria and Mongolia via loans to the new Chinese government for industrial development. Like Manchuria, Mongolia would soon be swept by the revolutionary wave arriving from European Russia after originating in the First World War.

The arrival of war and revolution

As the July 1914 crisis led towards the outbreak of that great conflict in Europe early in August, neither the assassination of the Austrian Archduke nor the ensuing widespread outbreak of hostilities caused immediate alarm in the Russian Far East.

Nevertheless, for other reasons, at the outbreak of the First World War, to quote Ian Nish, 'Manchuria was not at peace,' its citizens having been severely disturbed by pneumonic plague since its arrival in 1910. Because of the extreme cold in winter, windows were never opened and so there was poor ventilation. A Government Plague Prevention Service had been financed by some of the Chinese Maritime Customs revenues to suppress it, but some ill-feeling between the races ensued, partly because there was a mass influx of refugees from the provinces of North China which had been ravaged by famine brought about by severe drought.[35]

However, the economy was not severely hampered; indeed, there was a thriving trade in Moscow manufactures, sugar, tobacco, perfumes, footwear and rubber goods. Russians learned a lot about traditional Chinese agriculture in local conditions, while the Chinese benefitted from the arrival of tractors and other machinery. Here, as elsewhere, the CER had an important influence. General Khorvat himself was interested in agriculture, while the CER pavilion at the Russian exhibition in 1913 featured agriculture inter alia. Exports via Vladivostok consisted of locally grown agricultural produce, especially soybeans.[36] The Pacific sea route grew in importance as the overland railway experienced some difficulties. There was a considerable improvement in the streets and amenities of the city, paid for largely by the CER. Education was not seriously interrupted; indeed, new institutions were founded, including a flying school, just a few years after the first appearance of an aeroplane in 1911. The theatre and the newly arrived cinema thrived. A correspondent from the *Journal of the Ministry of Justice* (*Zhurnal ministerstva iustitsii*) reported:

> The physiognomy of Harbin is purely Far Eastern. One is struck by the variety of the population, the diversity in dress, the range of languages and speech. Here you can meet representatives of all the peoples of Europe, including Montenegrans, Serbs and Portuguese. On the streets of Harbin there are frequently to be found African negroes and a mixture of Indians, Persians and Turks.[37]

Some of these peoples, for example the Poles, had their own society and newspaper.

No doubt many of these immigrants joined in the patriotic demonstrations that greeted the outbreak of the war. And the Japanese joined their battle cry 'Banzai!' to the Russian 'Ura!' The Chinese officially remained neutral while many of the Germans left the city. Money and clothes were collected for the men at the front, and some of the CER employees were inspired to volunteer to join the war in the West. General Manager Khorvat later recalled:

> The officers especially were eager to join the ranks of the fighters, and some of them, without waiting for permission from Saint-Petersburg, left the railway secretly and were considered as deserters, until, much later, their names appeared in the lists of those who had distinguished themselves in battles in some army at the front.[38]

Khorvat himself was strongly against his forces being weakened by transfer to the battlefields, which would weaken the situation in Manchuria both economically and militarily. The response from the central government was insufficient to prevent a decline of Russian influence in the Far East. Although they themselves were far from united as well as under pressure from their Japanese rivals, the Chinese reinforced their presence in the region.

Meanwhile, growing concern about the infiltration of German spies centred on German tradesmen in Vladivostok along with breaking news of casualties and conscription led to a certain amount of apprehension. However, perhaps the most significant event of the early war years was the completion of a railway bridge a mile long over the Amur at Khabarovsk, making it possible for trains from St Petersburg to reach Vladivostok bypassing Manchuria from 1916 onwards. This realised the dream of transcontinental communication exclusively on Russian territory, but also promoted a nightmare. For, as John Stephan observes, 'the ribbon of steel linking the Far East to the Center served as a lightning rod for revolution.'[39]

In the shorter run, and nearer home, a friend aroused more apprehension than the enemy. Japan, allied to Russia, France and Britain, made Twenty-One Demands on China in January 1915. They included not only the acquisition of rights from Germany in Shantung Province which would include Kiaochow and elsewhere but also vast concessions to Japan in regions including Southern Manchuria and Inner Mongolia, along with an additional 99-year lease on Port Arthur, Dalny and South Manchurian Railways. Japan also asked for the right to continue and open mines as well as to build railways to the south. Japanese hospitals, temples and schools should be allowed to own land. Moreover, the Chinese government would be obliged to hire Japanese political, financial and military advisers, and to restrict the rights of other foreigners. B. L. Putnam Weale commented in June 1917:

> To study the original Chinese text is to pass as it were into the secret recesses of the Japanese brain, and to find in that darkened chamber a whole world of things which advertise ambitions mixed with limitations, hesitations overwhelmed by audacities, greatnesses succumbing to littlenesses, and vanities

having the appearance of velleities ... . One sees as it were the Japanese nation, released from bondage imposed by the Treaties which have been binding on all nations since 1860, swarming through the breached walls of ancient Cathay and disputing hotly the spoils of age-old domains.[40]

Putnam Weale's rhetoric was somewhat overblown, perhaps, but there could be no doubt about Japanese infiltration into China.[41]

The USA warned China and Japan that it would not recognise the Twenty-One Demands, but was hardly in a position to take any action. Partly in response to a perceived American threat, partly because the war in the West made its situation much weaker, Russia concluded a secret alliance with Japan in the summer of 1916 to counter any power 'harbouring hostile attentions' against them and their influence in China. The immediate prelude to the alliance was a mission to Japan by the Grand Duke Georgii Mikhailovich seeking supplies for the Russian army, which resulted in essential support for the Brusilov offensive against the Central Powers, on whom China was to declare war on 14 August 1917.[42]

This was a year after the Chengchiatun incident on 13 August 1916 when Japanese and Chinese troops clashed in a small but significant market town near the frontier between Manchuria and Inner Mongolia, each side blaming the other. Believing that their hold of Southern Manchuria and Inner Mongolia was essential to the balance of power in East Asia, the Japanese took advantage of the incident to consolidate their presence. The Chinese forces were commanded from Mukden by the 'Old Marshal,' Chang Tso-lin, who had been extending his power throughout Manchuria for some years.[43]

Large numbers of Russian soldiers, making the final sacrifice for their motherland on the European front, appeared to be enabling Japanese 'comrades' in ostensibly a common cause to extend their empire in China, reviving memories of their aggression in 1904–5. Putnam Weale observed in the summer of 1917: 'Now that the Romanoffs have been hurled from the throne, Russia must prove eager to reverse the policy which brought Japan to her Siberian frontiers and which pinned a brother democracy to the ground.'[44] In fact, as the former tsarist empire began to disintegrate, Russian soldiers and sailors too would find the expansionist activities of the Japanese forces ever more ambitious.

At the end of 1916, the *Kharbinskii Vestnik* (*Harbin Herald*) had observed:

> The approaching New Year will by common consent be the last year of the war. Will the general expectation of the end of the war in 1917 be justified? Most certainly, however, as the thirtieth month of the war comes close, the belligerent sides have accumulated great military resources exceeding those which they possessed at the war's beginning.

War losses had cooled the early ardour for war. Shortages cause some annoyance, exacerbated by smuggling and the illegal trade in drink and drugs. Moreover, the upkeep of troops involved huge expenditures.[45]

Some lines of verse were apprehensive about what a new war might bring:

Alarm spreads like the plague, –
The rumble of evil times …
Fate is bringing its mark
Close to you, Harbin … .

How many decades to wait
Who will be saved?
Children will quickly forget
The language of their fathers.[46]

In 1917 in Harbin in fact, the fall of the tsar led to a period of jostling for power as a series of meetings were held and committees formed. One speaker praised the counter-revolutionary General Kornilov as a patriot. But when news of the 'October' Revolution reached Harbin on 7 November soon after it occurred according to the New Style calendar, there were great celebrations by the police and soldiers, and the Executive Committee of the time was divided and therefore helpless. The situation crystallised as a straight fight between Khorvat, the director of the CER and the bourgeoisie on the one hand and the Bolsheviks supported by the lower classes on the other. The local foreign consuls sided with Khorvat. After further toing and froing, when Lenin ordered the Bolsheviks to seize power on behalf of the proletariat on 4 December, Khorvat invited a Chinese force about 500 strong to support him, and the Bolsheviks were reduced to asking for his collaboration. After several days of frenzied activity but virtual stalemate, Trotsky sent a telegram on the night of the 12–13 December demanding that the commander of the Chinese force be arrested, foreigners ordered to leave and Khorvat replaced by a people's committee. But Khorvat managed to hold out, helped by the decision of the railwaymen to begin a general strike against the Bolsheviks. On 16 December, advance units of a Chinese expeditionary force from the Old Marshal in Mukden began to arrive. Russian troops and militia were powerless to stop them, and Khorvat accepted a Chinese replacement, while the Bolsheviks were in disarray. Rosemary Quested concluded: 'The Chinese Army was now for a decisive moment the master of the CER zone. It was the first time that it had ever happened that a large body of Europeans had become reduced to anarchy and been brought under the control of Chinese troops.'[47]

The Russian Revolution and international relations

When tsarism fell in March 1917, the USA as well as Britain and France were quick to recognise the new Provisional Government. The USA joined in the war in April, with President Woodrow Wilson proclaiming that the overthrow of Nicholas II meant that the Allies were now fighting to make the 'world safe for democracy.' But when the Russian government was taken over by Lenin and his comrade Bolsheviks in November 1917 in the name of the socialist Soviets, both the USA and the Allies held back from recognition. Understandably enough, they were reluctant to have dealings with extremists who soon dissolved a Constituent

Assembly on the grounds that the Soviets represented a higher form of democracy, who were dedicated to the overthrow of world capitalism and demonstrated that they meant anti-business by repudiating tsarist foreign debts and nationalising foreign assets. And how could there be relations with a regime that was quick to issue a Decree on Peace abolishing secret diplomacy, annulling annexations, declaring an armistice and calling on workers involved in the war to support the movement for peace? If anything, the policy of the first People's Commissar for Foreign Affairs was even more radical. Describing his approach as 'active internationalism,' Leon Trotsky announced: 'I will issue a few revolutionary proclamations to the people of the world and then shut up shop.'[48] With the Central Powers bearing down on Soviet Russia, however, business had to be done. After lengthy negotiations necessarily quelling the appetite of some of Lenin's colleagues for revolutionary war, the Treaty of Brest-Litovsk making vast territorial concessions to the enemy, was finally signed on 3 March 1918.

Meanwhile, President Wilson had issued Fourteen Points for peace on 7 January 1918, acknowledging that the Russian representatives at Brest-Litovsk were 'sincere and earnest' while a voice calling for definitions of principle and purpose 'more thrilling than any of the moving voices with which the troubled air of the world is filled' was that of the Russian people. Wilson called for the evacuation of all Russian territory pending 'an unhampered and unembarrassed opportunity for the independent determination of her own political development and national policy' as well as for other readjustments capped by a 'general association of nations ... forced under specific covenants for the purpose of affording mutual guarantees of political independence and national integrity to great and small states alike.'[49]

On 20 January 1918, Acting Secretary of State F. I. Polk in Washington sent a telegram to the US ambassador in Japan, and copies to his counterparts in Britain, France and China. Polk declared that 'any movement towards the occupation of Russian territory would at once be construed as one hostile to Russia' opposing the occupation of Vladivostok in particular. On 8 February, the State Department sent a memorandum to these same representatives as well as to their counterparts in Belgium and Italy, opposing a British proposal to encourage and assist certain organisations in south and southeast Russia and to allow the Japanese army to take over the railway in Manchuria. On 5 March, Polk told the US ambassador in Japan to advise the Japanese government against intervention. Otherwise, he argued, 'the Central Powers could and would make it appear that Japan was doing in the East exactly what Germany was doing in the West.'[50]

After Japanese and British landings in Vladivostok early in April 1918, Trotsky's replacement as Commissar for Foreign Affairs G. N. Chicherin sent the first of many notes of protest to the US and other Allied governments. Nevertheless, the US government decided in June to send troops to Murmansk in Northern Russia with the aim of reinforcing the war against Germany, a step also taken by the British government. In July, under pressure from the Supreme War Council in Paris, the US government agreed to join in the Far Eastern intervention in Vladivostok, ostensibly for the protection of Czecho-Slovak troops formerly prisoners of war of the Central Powers and now located at different points along the Trans-Siberian Railway.[51]

The American government adhered to its avowed limited aims throughout the summer of 1918. However, on 24 October, Chicherin sent a long note to President Wilson accusing the USA of complicity in a Czecho-Slovak conspiracy (financed by France to control the Trans-Siberian Railway and cut off supplies to the peasants along the Volga and in Siberia) as well as participation in an invasion of the North. While pressing for the independence of European nations under the aegis of the League of Nations, the US President had said nothing about the liberation of Ireland, Egypt or India or even of the Philippines. The League of Nations should annul war loans and expropriate the capitalists of all countries. Only thus could peace be guaranteed and the exploitation of workers everywhere curtailed. In the light of these demands, the negative response to an offer of 8 November from Chicherin to negotiate with the USA and the other Allies for the end of intervention was hardly surprising. On 2 December, Chicherin made an even more vigorous protest against the intervention in support of the Czecho-Slovaks and the anti-Red White Guards.[52]

Of course, by this time the Armistice had been signed on 11 November 1918, the war was over and the stated aim of intervening to support the struggle against Germany no longer valid. On 27 November, Wilson's Secretary of War Newton D. Baker urged President Wilson to 'simply order our forces home by the first boat,' primarily because he feared that otherwise the USA might be

> rudely awakened some day to a realization that Japan has gone in under our wing and so completely mastered the country that Japan cannot be either induced out or forced out by any action either of the Russians or the Allies.[53]

However, despite Baker's exhortation, the USA became more deeply embroiled in the Russian Civil War. In spite of warnings from William C. Graves, the commander of the US expeditionary force in Vladivostok, about the reactionary nature of the Siberian regime led by Admiral Kolchak, the US government joined with the British, French and Japanese in lending him support. Little if any attention was paid to the observation by Graves that the peasant choice would be a more responsible and representative government, which, in the circumstances, would appear unobtainable anyway.[54]

Conclusion

To sum up, mourning their soldiers who had died in foreign fields, sometimes together, the Russians and Japanese had managed to avoid further conflict between the Revolutions of 1905 and 1917, largely because of different spheres of interest. Russia concentrated on Northern Manchuria and Mongolia, Japan on Southern Manchuria and Korea. However, both powers experienced tension with China, hardly surprising since they were trespassers on Chinese territory. The former adversaries managed to preserve good relations through much of the First World

74 *First World War and Russian Revolution*

War, even after Japan's notorious Twenty-One Demands on China, with which Russia acquiesced.

The capital of Russia in Manchuria, Harbin, continued to develop, although revolutionary activity continued after 1905. The outbreak of war in 1914 led in the short run to more anxiety than disturbance, but the situation deteriorated as October followed February in the Russian Revolution of 1917. As the Allies launched their military intervention in the Far East, the Western powers showed some concern about the intentions of Japan.

Notes

1 Quoted in Felix Patrikeef and Harold Shukman, *Railways and the Russo-Japanese War: Transporting War* (London: Routledge, 2007), p. 118; Rana Mitter, *China's War with Japan. 1937–1945: The Struggle for Survival* (London: Allen Lane, 2013), p. 25.
2 Hugh Seton-Watson, *The Russian Empire, 1801–1917* (Oxford: Oxford University Press, 1967), pp. 681–3.
3 See David MacLaren McDonald, *United Government and Foreign Policy in Russia, 1906–1914* (Cambridge, MA: Harvard University Press, 1992), for a distinctive and comprehensive approach.
4 John Stephan, *The Russian Far East: A History* (Stanford: Stanford University Press, 1994), pp. 96–7.
5 Vladimir Sokolov, 'Tropoiu Arsen'eva k istoricheskoi antropologii voennogo vostokovedeniia DV Rossii nachala XX veka', in Vladimir Klavdievich Arsen'ev, ed., *Sobranie sochinenii v 6 tomakh*, Tom III (Vladivostok: Rubezh, 2012), pp. 702, 712–3. Arsenev became Commissar for Alien Affairs of the Maritime Region in the early 1920s before falling under the suspicion of the Soviet authorities later in the decade.
6 Richard Storry, *Japan and the Decline of the West in Asia, 1894–1943* (London: Macmillan, 1979), pp. 82–3.
7 Ibid., p. 101; Michael H. Hunt, *Frontier Defense and the Open Door: Manchuria in Chinese-American Relations, 1895–1911* (New Haven: Yale University Press, 1973), pp. 204–16.
8 B. L. Putnam Weale, *The Coming Struggle in Eastern Asia* (London: Macmillan, 1909), 'Preface to the Second Edition' October 1908, pp. vii, ix, xiii, xiv.
9 Ibid., pp. 103, 159, 168–9, 205, 234.
10 Ibid., pp. 541–3.
11 Ibid., pp. 632, 637–8.
12 Quoted by Asada Masafumi, 'The China-Russia-Japan Military Balance in Manchuria, 1906–1918', *Modern Asian Studies*, Vol. 44, No. 6 (2010), p. 1294.
13 Quoted by J. O. P. Bland, *Recent Events and Present Policies in China* (London: William Heinemann, 1912), pp. 337–8.
14 Ibid., p. 338.
15 David Wolff, *To the Harbin Station: The Liberal Alternative in Russian Manchuria, 1898–1914* (Stanford: Stanford University Press, 1999), p. 158; Hugh Seton-Watson, *The Russian Empire, 1801–1917* (Oxford, 1967), pp. 656–7.
16 David Wolff, 'Russia Finds Its Limits: Crossing Borders into Manchuria', in Stephen Kotkin and David Wolff, eds., *Rediscovering Russia in Asia: Siberia and the Russian Far East* (London: Routledge, 1995), pp. 44–8.
17 G. V. Melikhov, *Man'chzhuriia: dalekaia i blizkaia* (Moscow: Nauka, 1991), p. 194. Melikhov does not give the leading journalist's name, nor for which of several newspapers he wrote.
18 Melikhov, *Man'chzhuriia*, pp. 188–9.

19 Ibid., pp. 204, 207–13, 256–7.
20 Ibid., pp. 199–201; Wolff, *To the Harbin Station*, pp. 142–3.
21 Wolff, *To the Harbin Station*, p. 143.
22 Ibid., pp. 143–5.
23 Ivan Sablin, *The Rise and Fall of Russia's Far Eastern Republic, 1905–1922: Nationalisms, Imperialisms, and Regionalisms in and after the Russian Empire* (London: Routledge, 2019), pp. 56, 66–7.
24 Melikhov, *Man'chzhuriia*, pp. 201–2.
25 Ibid., pp. 205–7.
26 Ibid., pp. 223–4; Raymond A. Esthus, *Double Eagle and Rising Sun: The Russians and Japanese at Portsmouth in 1905* (Durham: Duke UP, 1988), p. 198.
27 Masafumi, 'The China-Russia-Japan Military Balance', p. 1296.
28 Ibid., p. 1297.
29 Ibid., p. 1300.
30 Bland, *Recent Events*, pp. 339–41.
31 Ibid., pp. 341–2.
32 V. V. Grave, *Kitaitsy, Koreitsy i Iapontsy v Priamur'e: Trudy komandirovannoi po vysochaishemu poveleniiu amurskoi ekspeditsii, vypusk XI* (St. Peterburg: Tipografiia V.F. Kirshbauma, 1912), pp. 346–7.
33 Bland, *Recent Events*, pp. 343–6.
34 Ibid., pp. 347–9.
35 Melikhov, *Man'chzhuriia*, p. 187; Ian Nish, *The History of Manchuria, 1840–1948: A Sino-Russo-Japanese Triangle*, 2 vols. (Folkestone: Renaissance Books, 2016), Vol. 1, *Historical Narrative*, pp. 75, 87–8.
36 David Wolff, 'Bean There! Towards a Soy-Based History of Northeast Asia', *The South Atlantic Quarterly*, Vol. 99, No. 1 (2010), pp. 241–55.
37 Melikhov, *Man'chzhuriia*, p. 300. A local journalist in addition spotted people from Australia and Java.
38 Masafumi, 'The China-Russia-Japan Military Balance', p. 1305.
39 John J. Stephan, *The Russian Far East: A History* (Stanford: Stanford UP, 1994), pp. 108–9.
40 B. L. Putnam Weale, *The Fight for the Republic in China* (London: Hurst and Blackett, 1918), p. 71.
41 A. I. Krushanov and others, *Istoriia Severo-Vostochnogo Kitaia, XVII–XXvv.*, kniga 1 (Vladivostok: Dal'nevostochnoe izdatel'stvo, 1987), pp. 342–3, 360–1.
42 B. A. Romanov, *Russia in Manchuria (1892–1906)* (Ann Arbor: American Council of Learned Societies, 1952), first published in Leningrad in 1928, p. 25.
43 Putnam Weale, *The Fight*, pp. 221–5, 227–8.
44 Ibid., p. 279.
45 P. T. 'K voprosu o denezhnem krizise v Severnoi Man'chzhurii', *Vestnik Azii*, No. 11–12 (1916), pp. 43–4.
46 Melikhov, *Man'chzhuriia*, p. 315.
47 R. K. I. Quested, *"Matey" Imperialists? The Tsarist Russians in Manchuria 1895–1917* (Hong Kong: Centre of Asian Studies, University of Hong Kong), p. 324 after her summary of events of the Revolution in Harbin, pp. 308–24. See also A. I. Krushanov and others, *Istoriia svero-vostochnogo Kitaia XVII–XX vv.*, Vol. 2, *Severo-Vostochnyi Kitai 1917–1949gg.* (Vladivostok: Dal'nevostochnoe knizhnoe izdatel'stvo, 1989), pp. 14–5.
48 Quotation from E. H. Carr, *The Bolshevik Revolution*, Vol. 3 (Harmondsworth: Penguin, 1966), p. 26, note 2, with the additional explanation given by Trotsky as quoted by one of his associates: 'I wanted to have more time for party affairs.'
49 Harold J. Goldberg, ed., *Documents of Soviet-American Relations*, Vol. 1, *Intervention, Famine Relief, International Affairs, 1917–1933* (Gulf Breeze, Florida: Academic International, 1993), pp. 262–3.

50 Paul Dukes, *The USA in the Making of the USSR: The Washington Conference, 1921–1922, and 'Uninvited Russia* (Abingdon: RoutledgeCurzon, 2004), pp. 7–8.
51 Ibid., pp. 71–91. Since Czechoslovakia was not officially created before 28 October, I have adopted the term 'Czecho-Slovak' widely used before and even after that date.
52 Ibid., pp. 112–22.
53 Arno J. Mayer, *Politics and Diplomacy of Peacemaking, Containment and Counter-Revolution at Versailles, 1918–1919* (New York: Knopf, 1967), pp. 329–30.
54 Goldberg, Documents, Vol. 1, pp. 122–8; David S. Foglesong, *America's Secret War against Bolshevism: U.S. Intervention in the Russian Civil War 1917–1920* (Chapel Hill: North Carolina UP, 1995), pp. 179–87.

5 Soviet Russia, Imperial Japan and the USA
Harbin, 1918–29

The Paris Conference: revolution, civil war and intervention in the Far East

Soon after the Armistice of November 1918, the Peace Conference opened in Paris in January 1919, with US President Wilson keen to push his Fourteen Points for peace in the face of the scepticism of British Prime Minister Lloyd George and the French Premier Clemenceau, who complained that God Almighty had made no more than Ten. The Japanese delegation failed to get support for its suggestion that the equality of nations be recognised. It also found acceptance of the takeover of German rights in the Shantung peninsula and the Pacific Islands difficult to obtain until it revealed that Britain, France, Italy and the USA had pledged them in secret treaties of 1917; it threatened to stay out of the League of Nations if the promise was not kept. China, which had entered the war after much Allied pressure in February 1917, acquiesced with reluctance.

Regarding the other Far Eastern power, Russia, on 22 January the Big Three adopted a proposal for every organised group exercising political authority or military control anywhere in Siberia or Europe to come to Prinkipo Island near Istanbul for discussion with representatives of the Allies about achieving 'happy co-operative relations' between the Russian peoples and the other peoples of the world. Commissar for Foreign Affairs Chicherin, who had been continuing his denunciation of intervention along with his appeals for peace, gave a positive response on 4 February to the invitation that had been broadcast by radio to the Soviet government and its opponents, offering to repay the tsarist foreign debts among other concessions. However, the White opposition in Paris joined the sceptical French and American representatives to speak out against any dealings with the Bolsheviks. Woodrow Wilson, who insisted that he was not looking for 'a rapprochement with the Bolsheviks,' nevertheless later in February sent a representative from the State Department, William C. Bullitt, to Moscow to explore the possibilities of peace with Lenin and his comrades. In return for the cessation of the Allied Intervention in Russia and recognition of de facto governments on the territory of the former Russian Empire, the Bolsheviks were prepared to offer a general amnesty while reiterating their readiness to repay tsarist foreign debts although insisting that, because of their parlous financial position, the Russian

DOI: 10.4324/9781003161769-5

gold seized by the Czecho-Slovaks in Siberia or taken from Germany by the Allies would be regarded by them as part payment. Disappointed by Wilson's reaction to the Bolshevik concessions, Bullitt resigned from the State Department on 17 May, observing that Russia had not been understood while the USA had not acted in the spirit of Wilson's Fourteen Points. In spite of Bullitt's remarks and further reservations by General Graves about the lack of popular support for Admiral Kolchak in Siberia, Wilson joined the Allies in an invitation of 26 May to the White leader 'to form a single government and army command' as soon as the military situation made it possible and provided that he accepted the principle of democracy. Kolchak's response was accommodating, but his subsequent behaviour was far from democratic.[1]

Meanwhile, in March 1919, excluded from the League of Nations and disappointed by the way negotiations with the Allies were failing, the Soviet Government set up the Communist International or Comintern. Trotsky wrote on May Day 1919 that the movement would soon spread to Berlin, Paris and London, but in fact, such wild hopes were attended by deep fears as Kolchak and other opponents, both Russian and interventionist, presented dire threats. The mood was to become even more excited in early September 1920, when the Comintern President G. E. Zinoviev told the First Congress of the Toilers of the East meeting in Baku that 'The real revolution will blaze up only when we are joined by the 800,000,000 people who live in Asia, when the African continent joins us.'[2]

Also in 1919, under the impact of the First World War, Halford J. Mackinder declared that a lasting peace would include 'a balance between German and Slav, and the independence of each.' For:

Who rules East Europe commands the Heartland:
Who rules the Heartland commands the World-Island:
Who rules the World-Island commands the world.[3]

But was he right to give such emphasis to East Europe when developments in the Far East were also of key importance for the whole world? Certainly, along with the ideas of Captain Mahan concerning the influence of sea power in history, those of Mackinder on continental significance played a leading part in geopolitical thought in the twentieth century through the Second World War and Cold War.[4]

It is high time indeed that we switch our attention from the diplomatic deliberations in Europe to the broader developments in Asia with a search for 'the real revolution.' After the October Revolution in the Russian Far East, while the Governor-General and his entourage, officials both secular and ecclesiastical, along with officers in the armed forces, were dismayed, much of the rest of the population, soldiers, sailors and Cossacks, along with merchants, workers and peasants, teachers and exiles, were enthusiastic. New organisations ranging from moderate zemstvos to radical political parties sprang up.

Party alignments were at first more fluid in the Far East than at the centre as Social Democrats often collaborated irrespective of Bolshevik or Menshevik affiliations. Mensheviks predominated in the major cities, Vladivostok, Khabarovsk and Harbin, but the Bolsheviks established their control after the October Revolution, easily in Vladivostok, with some difficulty in Khabarovsk. In Harbin, however, Chinese intervention in the shape of the forces of the Old Marshal based in Mukden forestalled a takeover by Lenin's supporters, as we have seen.

A feature of Bolshevik activity in the Far East was the participation of several Russian-born immigrants from Chicago. One of them, Alexander Krasnoshchekov was made chairman of the People's Commissariat of the Far East or *Dal'sovnarkom*.[5] But Krasnoshchekov in Khabarovsk could not control the region assigned to him or even the Bolsheviks in it, let alone other radical parties. The Socialist Revolutionaries were more popular in rural areas, and the call for the reconvention of the Constituent Assembly which had been dissolved back in Petrograd in January 1918 gave them a rallying cry. To be sure, most peasants, more locally focussed on their rights to their own land, would not have much interest in the niceties of the subject, and in any case, there were soon other organisations seeking their support who rejected the October and even the February Revolutions. Indeed, the Far East including Manchuria became a battlefield in which some of the most powerful forces were composed of monarchists or right-wing nationalists.

Prominent among them was Grigorii Mikhailovich Semyonov, who was ideally qualified for leadership in the region. The son of a Buryat Mongol mother and a Transbaikal Cossack father, he had served the tsar on the European front before being ordered by the Provisional Government in June 1917 to raise a force of Buryats and Cossacks for service on that same front. After the October Revolution, Semyonov made use of this force in an attempt to overthrow the Soviet regime. He failed, and retreated into Manchuria, where the Director of the Chinese Eastern Railway (CER), General Khorvat and the local Chinese authorities gave him asylum in Harbin. Subsidised by the Japanese, and with a force composed of Buryats, tsarist officers and cadets, Semyonov formed a Special Manchurian detachment, which invaded Transbaikalia in January 1918 with the avowed aim of liberating Buryat Mongolia. Attracting support from Cossacks, peasants and anti-Bolshevik socialists, as well as some Chinese, Korean, Japanese, Tatars and even Serbs, he advanced towards Chita. Driven back to Manchuria by Red Guards and 'internationalists' under Sergei Lazo, Semyonov counterattacked in April and was able to set up a 'Provisional Transbaikalian Government' before Lazo pushed him out again.[6]

The Civil War continued to ebb and flow through a porous frontier. A White force supported by Chinese and Japanese militia crossed the Amur from Manchuria to occupy Blagoveshchensk in March 1918, only to be overwhelmed by their Red enemies after a siege of three days, and then routed across the river. Also in March, another White force came from Manchuria with the aim of taking Grodekovo, about 90 miles to the north of Vladivostok. Again, a force of Red guards and 'internationalists' hurried to the defence of the town; several months of fighting ensued.

Soon, the pro-Soviet 'internationalists' found themselves along with their comrades in a wider conflict involving 'interventionists,' in particular with the Czecho-Slovak ex-POWS of the Central Powers supporting the anti-Bolshevik secessionist cause and going on the rampage throughout Siberia, the Far East and Manchuria in May and June 1918. As John Stephan puts it, 'the Czech coup set the stage for a Red victory by staining the White cause with Russian blood drawn by foreign bayonets.'[7]

In spite of all warnings, the British and Japanese forces landed in Vladivostok in early April 1918. In July, the US government agreed to join in the Far East intervention, ostensibly to collaborate with other interventionists for the protection of the ex-POW Czech troops located at various points along the Trans-Siberian Railway as well as of Allied military stores in Vladivostok. For its part, preoccupied with the sequel to the negotiations with the Central Powers at Brest-Litovsk, which included drastic withdrawal, the Soviet government had little power to resist Allied intervention with anything other than words.

A number of governments in and near Manchuria jostled for power in the aftermath of the Bolshevik collapse in the Far East, including, among others, Semenov's Buryat Mongol Republic in Chita and Khorvat's CER regime in Harbin. General D. L. Khorvat, General Manager of the CER from 1902, succeeded in holding Harbin against all rivals until March 1920, supported by the CER shareholders and the Russo-Asiatic Bank. Although his supporters talked of 'happy, blessed Khorvatiia,' the General's dictatorial policies led to a general strike on the CER ordered by the Soviet government and to the Chinese Government's protests at the threat to its sovereignty, and he was obliged to resign. The Soviet government made several disavowals of its rights in Manchuria, for example on 24 April 1921 renouncing 'all mining and lumber concessions in Manchuria,' and returning 'to China without compensation the Chinese Eastern Railway and everything that was forcibly seized by the tsarist government, the brigands Kolchak and Semyonov and the Russian bourgeoisie.'[8] However, until October 1922, the administration of the CER was taken over by an Inter-Allied Technical Board.

The continued uncertainty in Vladivostok during the period of Intervention was well caught by William Gerhardie in his novel *Futility*, in which a British Admiral, hailed as the 'new Lafayette,' jokingly works out a timetable for seeing clients:

> Dictators, say, from 7 to 10; supreme rulers between 10 and 1; prime ministers could be admitted between 2 and 5. Then till seven he would be free to cabinet ministers of the rank and file. Supreme commanders-in-chief could come from 8 to 1.

In return, four joint deputations representing the heads of four separate All-Russia Governments had apparently conferred on the fictional British Admiral something like 'the title of Supreme Commander-in-Chief of All the Armed Military and Naval Forces operating on the Territory of Russia.'[9]

Figure 8 General Dmitry Khorvat, military engineer and manager of the Far Eastern Railway, in the company of fellow officers from interventionist forces in Vladivostok in 1918. (Wikipedia)

The regime of the real Russian Admiral Kolchak, self-styled 'Supreme Ruler of the Russian State,' which at first promised to be the most formidable anti-Red force and received wide support from the Allies, was already in full retreat before the leader was executed by the Bolsheviks in Irkutsk at the beginning of 1920. A wide variety of partisan movements were to be found throughout the region, carrying out all kinds of atrocities, some of which were also perpetrated by the American, British and Japanese interventionists. By early 1920, the American and British Expeditionary Forces had left for home, while the Japanese lingered on until 1922, making use of local allies. Semyonov in Chita and Khorvat in Harbin received subsidies from them, while, to give another example, the Baltic Baron R. F. Ungern-Shternberg, formerly an officer with Semyonov, created his own force with Japanese patronage and participation and became 'military adviser' to an 'Independent Government' of Mongolia and launched an abortive offensive on Kiakhta in Soviet territory in May 1921.

The Soviet government had to do something about its fragile hold on the Far East. One useful stratagem was initiated on 7 March 1920 by the former chairman of the defunct *Dal'sovnarkom* A. M. Krasnoshchekov in the shape of a 'Provisional Government of Pribaikalia,' Lenin and Trotsky believing that such a buffer state could be controlled by themselves and their party. In April, a Far Eastern Republic (FER) was created in Verkhneudinsk near Lake Baikal with Krasnoshchekov as President, his fellow Chicagoan Bill Shatov as Minister of War and a declaration of independence in English. In 1921, a Special Far Eastern

Army was created: the NRA (People's Revolutionary Army), the military wing of the FER, was put under the command of V. K. Bliukher, an officer with experience in the Civil War. When Japan indicated that it would not object, Bliukher led a cosmopolitan force consisting of Buryat Mongols and Koreans as well as Russians and even Volga Germans on a series of sorties deep into Manchuria in October and November.

The FER did indeed perform an important role as a buffer state, keeping the Japanese and their White allies at bay until Vladivostok was retaken in October 1922. But Krasnoshchekov and his comrades by no means followed all instructions from Moscow, which was soon to incorporate the FER into the Soviet state. As John Stephan, whose account we have mostly followed here, aptly observes: 'Successful in expediting a Japanese withdrawal, Lenin's buffer state returned to haunt Moscow, for the independence charade had infected some players with a regionalist virus.'[10] Krasnoshchekov left for Moscow where, after a period of imprisonment, he became a government official until arrested and shot in the purges of 1937.[11]

The Washington Conference: Harbin and North Manchuria

The contribution of the FER was made not only within the confines of the Soviet Republic but also in the international sphere through the lobbying activity of its Trade Delegation at the Washington Conference on the Limitation of Armament and on the Pacific and Far Eastern Questions from November 1921 to February 1922, a little-known episode in 'one of the most significant, and overlooked diplomatic meetings in American history' according to a leading authority Walter LaFeber.[12] Through a series of treaties, the Conference established the USA as the world's major power, bringing to an end the special relationship between the United Kingdom and Japan, affording protection for China and limiting the size of the world's leading navies. Soviet Russia was excluded, but, although the FER Delegation failed to gain official recognition at the Conference, its members managed to meet Senators and other leading figures to put their case. Moreover, the FER's participation in conferences with Japan taking place in Manchuria, in Dairen and Changchun, albeit under increasing Soviet tutelage, helped to bring Japanese intervention to an end and put Japanese–Soviet relations on a more secure footing than might otherwise have been the case. However, towards the end of 1922, in November, the FER became an 'inseparable part' of the Russian Republic on the eve of the creation of the Union of Soviet Socialist Republics. In May 1923, the Buryat Mongol Autonomous Soviet Socialist Republic was created. The Far Eastern Territory (krai) was set up in 1926.[13]

By this time, the Soviet government had achieved a little publicised but extremely significant consolidation of its external relations in the shape of a treaty of mutual recognition with the Mongolian People's Republic (MPR) of 5 November 1921. Then, as E. H. Carr described the sequel, after the rear-guard action by 'a conservative pro-Chinese group drawn from the old lama class,' a further Soviet–Mongolian treaty of 31 May 1922 'made still more apparent the resumption by the Soviet government of the paramount role successfully asserted in Outer Mongolia by the last tsarist government.'[14] In effect, the MPR became a Soviet satellite, with a strong Red Army presence helping to maintain order on Manchuria's Western flank.

Soon after the Washington Conference closed, another was held in Genoa. The USA did not attend, while Russia reached an accommodation with Germany in nearby Rapallo in April 1922.

Regarding Manchuria itself, after tortuous negotiations, on 31 May 1924, the central Chinese government officially recognised the Soviet Union, which gave up in return the privileges previously enjoyed by itself and its citizens in China. In a temporary agreement on the administration of the CER, a joint Soviet and Chinese management was to exercise control with equal representation from both sides until China was able to purchase the railway, with the Soviet government assuming the role previously played by the Russo-Asiatic Bank. This agreement lasted, albeit not without difficulties, until a complete break in Sino-Soviet relations in 1929 led to outright hostilities.[15] Yet, on the frontier far away from Moscow and Peking, the edicts of the central government were not always implemented at once and in full.

The centre of the Soviet hold on Northern Manchuria was to become Harbin. We can follow the developments there through the diary of a participant in the public life of the city, Petr Vasil'evich Vologodskii, who provides much information and many insights. Born in a village in Tomsk province in 1863, he later lived in Tomsk itself soon after being expelled from St Petersburg for student political activity in 1887. Working in a number of administrative posts, he showed a major interest in Siberian regionalism, which brought him to the fore in 1918 as Chairman of the Council of Ministers of the Provisional Siberian Government (PSG) in Omsk. Soon, in order to gain wider recognition for the PSG's authority, he led a mission to the Far East from September to October 1918.

In Harbin, he made General Khorvat the PSG's Viceroy in the Far East as a means of achieving supreme authority for it. He met the British High Commissioner for Siberia Sir Charles Eliot, who suggested that official recognition might soon be given to the PSG; he discussed with the leading Japanese diplomat in Siberia, Count Tsuneo Matsudaira, the possibility of joint action against the Bolsheviks. However, when Admiral Kolchak seized power in Omsk in November 1918, Vologodskii found it difficult to maintain his position until Kolchak dismissed him in November 1919. Sensing danger, and taking advantage of an offer of places on a departing Japanese train, he went into exile with his wife and daughter, arriving again in Harbin on 29 January 1920. Just over a week later, on 7 February, his replacement as Chairman of the Council of Ministers of the PSG was shot along with Admiral Kolchak by the Bolsheviks.

In March 1920, Vologodskii moved on to Shanghai, hoping to use his legal expertise as a source of income from the local Russian community. His hopes dashed there, and then in Tianjin and Peking, he moved back to Harbin in the summer of 1922 after a friend had secured for him a post as an agent in the Juridical Department of the Main Administration of the CER.[16]

At this time, although Chinese officials were to be found in its higher levels, the CER was largely in the hands of Russians, who also constituted by far the greatest number of its 16,000 employees. As Semion Lyandres and Dietmar Wulff point out:

> the CER was still by far the largest employer in the region. It oversaw numerous repair shops and related facilities, and it owned land, health resorts, buildings, steamships, hospitals, printing houses, schools, and property all across the former right-of-way zone. No company, bank, or legal firm could hope to succeed without maintaining some sort of business relationship with the CER Administration and its offices. A variety of periodical publications depended almost entirely on subsidies from the CER, as did many educational, cultural, and charitable institutions.[17]

With a limited income, Vologodskii was not able to enjoy all that Harbin offered, but he went to the theatre, attended public lectures and even on occasion had a day at the races or enjoyed a game of billiards. He read avidly the news about the Soviet Union, hoping that it would collapse, and studied the Russian Revolution, comparing it with the French. He also tried to keep abreast of developments in China, and to understand them. He earned a little more money by writing book reviews for the newspaper *Russkii Golos* or *Russian Voice*.

On 1 May 1923, workers celebrated and Vologodskii witnessed a demonstration. He confessed on 6 May how difficult it would be for him to give up the 'rich, wide-ranging and happy' bourgeois life that he was used to, with amusements varying from the opera to the lotto. In fact, many of the old ways continued for a year or so in spite of all kinds of rumours and some threats.

In the fluid situation existing in Harbin, Vologodskii became concerned for his future. His anxiety grew when, on 24 September, the Soviet government signed a further agreement in Mukden with the Autonomous Provisional Government of the Three Eastern Provinces of the Republic of China under the Old Marshal Chang Tso-lin, confirming the loss by the Russians of their previous privileges. Almost immediately, the Chinese authorities replaced the chief manager of the CER with a Chinese official, and Vologodskii and many of his associates had to endure months of uncertainty. While he hesitated about applying for Chinese citizenship, his previous record making it impossible to apply for Soviet citizenship, a Chinese lawyer was given his position in the CER's Juridical Department.

From 9 April 1925, all Russian émigrés were to be dismissed from employment in the CER.[18] This was, so to speak, one of the last nails in Vologodskii's coffin. After a few failed attempts at making an alternative living, he went into a steep decline and died on 19 October 1925. Fortunately, through the devotion of his wife and daughter and the help of friends, his diary survived for later publication.[19]

The press in Harbin

The context of Vologodskii's life in Harbin may be illustrated through a survey of its press, which included a range of journals and newspapers, although most of them were of an ephemeral nature owing to a range of circumstances, varying from the political to the financial. Yet, other forms of cultural activity such as the theatre are even more ephemeral and evade description.

While there was some press activity before the Civil War, in the following years, there were no fewer than about 300 titles, 90% of which were in Russian. No other town beyond the frontiers of Russia produced anything like as many such publications. And, of course, there was an intermittent stream of publications reaching Harbin and the Far East from Moscow, Petrograd and other sources. The level of journalistic activity in Harbin in the 1920s may be a little surprising for a town with approximately 400,000 Russian inhabitants, but there was a range of other nationalities, too, many Chinese, some Japanese and at least a few Europeans.[20] Moreover, this was a frontier territory, a kind of Klondyke, with all kinds of adventurers seeking their fortune in any possible way as well as a large number of refugees from the Revolution and its sequel. For example, Ataman Semyonov put out a newspaper with the title *Svet* meaning *Light* or *World*, with a former Socialist Revolutionary as its editor but its content was ultra-reactionary. In spite of subsidies from the White government in Vladivostok, *Svet* collapsed in 1924.

First issued in 1920, *Zarya* or *Dawn* reached its zenith from 1922–3. It imported the title from Omsk, but soon lost the ideological baggage of support for Admiral Kolchak. Becoming the vehicle for light entertainment, it talked of its 'ringing' appeal. But it maintained a close connection with the local police authorities, who were largely White Guards, thus becoming the purveyor of piquant details concerning cases under confidential investigation. Indeed, *Zarya* became a popular scandal sheet, with many revelations concerning secrets of the boudoir and personal feuds. It was anti-Soviet, even anti-Russian, but maintained its existence up to 1945. The unslaked thirst of readers as well as the desire for work of unemployed journalists led to the foundation of a rival newspaper, *Rupor* or *Megaphone*, which was published from 1921 to 1938.

After the demise of *Svet* in 1924, a new right-wing organ was created. *Russkoe Slovo*, or the *Russian Word*, nursed the hope of a crusade against Moscow and the reintroduction of monarchy. First appearing in 1920 as *Russkii Golos*, or the *Russian Voice*, it originally took a constitutional monarchist position in contrast to the ultra-reactionary *Svet*. But almost immediately it began to support Semyonov, then other White leaders such as Baron Wrangel. At the same time, it also expressed its agreement with Russian émigrés in Paris, Berlin and Prague, at first including the former Foreign Minister of the Provisional Government Pavel Miliukov. But when Miliukov lost support, *Russkii Golos* moved to the right at about the time that Vologodskii was writing for it, from 1923 favouring the revival of monarchy in Russia under the aegis of the Grand Duke Nikolai Nikolaevich. Edited by a former member of the State Duma S. V. Vostrotin, it received support from Paris, and later from Vladivostok. When Vladivostok fell to the Bolsheviks in 1924, it lost the patronage of the White administration of the CER, although giving its support to the Union without Party which opposed the *Dorprofsozh* or Union of Railway workers and employees. After the formation of the Soviet-Chinese administration of the CER, the Union without Party went into decline along with *Russkii Golos*. Because of debts and litigation, its editor Vostrotin had to seek refuge in the Japanese concession in Mukden. In order to keep going in reduced circumstances, the newspaper reverted to its former title *Russkoe Slovo* and took on the form of a leaflet.

According to Neverov and G-vich, the authors of the lively, if somewhat tendentious, survey of the press of Northern Manchuria in the first half of the 1920s that we are following here, a large number of 'reactionary rags' [*bul'varno-chernosotennykh listkov*] appeared in 1922 'like mushrooms after rain.' The 'ultra-yellow' *Kopeika* or *Kopek* appeared in 1923 when the old administrators of the CER were looking for support and were able to secure financial subsidy from the Russo-Asiatic Bank. Although *Kopeika* had its own printing press and paid its workers just enough for a crust of bread, it soon ran into considerable debt. The Chinese court rejected complaints from the workers and supported the editor, V. A. Chilikin, who also managed to survive several scandals in his single-minded pursuit of self-aggrandisement. However, his reactionary stance, in particular his harsh criticism of the local Soviet authorities, led to Chilikin being deprived of his citizenship in 1925. Then, because of his attacks on the Chinese authorities, he was sent into exile.

Apart from the reactionary press, there were other organs that to various degrees supported the Soviet order, concentrating on wider political issues rather than local gossip. In the spring of 1920, 'The United Conference of the Professional Unions of Political Parties and Social Organizations of the Special Region,' which was seen by Chinese and Soviet authorities alike as a left-wing parliament, produced a newspaper with the title *Vperëd* or *Forward*. While this paper closed in June 1921 owing to the harassment of what Neverov and G-vich call 'police scorpions,' another began three weeks later with the title *Rossiia*. Again, however, there was much opposition influencing the Chinese authorities although the newspaper made no mention of politics. After a series of fines and other tribulations, the police forced it to close.

After a couple of false starts, another new beginning was made with *Tribuna* or *Tribune*, which increased its circulation considerably in 1924. Falling under suspicion because of its discussion of Chinese politics and support of Japanese workers, *Tribuna* was closed in March 1925. An eight-page replacement, *Ekho* or *Echo*, was published weekly but concentrated too much on world politics at the expense of the interests of the local readership.

As well as right-wing and left-wing newspapers, there was also a liberal press attempting at least at first to adhere to the middle of the road. For example, *Novosti Zhizni*, or *News of Life*, founded in 1914 and supporting the war, then the fall of tsarism, began to be suspicious about the course of events in Petrograd later in 1917. After the October Revolution, it dubbed the Bolsheviks 'usurpers of Russia' and 'enemies of the Russian people' but held back from full recognition of the Khorvath regime. And, from the autumn of 1919, it began to accept the new Soviet order. When Professor N. V. Ustrialov joined the editorial board in the spring of 1920, *Novosti Zhizni* carried on an interesting discussion about future directions. However, at the end of 1923, with Ustrialov's departure, it lost its connections with like-minded émigrés in Berlin, and much of its interest for the local intelligentsia, becoming a loyal supporter of the Soviet regime, without much further original thinking, as well as reducing its size to two pages. In 1926, a four-page paper entitled *Molva* or *Rumour*, was being published, but without a clear point of view and without many readers.

The Japanese made several attempts to publish newspapers in the Russian language but reflecting Japanese national interests. As early as 1920, *Mir* (*The World* or *Peace*) attempted to capture the attention of the Harbin public. Its failure did not deter the Japanese from several further ventures, all costly failures, especially as Soviet power began to establish itself more firmly in Harbin.

Apart from daily newspapers, there was a range of periodical publications in the region. *Kommercheskii Telegraf* (*Commercial Telegraph*) was founded in 1921 by V. A. Chilikin, the editor of *Kopeika*, and with much the same kind of contents, aiming to satisfy the conservative tastes of the businessmen who advertised in it. It ceased to appear after the disgrace of Chilikin.

Evreiskii Zhizn or *Jewish Life* with the subtitle *Siberia-Palestine* was edited by Doctor A. I. Kaufman and published for about seven years with a print run of 800. It promoted the Zionist cause and complained of the treatment of Jews in the USSR.

Vestnik Zheleznodorozhnikov or *Railwaymen's Herald* had a somewhat miserable look but was published monthly in 1925 under the editorship of General Zagoskin. It, in fact, had no connection with railwaymen but bore at first the subtitle *Vestnik Bezhentsev*, or *Refugees' Herald*, then *Vestnik Fashisma*, or Herald of Fascism. Characteristically, in its first number, it printed the Manifesto of Nikolai Nikolaevich and other monarchist material.

First appearing in 1909, *Vestnik Azii* or the *Herald of Asia* aimed at bringing Orientalists together under seven headings: socio-political; economic; Russia and the Far East; ethnography, travel, history and linguistics; chronicle of the East; science and method; and bibliography. Financial problems meant that it appeared not more than 50 times in 17 years with a small print run, and by 1926 was losing its significance as an organ of learning.

Izvestiia Obshchestva Izucheniia Man'chzhurskogo Kraia, or the *News of the Society for the Study of the Manchurian Land*, presented an annual digest of the society's activities, sometimes with a special emphasis. No. 6 in 1926 was especially full with reports from the various sections and many photographs.

Izvestiia iuridicheskogo fakul'teta, or *News of the Juridical Faculty*, first appeared in 1925 as the substantial organ of one of the most important educational institutions of the Far East and published appropriate material. It was, however, somewhat isolated from Soviet society.

The journal of Harbin's Esperantists, *Oriento: Monata ilustrita revuo en Esperanto*, appeared irregularly under the editorship of I. I. Seryshev who attempted to make contact with the local Chinese and their culture before emigrating to Japan and then Canada from which he sent contributions to *Russkoe Slovo*.

Humanitarian and religious organisations in the USA extended their influence to Northern Manchuria, especially the Methodists and YMCA, who opened schools and libraries and encouraged sports among other activities. *Metodistskii Khristianskii Pobornik*, or the *Methodist Christian Champion*, had no more than a brief existence in 1924, however, while *Biulleten' Sib.-Man'chzh. Missii Metodistskoi Episkopal'noi Tserkvi Iug*, the *Bulletin of the Siberian-Manchurian Mission of the Methodist Episcopal Church South*, was little more than a free leaflet. Methodist teachers published a teaching journal *Utro* or *Morning* and sold it cheaply. The YMCA also sold publications at low cost, including a special *Rozhdestvo* or *Christmas* number dated 25 December 1925 Old Style. Among a number of other sects and movements, the Kazan Mother of God Monastery brought out *Khleb Nebesnyi, Dukhovno-Nravstvennyi Pravoslavnyi Zhurnal*, or *Bread of Heaven, a Spiritual-Moral Journal*, in 1926. From 1925, a Deacon Kislovich brought out a weekly leaflet entitled *Put' Khristov*, the *Way of Christ*, which had a somewhat commercial slant. From 1925, too, a *Bulletin de la mission Catholique* entitled *Edinstvo* or *Unity* was published with the rubric 'Christians of All Countries Unite,' but its archpriest (*protoierei*) editor soon died.

Finally, there were a number of English-language journals, for example the *Harbin Daily News*, which began its existence in Petrograd under the editorship of Kh. Kestis Vizi [? Custis Vesey?], an American in government service. Vizi moved the paper to Harbin, and from 1919 to 1921 supported Kolchak and then Semyonov throughout Manchuria and China, albeit with a small print run. *The Harbin Observer* was an evening newspaper edited by an Englishman, B. Flit [Fleet?], saying little about political questions with, again, a small print run, owing to the fact that there were few English-speakers in the town. Flit had previously acted in various capacities in Nikolaevsk-na-Amure and had some knowledge, therefore, of the Russian Far East.[21]

The survey of the Harbin press in the mid-1920s by Neverov and G-vich probably reflects too closely the prejudices of its authors; with 300 titles to choose from, their selection may have been partial. Of particular significance among their omissions would appear to be *Kharbinskie Vedomosti* or *Harbin News*, the Russian version of the Chinese daily newspaper *Gun-Bao* that appeared from 1926 to 1937.[22] However, Neverov and G-vich certainly manage to convey the variety of the Harbin press in the first half of the 1920s and thus to reflect the liveliness of the city's culture at that time.

More was to follow later in the decade. To give just two examples, both of literary journals founded in 1926 by editors of *Zaria* and *Rupor*, *Rubezh* or *Boundary* provided an outlet for Harbin's writers while *Lastochka* or *Swallow* served the same purpose aiming at a younger readership. Both journals survived the Japanese occupation but collapsed in 1945 with the Soviet 'liberation.'[23]

Ideology in Harbin

The range of ideas to be found in post-revolutionary Harbin can be further illustrated by a consideration of the outlooks of two frequent contributors to its press, one of whom was P. V. Vologodskii, who came to favour the revival of tsarism under the Grand Duke Nikolai Nikolaevich. He was aware of monarchists in Vladivostok, who were supported by conservatives from Harbin, although he disapproved of two of their leading lights, the Merkulov brothers. On Sunday 22 August 1921, he wrote in his diary that to send congratulatory telegrams to the Grand Duke and the widow of Alexander III, Mariia Fedorovna, on the occasion of the *tezoiminetstvo* (celebration of the name-day of the tsarist family) was a 'sign of the times.' He noted the existence of a Monarchical Union in Germany. However, Vologodskii's support for the return of tsarism was somewhat lukewarm, a case of *faute de mieux*.[24]

On the left was Professor Nikolai Vasilevich Ustrialov, a former member of the moderate Constitutional Democratic Party, and a supporter of the White cause during the Civil War, indeed in the service of Kolchak. Then, however, he moved towards an amalgam of nationalism with Bolshevism, which he saw as the best hope for the Soviet Union in the international arena. In 1921, he published in Prague a collection of articles, *Smena vekh* or *Change of Landmarks*, in which he spelled out his views of support for the Bolsheviks as the guarantors of Russian security. He came to call himself a National Bolshevik and returned to the Soviet Union in 1935. However, his past told against him, and he was sent to a Gulag camp, then shot in 1937.

To the far right was the Russian Fascist Organisation (RFO) founded in 1925 and first publishing in 1926 a tabloid with the title *Nashe Trebovaniia* or *Our Demands*. The RFO was to make a considerable impact under Japanese protection in the 1930s, as we shall see in the next chapter.[25]

Then, there were the Eurasians, cultural rather than political, emanating like the *Smena vekh* movement from Prague. Towards the end of the First World War in 1918, Oswald Spengler published his *Decline of the West* owing much to the emergence of German and Austrian Orientology in the late nineteenth century. He used the term 'Abendland' (literally 'evening land') rather than 'West,' hinting at the setting sun giving way to the rising sun, and largely rejecting the term 'Europe.' Meanwhile, Eurasianism drew heavily on Russian Orientology as well as Slavophilism.

What might be called 'classical' Eurasianism was enunciated in the years following the Revolutions of 1917. It was indeed a geographical ideology, influenced by Mackinder, but also looking to the United States of America with its strong economic nationalism, its Monroe Doctrine, unifying the north and south of the continent and its continental consciousness before exercising its seapower in a manner recommended by Mahan. But its devotees looked beyond geography to ideology, with the belief that the West was in terminal decline and that a new centre of world culture would be found in the East. Peter the Great's Window on the West had changed the outlook of the elite but kept the people looking on, so to speak, and that a new unifying movement must be created on the basis of Orthodoxy. Eurasianism was influential in Japan, where it contributed to the formulation of Pan-Asianism.[26]

In 1926, V. N. Ivanov, a journalist from Omsk, drew on Eurasian thought in a book with the title *My: kul'turno-istoricheskie osnovy russkoi gosudarstvennosti*

(*We: cultural-historical foundations of Russian statehood*) published in Harbin by *Zarya*. He declared in his Preface:

> In Asia, we are at home, we must be conscious of this, and from this short phrase arise perspectives for our personal relationship with the Pacific Ocean which will occur during the course of the next century, when our great civilisation will develop beyond the Urals, completing with this 'Window on Asia' the cause of Tsar Peter, and completely European in spirit: indeed our Asian aspiration will be the result of European critical response to our spirit. Eurasians seek actions in practical application of their doctrine, but they do not draw such huge perspectives as will appear before our people as soon as we make an approach from the Asian side: where there are the results of the ideology, there will be a path for everybody, one following the other and with evident clarity and justice, and which, DV, will erase the contradictions resulting from our revolution.[27]

A further perspective on the Russian Far East was provided by the anthropologist Sergei M. Shirokogoroff, who had done fieldwork in Manchuria and elsewhere. He was also a political activist searching in Vladivostok and beyond for an ideology appropriate for an empire in dissolution. He put forward the concept of 'ethnos' which envisioned 'the "people" being animated by a popular "will" which manifested itself within a broad "national" movement,' combining monarchy with democracy in a new version of the old *zemskii sobor* or Assembly of the Land.[28]

Generally speaking, a range of suggestions for the future of Russia in the Far East were put forward in the years following the Russian Revolution. Needless to say, the Bolsheviks adhered strongly to Marxism, becoming Marxism-Leninism under Stalin.

A reading and thinking public was provided by a variety of schools, from higher to lower levels. As Viktor Petrov observed of the early 1920s:

> With the influx of a cultured population Harbin became a university town. Professors arrived, refugees from Russia, and this made it possible to found institutes of higher education. Because Russia was now under the domination of the Bolsheviks, all contact was broken and all communication severed, so Harbin's youngsters had nowhere to go to complete their education, unless they went abroad.

But most students found it difficult to pay even for a local completion of their education.

Petrov tells us of a short-lived Medical School, an Institute of Oriental and Commercial Studies, and a separate Legal Faculty, as well as a technical institute that grew into a complete Polytechnic. Petrov asserted: 'Harbin's young students set the tone of the town's life with their youthful exuberance, enthusiasm, sincere good humour and corporate spirit.' Non-classical schools, then other high schools, were created to supplement the work of the previous commercial institute – the General

Horvath High School, and various private academies for boys and girls. Religious education and life flourished too under the guidance of the local church dignitaries, many of them exiles. The church would probably not approve some of the entertainments on offer in Harbin, which included a nightlife entirely appropriate for the roaring 1920s, with a strong hint of impending doom reminiscent of Weimar Germany.[29]

New diplomacy?

Having come to terms with China in 1924, the Soviet Union addressed the problem of a settlement with Japan in 1925. Was this the beginning of a new diplomacy in the Far East?

Early in 1923, the Soviet diplomat A. A. Ioffe was instructed regarding negotiations with Japan:

> The forcing of the pace of the talks and the conclusion of an agreement with Japan acquires exceptional significance in connection with Anglo-Russian conflicts and the possible further complication of our international situation in Europe. Therefore you must take all measures to accelerate the official talks.

One formula for the agreement could follow that concluded with Germany at Rapallo in 1922.[30]

The Japanese offered to buy the north of the island of Sakhalin, but the Soviet price was too high. For already, because of their intervention in the Far East, the Japanese had incurred not only international unpopularity but also a heavy financial burden of about 600 million yen, the equivalent of the same amount of gold roubles according to one account. And so, there was no great opposition to bringing intervention to a formal end without the fulfilment of a long-held aim, the acquisition of all Sakhalin.

A 'Convention embodying the basic principles of the relations between Japan and the Union of Soviet Socialist Republics' was signed on 20 January 1925 after a period of ups and downs in 1923 and 1924. There were seven clauses: (1) Japan gave full recognition to the USSR; (2) The USSR expressed its 'sincere regrets' for a 'massacre' occurring in 1920, Japan having withdrawn its claim for reparations and promising to withdraw its garrison from northern Sakhalin by 15 May 1925; (3) The USSR recognised the doctrine of private ownership in anticipation of future relations; (4) There was to be no overt or covert propaganda by the governments and their agents; (5) Regarding natural resources, the USSR signified its willingness to grant to Japan concessions for the exploitation of minerals, forests and other natural concessions in all Soviet territories, including for oil in Sakhalin in particular; (6) Fishery rights in Soviet waters were granted to the Japanese in principle; (7) As for debts and obligations, 'a settlement was reserved for further negotiations on condition that the Japanese government and people would not be placed in any position less favourable than that which might be accorded to other governments or nationals.'[31]

In a letter of 18 March 1926, the Soviet *Narkomindel* (People's Commissar for Foreign Affairs) G. V. Chicherin compared Soviet policy in Manchuria and Mongolia to that in Iran and Turkey, writing:

> The main reason for our failures everywhere in the East is the contradiction between our historical [Soviet] nature and our actual imperialist methods. In economic affairs, these imperialist methods appear in the work of our economic agencies in both Manchuria and Mongolia … . Nowhere does this contradiction appear as clearly as in the CER and nowhere therefore is our policy subject to such danger. But our whole Chinese policy is subject to danger as a result of this deep contradiction arising from our work in the CER … . On the one hand, we make statements emanating from our historical nature, about solidarity with oppressed peoples and on the other hand in practice we follow a line in the spirit of tsarist governors.[32]

The leading authority Akire Iriye argued in 1965 that, following the lead of the USA at the Washington Conference, the Western Great Powers 'took cognisance of the passing of the old order and tried to bring about a new era of "economic foreign policy" as a basis of reconciling and promoting their interests.' However, anti-imperialist Soviet diplomacy frustrated this attempt from the beginning as it worked towards an alternative system of relations with China in particular. From 1922 to 1927, 'the Soviet Union was the most active agent of change in the Far East, and the Russian-inspired Nationalists conquered half of China.' In Iriye's estimation, the USA, Great Britain and Japan were coming to realise 'the futility of basing their policies on the framework of the Washington Conference.'[33]

Is this how a range of commentators in Harbin viewed the international situation in the 1920s? G. Diky, writing on 'Ominous Flashes in Eastern Asia' in 1925, considered that

> It is difficult to overestimate the political and military significance of the Washington Conference … . Undoubtedly, the Washington Conference merely served to secure for the further active policy of the United States a base from which the further offensive might be launched.

Although economic crisis and political uncertainty had caused a certain delay, there was no doubt that the decisions of the Washington Conference together with the operation of the Open Door Policy would promote American expansion. Diky added: 'China has been and will always continue to be the object of the closest attention on the part of the World Powers in the Far East.' Chinese unification would be good for the USA but not for 'European Oppressors.' In particular, it would promote the idea of a struggle for the emancipation of India from the yoke of Great Britain, already weakened by becoming a debtor to the USA. In bold type, Diky added, 'In its fundamental nature, this phase of Soviet diplomatic activity is not contrary to American interests in China.' In these circumstances, 'it becomes possible for the United States to wage war against

Japan.' Japan had taken advantage of the USA's inaction. On the other hand, the resumption of diplomatic relations between Soviet Russia and Japan was to be welcomed, although 'Russia has ceased to be a World Power and has passed from the stage.'

Professor N. V. Ustryalov, the National Bolshevik already introduced, began his discussion of 'Russia in the Far East' with an assertion in bold type expressing disagreement with Diky concerning the strength of Soviet Russia: 'The last five years (1920 to 1925) have witnessed a persistent and systematic if slow recovery of her Far Eastern position by Russia.' He continued:

> Only when on the one hand news began to come from Europe to the effect that the Great Powers had started negotiations with Moscow, and, on the other hand had extended as far as Possiet Bay, thereby surrounding Manchuria on three sides, did the Peking government begin to hold more serious and more circumstantial talks with Russia.

Ustryalov added 'The vernal season of the revolution had become a thing of the past.' The Soviet Union had become more realistic at the same time as no more imperialistic. And so, the joint administration of the CER by China and Soviet Russia agreed in 1924 should proceed smoothly, while the Japanese had made a friendly gesture at the time of the agreement with Soviet Russia by marking it with the anniversary of Lenin's death.

E. E. Yashneff agreed with Diky that war between the USA and Japan was a considerable possibility. This would be accompanied by a blockade on Japan. Therefore, he observed 'Under the circumstances created by the Washington Conference it remains for Japan merely to effect a political, economic and metallurgical preparation for the possible war and, in particular, to strengthen her position in China.' Japan would develop the South Manchurian Railway, and resist any competition with it, thus posing a threat to the CER.

V. I. Surin expanded on the Japanese situation in an article entitled 'The "Pacific" Problem and Northern Manchuria.' Faced by opposition not only from the USA but also from its former ally Great Britain and others, Japan felt the necessity to occupy Korea, all of Manchuria and even Primor'e [the Russian littoral]. The railway could be used to take over Mongolia, too. But the Russian Far East was priceless from both military and economic points of view, and Japanese expansion must be resisted.

The railway in particular was the subject for several further articles in *Manchuria Monitor*. For example, on 'The Chinese Eastern Railway,' A. F. Iakolkovsky asserted that North Manchuria was 'almost desert territory' before the coming of the railway, while for the Chinese on the other side of the Great Wall, it seemed 'an empty northern space.' The construction of the CER had encouraged the cultivation of [soy] beans, the felling of trees and the extraction of coal, but there had been no development of manufacturing. 'Therefore,' he claimed, 'the economy of the country still remains typically colonial.' An anonymous article of 1926 declared that 'North Manchuria has become in our days the centre of the world's interest, and no less attention is being actually devoted to it, than to Versailles and Locarno at the respective period.'[34]

Something of an exaggeration here, perhaps, if there can be little doubt that the Manchurian question attracted wide international interest in the late 1920s. In June 1928, the Old Marshal Chang Tso-lin was killed, probably by the Kwantung Army with the help of Soviet special services, as he was returning to Mukden from Peking where he had held sway for several years but had just been threatened by the Japanese with the withdrawal of their protection. His son, the Young Marshal Chang Hsiuhliang took over, like his father looking south rather than north for support.[35] But the cause of Chinese unification seemed as hopeless as ever.

Conclusion

After the turmoil of the Civil War in the Far East and the end of the Japanese intervention, life in Russian Manchuria could hardly be called settled; indeed, the cosmopolitan city of Harbin experienced a distinctive decade of turmoil. However, the 1920s also managed to produce there a lively press, animated political discussion and varied culture; the spirit of the times was caught in a satirical song:

> The Japanese howl
> The Chinese seethe
> The Mongols graze
> The Koreans trade
> But the Russians dance![36]

In the early 1920s, the Manchurian frontier was still very much open, even if the 'Open Door' was not as the Americans would have liked it, since the Chinese, Japanese and Russians enjoyed freer entrance as borders became more defined later in the 1920s.

Nevertheless, the most noteworthy feature of international relations in the region was the emergence of the USA as the dominant Western power, although the Soviet Union built up its strength, too, with Stalin taking more of an interest after the consolidation of his power in Moscow. Japan was under great pressure, more from the USA than the USSR, and increasingly felt the need to strengthen its hold in Manchuria. The possibility of war between the USA and Japan was already perceived.

Notes

1 David S. Foglesong, *America's Secret War against Bolshevism: US Intervention in the Russian Civil War, 1917–1920* (Chapel Hill: University of North Carolina Press, 1995), p. 280; Harold J. Goldberg, *Documents of Soviet-American Relations*, 3 vols., Vol. 1, *Intervention, Famine Relief, International Affairs* (Gulf Breeze: Academic International, 1993), pp. 132–40, 150, 153–6. For a thorough and judicious appraisal, see J. D. Smele, *Civil War in Siberia: The Anti-Bolshevik Government of Admiral Kolchak, 1918–1920* (Cambridge: Cambridge UP, 1996).
2 The preceding paragraph from Paul Dukes, *October and the World: Perspectives on the Russian Revolution* (London: Palgrave Macmillan, 1979), pp. 98–101.

Soviet Russia, Imperial Japan and the USA 95

3 Halford J. Mackinder, *Democratic Ideals and Reality: A Study in the Politics of Reconstruction* (Harmondsworth: Penguin, 1944), pp. 112–3.
4 See, for example, Paul Kennedy, 'Mahan versus Mackinder: Two Interpretations of British Sea Power', in *Strategy and Diplomacy, 1870–1945* (London: Allen and Unwin, 1961), pp.43–85. On the spread of similar ideas in Germany and beyond throughout the twentieth century, see Holger H. Herwig, 'Geopolitics, Haushofer, Hitler and Lebensraum', in Colin S. Gray and Gordon Sloan, eds, *Geopolitics, Geography and Strategy* (London: Psychology Press, 1999). German ideas were especially influential in Japan.
5 John J. Stephan, *The Russian Far East: A History* (Stanford: Stanford UP, 1994), pp. 110–5.
6 Ibid., pp. 118–9.
7 Ibid., p. 125.
8 *Biulleten Dal'ne Vostochnogo Kominterna*, No. 5, p. 3, quoted by Bruce A. Elleman, 'The Soviet Union's Secret Diplomacy Concerning the Chinese Eastern Railway, 1924–1925', *The Journal of Asian Studies*, Vol. 53, No. 2 (1994), p. 461.
9 William Alexander Gerhardie, *Futility: A Novel on Russian Themes* (Memphis: New Beginnings, 2010), p. 47. The novel was originally published in 1922.
10 John J. Stephan, *The Russian Far East: A History* (Stanford: Stanford University Press, 1994), pp. 147–51, 155, 175–6, 179. On Semyonov and Ungern-Shternberg, see Alan Wood, *Russia's Frozen Frontier: A History of Siberia and the Russian Far East. 1581–1991* (London: Bloomsbury, 2011), pp. 179–82.
11 V. N. Mukharev, *Aleksandr Krasnoshchekov: istoriko-biograficheskii ocherk* (Vladivostok: DVO RAN, 1999), pp. 210, 221. I have had the privilege of a meeting in St. Petersburg with Aleksandr's daughter Luella, whose spirited conversation included memories of the Russian poet Mayakovsky, who sometimes took her to school in Moscow, and of Benny Goodman, the American musician, who was a family friend in Chicago. Bill Shatov later worked on the Turksib Railway before being executed in 1941.
12 Walter LaFeber, *The Clash: US-Japanese Relations throughout History* (New York: WW Norton & Company), 1997), p. xix.
13 Paul Dukes, *The USA in the Making of the USSR: The Washington Conference, 1921–1922, and 'Uninvited Russia'* (London: RoutledgeCurzon, 2004), pp. 93–9, 120–2; Ivan Sablin, *The Rise and Fall of Russia's Far Eastern Republic, 1905–1922: Nationalisms, Imperialisms, and Regionalisms in and after the Russian Empire* (London: Routledge, 2019), p. 235.
14 E. H. Carr, *The Bolshevik Revolution, 1917–1923*, 3 vols. (London: Macmillan, 1953) Vol. 3, pp. 515–6.
15 E. N. Nazemtseva, 'Na poroge voiny: prichiny i posledstviia uvol'neniia russkikh sluzhashchikh s Kitaiskikh Vostochnoi zheleznoi dorogoi v 1925', *Rossiiskaia istoriia*, Vol. 1 (2018), pp. 109–18.
16 Semion Lyandres and Dietmar Wulff, intro. and eds., *A Chronicle of the Civil War in Siberia and Exile in China: The Diaries of Petr Vasil'evich Vologodskii, 1918–1925*, 2 vols. (Stanford: Stanford UP, 2002), Vol. 1, pp. 14, 24, 44–64.
17 Ibid., Vol. 1, p. 65.
18 Nazemtseva, 'Na poroge', p. 110.
19 Lyandres and Wulff, *A Chronicle*, Vol. 1, pp. 67–70. Quotation from Vol. 2, p. 126.
20 Ibid., Vol. 1, pp. 60–1.
21 Neverov and G-vich, 'Pressa Severnoi Man'chzhurii', *Vestnik Man'chzhurii*, Tipografiia Kit. Vost. Zhel. Dor., Harbin, No. 7, 1926, pp. 148–58.
22 A. A. Khisamutdinov, *Russkie volny na Pacifike: iz Rossii cherez Kitai, Koreiu i Iaponiiu v Novyi Svet* (Pekin-Vladivostok: Rubezh, 2013), pp. 193–4.
23 Ibid., pp. 196–8. See also A. N. Kravtsov, 'Liubimye avtory zhurnala "Rubezh": Lovich i drugie', in Li Ian'lin, ed., *Liubimyi Kharbin – Gorod druzhby Rossi ii Kitaia:*

Materialy mezhdunarodnoi nauchno-prakticheskoi konferentsii, posviashchennoi 120-letiiu russkoi istorii g. Kharbina, proshlomu i nastoiashchemu russkoi diaspory v Kitae, Kharbin 16–18 iiunia 2018g. (Kharbin-Vladivostok: VGUES, 2019), pp. 276–82. *Rubezh* was revived in 1992 in Vladivostok under the editorship of A. V. Kolesov.

24 Lyandres and Wulff, *A Chronicle*, Vol. 2, pp. 93–4, 133.
25 John Stephan, *The Russian Fascists: Tragedy and Farce in Exile, 1925–1945* (London: Hamish Hamilton, 1978), pp. 51–3.
26 Mark Bassin, Sergey Glebov, and Marlene Laruelle, *Between Europe and Asia: The Origins, Theories, and Legacies of Russian Eurasianism* (Pittsburgh: University of Pittsburgh Press, 2015), pp. 6–12; Catherine Andreyev, *Vlasov and the Russian Liberation Movement: Soviet Reality and émigré Theories* (Cambridge: Cambridge University Press, 1987), pp. 175–6.
27 Khisamutdinov, *Russkie volny*, p. 203. *My* was republished in 2005.
28 Dmitry V. Arzyutov, 'Order Out of Chaos: Anthropology and Politics of Sergei M. Shirokogoroff', in David G. Anderson, Dmitry V. Arzyutov, and Sergei S. Alymov, eds, *Life Theories of Etnos Theory in Russia and Beyond* (Cambridge: Open Book Publishers, 2019), pp. 267–70. Shirokogoroff's ideas were taken up in Britain by Sir Arthur Keith, a racist anthropologist.
29 Viktor Petrov, *The Town on the Sungari* (Washington, DC: The Russian-American Historical Society, 1984), as in Michael Glenny and Norman Stone, eds., *The Other Russia* (London: Faber and Faber, 1990), pp. 218–9.
30 Dukes, *The USA in the Making of the USSR*, p. 123.
31 Ibid., pp. 123–4.
32 From a paper of A. I. Kartunov cited by Marina Fuchs, *Regional'naia elita Dal'nego Vostoka v mekhanizme sovetskoi vneshnei politiki: Dokumental'naia istoriia voennogo konflikta na KVZHD mezhdu SSSR i Kitaem, 1929* (New York: South Eastern Publishers Inc., 2020), p. 5.
33 Akire Iriye, *After Imperialism: The Search for a New Order in the Far East, 1921–1931* (Cambridge, MA: Harvard UP, 1965), pp. 2–3.
34 G. Diky, 'Ominous Lightning Flashes in Eastern Asia', *Manchurian Monitor*, No. 1–2 (1925), pp. 3–11; Professor N. Ustrialoff, 'Russia in the Far East', *Manchurian Monitor*, No. 1–2 (1925), pp. 12–6; E. E. Yashnoff, 'The Problem of the Pacific', *Manchurian Monitor*, No. 3–4 (1925), pp. 1–7; V. I. Surin, 'The "Pacific" Problem and Northern Manchuria', *Manchurian Monitor*, No. 5 (1926), pp. 1–11; A. F. Iakolkovsky, 'The Chinese Eastern Railway', *Manchurian Monitor*, No. 5–7 (1925), pp. 15–26. The Locarno Treaties of 1925 fixed the frontiers of Germany.
35 Ian Nish, *The History of Manchuria, 1840–1948: A Sino-Russo-Japanese Triangle*, 2 vols (Folkestone: Renaissance Books, 2016), Vol. 1, *Historical Narrative*, pp. 116–20.
36 E. M. Antashkevich, 'Grad Kitezh v Kitae (Slovo pisatelia o Kharbine)', in Ian'lin, ed., *Liubimyi Kharbin*, p. 19. Antashkevich compares Kharbin to the fabled city of Kitezh.

6 Conflict with China
Manchukuo and the Second World War, 1929–45

Conflict with China

Just before Christmas 1922, the American diplomat George C. Hanson was transferred to Harbin in the midst of its severe winter. Appropriately, however, Hanson had something of the frontiersman about him, being a keen hunter, and soon made himself at home and became popular among the expat community, among which he was known variously as 'mayor of Harbin,' 'Mr. Manchuria' and even 'king of Manchuria' during a ten-year stay in the northern city. He developed a talent for dealing with bandits, rescuing 'pigheaded missionaries' by drinking with their captors and telling them dirty jokes in Chinese. His disregard for protocol resulted in less than high ratings for his performance and a slow rate of increase in salary and promotion, even though American businessmen who had completed good deals and made useful connections with his help sent supportive letters to the State Department.

Hanson dutifully sent monthly reports to the State Department, for example describing the predicament of the Japanese in Harbin early in 1928. They were taxed heavily, he wrote, while the Mukden warlord, the Young Marshal Chang Hsueh-liang, insisted that transactions were carried out in the hated local currency rather than the more reliable yen or dollar. Local Chinese officials were anti-Japanese, turning a blind eye to the warlord's installation of telegraph and rail lines in contravention to treaty agreements and his cancellation of Japanese leases on the local racecourse. As Kathryn Meyer suggests, these complaints could well have been listed by the Japanese consul himself.[1] They certainly indicate why the Japanese in Harbin were delighted in 1931 when the Kwantung Army took over the city with the rest of Manchuria which became known as Manchukuo. Before then, there was a serious clash between China and Russia paving the way for the Japanese takeover.

On 31 December 1928, Hanson reported to the American Minister in China MacMurray that the Chinese Nationalist flag had just been hoisted at Harbin, along the Chinese Eastern Railway and at other places in North Manchuria. No particular enthusiasm had been observed among the local Chinese residents, while the Nationalist Government in Nanking would have little effect on the administration of Harbin and the Special Area of the Eastern Provinces whose officials had

DOI: 10.4324/9781003161769-6

98   *Conflict with China*

been appointed by Mukden. But Hanson estimated that Nanking and Mukden would present a united front to the outside world on foreign affairs.

The Board of Directors of the CER were discussing a new flag to replace the current combination of the Chinese flag above the Soviet, perhaps with the exclusion of the latter. The representative of the Young Marshal had insisted that local Soviet citizens should be completely loyal to China and that Chinese citizens should be given full parity of employment. However, local Soviet officials did not appear to be worried, while Hanson recalled the agreements of 1924 between Soviet Russia on the one hand and the Nanking and Mukden governments on the other. The Harbin consul expected that the Soviet regime would come to an understanding with the Nanking Government which would represent China as a whole in foreign affairs.

On 9 January 1929, changing his tack, Hanson reported to MacMurray that Soviet officials in Harbin had received a shock when the local Chinese authorities had taken over by force [on 22 December 1928] without compensation the city's telephone system. The Soviet officials could not take strong action, however, because of their fear of complications with nearby Japan and, for a reason not made clear, distant Poland. On 7 February, the American consul in Mukden reported to MacMurray that the Chinese were thinking of taking over the CER as a whole.[2]

On 27 May, the Young Marshal's forces raided the Soviet consulate-general in Harbin and seized some documents that they considered subversive. On 10 July, they closed the Soviet trade and marine offices. They took over the CER, adding insult to injury by replacing Red Russian officials with White. Chiang Kai-shek's government in Nanking was not directly affected at first, but then the Soviet Union broke off relations.

Determined to accept no other solution than a return to the status quo in its dispute with China, the Soviet government set up in August 1929 a Special Far Eastern Army under the Civil War veteran General Bliukher. Soviet troops were prepared for action along the Siberian border with Manchuria while Bliukher managed to survive several threats to his authority including a temporary arrest for conspiracy against the Party. On 21 August, MacMurray in Peking communicated to Secretary of State Stimson in Washington that the Chinese Commissioner for Foreign Affairs had telegraphed all consuls that regular Soviet troops perhaps including Koreans, Buriats and Magyars had raided Chinese territory. On 22 August, MacMurray passed on a communication from the Tass news agency in Moscow of 20 August that, owing to frequent attacks on Soviet territory by White Guard detachments organised on Chinese territory, the Soviet Commissariat of Foreign Affairs had sent a statement to both Mukden and Nanking Governments asserting that crossings of the border by the Red Army were in response to the White Guard attacks. On the same day, MacMurray passed on to Washington DC the observation from Hanson that there was nothing special to report from the frontier, although there were allegations from both the Soviet and Chinese sides of cruel treatment of prisoners.[3]

On vacation at the beginning of the crisis and not wanting to be disturbed, Stalin wrote to Molotov on 7 October:

We need to organise two regiments of two brigades each, mainly from the Chinese, supply them with everything necessary (artillery, machine guns etc.), put Chinese commanders at the head and let them go to Manchuria, while giving them a task: to provoke revolt in the Manchu troops, attach to themselves reliable soldiers from these troops (the rest should be disbanded, removing the commanders beforehand), organise military division, capture Harbin and gathering strength, announce Zhang Xueliang [the Young Marshal] deposed, establish revolutionary power (plunder landlords, persuade peasants to establish Soviets in towns and villages etc.).[4]

This was more revolutionary advice than traditionally imperial. However, in any case, Stalin's instructions could not be carried out for a number of reasons: the ineptitude and rivalry between Bolshevik officials in Harbin, as well as confusion there between them, diplomatic officials and representatives of the Third International; an imperfect chain of command from Moscow to Harbin via Khabarovsk; concern about the provocation of the Japanese; and the lack of enthusiasm on the part of the Chinese. Moreover, in Moscow, there was more interest at the time in Afghanistan.[5]

Full hostilities broke out in the Far East in November after a broadcast of the aims of the Red Army from Khabarovsk, and the Chinese forces were driven back with heavy losses partly inflicted by Soviet aircraft. Attempts by the USA to activate the Kellog-Briand Pact of 1928 officially coming into effect on 24 July 1929 and aimed at the abolition of war as a means of settling international disputes failed, with France the only other great power in favour. The British point of view expressed to a Chinese legal official on 29 October was that the 'experience of the Russians in Manchuria was a grave warning of the disastrous results of the hasty abolition of extraterritoriality before adequate arrangements had been thought out for meeting the situation.' The USA and France argued along similar lines. Nevertheless, Sir Miles Lampson, the British Minister to Peking, pointed out that,

> on this occasion, in 1929, the Far Eastern public was presented with the singular spectacle of armed action by the Union of Soviet Socialist Republics which was held up by the 'Imperialist' press of Treaty Ports as an example of how to deal with the Chinese.

Certainly, the Mukden authorities were sufficiently impressed by Soviet military success to sign a protocol at Khabarovsk on 22 December restoring 'the former co-relation of the departments headed by Soviet and Chinese citizens,' although the Nanking Government would not ratify it.[6]

After much delay, a Moscow Conference for the settlement of the CER problem as provided for in the Khabarovsk Protocol opened on 11 October 1930. The Chinese side representing Nanking wanted to revert to the agreements of 1924; the Soviet side procrastinated while protesting about the activities of White Russian activities in Manchuria. In December, the Soviet Foreign Minister Litvinov declared that even if the 'highly probable supposition' that China had been pressured into its activities by some imperialist power or powers were set aside, the Nationalist Government remained confident that it could still rely on the hostility of the capitalist powers to the Soviet Union. Marshal Voroshilov completed an extensive tour of Siberia and the Far East in July 1931 to bolster up the army via a public acknowledgement of Bliukher (to whom he had already given the Order of the Red Star in Moscow in June 1930) and other complimentary gestures as the Japanese invasion of Manchuria threatened.[7]

Then, the proceedings of the Moscow Conference were brought to an inconclusive halt by that invasion on 18 September 1931. The Japanese Kwantung Army had been encouraged by the restraint of the Soviet forces and the failure of the Chinese to contemplate the takeover of the whole of Manchuria as well as by the belief of the Japanese government that it could form a solid hinterland for any action in the Pacific.

Owen Lattimore was an informed visitor to Manchuria just before the Japanese takeover. He met many interesting people, for example including some Russians indicating three fingers cut off their right hand as an indication that they had been bandits but were now rendered incapable of holding a rifle. (Was this a contrast to medieval English archers allegedly showing two fingers as proof that they could still use their bows?) However, the main emphasis of his subsequent book was on historical analysis rather than current description. He wrote of the three zones, the southern which he called the 'Old Chinese,' the middle and northern mostly Manchu zone with a Mongol zone to the west. They had formed a series of defences against threats to China from the north. But now, to

> the rapid destruction of old Manchurian tradition brought about by the sudden, vigorous onslaught of machine civilization, can be traced the tidal influence of the ineluctable Manchurian relation to China, to Mongolia and to Russia – and also to China and Japan. The old forces persist through altered activities.

The advent of the railway was bringing the frontier to an end as it had done so in the USA. The Russian army was 'an engine of unknown power but very great importance.'[8]

Manchukuo and the Lytton Commission

Most of the period from 1931 to 1945 saw Soviet Russia excluded completely from Manchuria. Then, in an extraordinary turnabout taking less than three weeks, the Red Army was to achieve an aim that had been no more than a dream of Russian patriots for many years, the occupation of the entire region, and more.

On 18 September 1931, Japanese forces launched an attack on Manchuria, giving the justification that a bomb exploded on the South Manchurian Railway in Mukden had killed Captain Nakamura and several soldiers. This incident was the spark that lit an already threatening conflagration. The Japanese army based in the Kwantung peninsula, having already been restrained with difficulty by diplomats in Tokyo, was raring to go as it perceived the Soviet victory over the Chinese army. As David M. Glantz describes it:

> The Kwantung Army was a venerable force whose name had, for years, evoked respect and fear on the part of its prospective foes. Formed in 1919 to defend Kwantung territory ... [it was] responsible for the defence of all Manchuria after the Japanese seized the region in 1931.'[9]

However, considerations were by no means exclusively military: Japan was dependent on Manchuria for raw materials and trade, as well as an outlet for population, especially after the onset of the Depression, and so the Japanese government came round to accepting the Kwantung Army's action. From the Soviet point of view, the threat to the CER was of prime concern.

The first public Soviet comment on the Japanese takeover of Manchukuo was in *Pravda* on 25 September 1931, declaring that the sole force capable of reversing the outrage would be 'the victory of the worker-peasant revolution in China under the leadership of the Chinese Communist Party.' Then, on 18 October, *Pravda* put forward the view that 'the Sino-Japanese conflict is changing into a US-Japanese one.'[10] However, largely because of their pressing economic problems stemming from the Depression, neither the USA nor the UK wanted to become involved, while the Chinese were deeply committed to their civil war. The first Soviet government reaction to the creation of Manchukuo was to offer in vain a non-aggression pact with Japan. However, the Soviet government also pointed out that the Japanese demands in Manchuria infringed the Portsmouth Treaty at the end of the Russo-Japanese War of 1904–5. As Jonathan Haslam observes: 'Henceforth the Russians were to pursue a policy of de facto recognition, dictated by the concern to deprive the Japanese military of any opportunity to further infringe Soviet interests in the region.'

There was a considerable amount of opposition in Moscow to such a policy of appeasement. On 10 December 1931, for example, *Kommunisticheskii Internatsional* criticised fraternal foreigners in particular, declaring:

> Even when Japanese guns thundered in the immediate neighbourhood of the Soviet Union, many comrades failed to understand the intimate connexion between the Japanese attack on Manchuria and the preparation of a great anti-Soviet war. This obliges us again and again to focus the attention of all Communist Parties and the whole of the international proletariat on the burning question.[11]

On the very same day, 10 December 1931, the Council of the League of Nations resolved to create a Commission to contribute towards 'a final and fundamental solution' by the governments of China and Japan of the questions at issue between them. Named the Lytton Commission after the English Earl elected as its chairman, its other members were from France, Germany, Italy and the United States. While the fact that Lytton's private secretary was the Honourable W. W. Astor could only have increased the suspicion of some republicans, the Commission normally named after the Earl could be said to have carried out its mission in an efficient manner even if it reflected Western prejudices of the time concerning the Soviet Union in particular. Publicly, it made little or no criticism of Japan, although Lytton was less guarded in a private letter to his sister, observing that 'The Manchukuo is a very patent fraud.'[12]

The Soviet Government did not co-operate with the 'capitalist' Commission. For example, on 22 April 1932, the Commissar for Foreign Affairs Litvinov rejected a request from the League Secretary-General for the assistance of the Soviet consuls in Manchuria.[13]

On 30 April 1932, after a six-week visit to Manchuria and Japan, the Commission issued a summary Memorandum, beginning with a description of China as 'a nation in evolution' whose reconstruction had previously been complicated by 'such factors as lack of communication, war lords and banditry.' But now 'a new menace has arisen in the form of communism' which has become 'an actual rival of the national government.' 'The relation of Manchuria to the rest of China' the Memorandum continued, 'was never one of independent sovereignty,' adding:

> The strength of Manchuria, however, rested far more on its own armies than on the alliance with the Chinese Government, a point which is illustrated by the fact that 80% of public expenditures in Manchuria were for military purposes. Nepotism, corruption and maladministration were unavoidable consequences of such a state of affairs, but these conditions were not peculiar to Manchuria as they also existed in other parts of China.

The memorandum asserted that 'The balance of forces in Manchuria ... was upset by the Russian agreements with China in 1924 which shattered the basis of Russo-Japanese cooperation in the area and bolstered China's nationalistic aspirations.' Moreover, 'The growth of communist influences in North Manchuria and bordering territories and in the rest of China increased Japan's desire for a Manchuria free from all such influences.'

The memorandum went on to an analysis of the events of 18–19 September 1931, including 'the slaying of Captain Nakamura,' that somewhat sat on the fence before reporting:

> The evidence received from all sources has satisfied the Commission that while there were a number of factors which contributed to the creation of 'Manchukuo' the two which in combination were most effective and without which in our judgment the new state could not have been formed were the presence of Japanese troops and the activities of Japanese officials, both civil and military. For this reason the present regime cannot be considered to have been called into existence by a genuine and spontaneous independence movement.

The Commission could find no indication that the government of Manchukuo would be able to carry out any reform programme nor that there was any general local Chinese support for it. On the other hand, the boycott of Japanese goods encouraged by the Chinese Nationalist Kuomintang should be a problem of international law. Moreover, the principle of the Open Door should be maintained 'not only from the legal point of view, but also in the actual practice of trade, industry and banking.' The Commission recognised the great importance of Manchukuo in the economic development of Japan but doubted that military occupation, expensive for Japan and provocative for China, would be in Japan's best interests. At the same time, any loss of confidence in the principles of the League's Covenant decisions could be a threat to the peace of the world, while any solution of the Sino-Japanese conflict that ignored the interests of the USSR 'would risk a future breach of the peace and would not be permanent.' Part of the solution could be an Advisory Conference including the governments of Japan and China which would arrange 'the constitution of a special regime for the administration of the Three Eastern provinces' including observance of the principle of 'the maintenance of the territorial and administrative integrity of China and the grant of a large measure of autonomy in Manchuria.' The final proposals of the Advisory Conference would be transmitted to both the League of Nations and the signatory Powers of the Nine Power Treaty drawn up at the Washington Conference. In fact, the Advisory Conference was never met.[14]

Two sections of the full Report of the Commission of Enquiry in response to the Appeal of the Chinese Government to the League of Nations (the final Lytton Report), dated 1 October 1932, invite particular comments. 'Relations with Russia' began with a summary of developments from the war between China and Japan of 1894–5 and continued through the war between Japan and Russia of 1904–5 to the Russian Revolution of 1917 and beyond. It noted the agreements with China of 1924 before a summary description of the hostilities of 1929 leading to the Protocol of Khabarovsk of 22 December. The Report noted:

> During the dispute, the Soviet Government had always taken the position, in answer to various memoranda from third-Power signatories to the Pact of Paris [Versailles], that her action had been taken in legitimate self-defence and could in no way be interpreted as a breach of that agreement.

As for China and Japan, 'Relations with Russia' asserted that after the end of the Japanese intervention of 1920–2:

> The attitude of the Soviet Government gave a strong impetus to China's nationalist aspirations. As the Soviet Government and the Third International had adopted a policy opposed to all imperialist Powers which maintained relations with China on the basis of the existing treaties, it seemed probable that they would support China in the struggle for sovereign rights. This development revived all the old anxieties and suspicions of Japan towards her Russian neighbour. This country, with which she had once been at war, had, during the years which followed that war, become a friend and ally. Now the relationship was changed, and the possibility of a danger from across the

104 *Conflict with China*

> North-Manchurian border again became a matter of concern for Japan ... . Japanese misgivings have been still further increased in the last few years by the predominant influence acquired by the U.S.S.R. in Outer Mongolia and the growth of Communism in China.[15]

This analysis was in a chapter entitled 'Manchuria: Description: Relations with the Rest of China and with Russia.' From the Soviet point of view, of course, it would seem a less than objective account of the Soviet policy towards what the Commission called a 'new state' with which it shared a long frontier.

In a Chapter on 'Manchukuo,' Part III on 'The Opinions of the Inhabitants of Manchuria' observed that the small community of White Russians, about 100,000 in number living in and around Harbin, had suffered the most in recent years: 'Because they are a minority community with no national Government to protect them, they have been subjected to every kind of humiliation by the Chinese officials and police.' While the poor suffered the most, 'The richer and more educated members of their community can earn a livelihood, but they have been liable to suffer whenever the Chinese authorities have thought some advantage was to be gained from the U.S.S.R. at their expense.' The Commission had gathered from the White Russians that they would support any regime which would guarantee them the right of asylum, fair police, justice and taxation, along with rights of trade and settlement without bribes and facilities for educating their children. For their part, of course, the Chinese did not approve of Manchukuo which they saw as the instrument of the Japanese, but the Kuomintang leader Chiang gave de facto recognition following Manchukuo's 'declaration of independence' in February 1933, and was sometimes seen as an appeaser.[16]

Lytton's own conclusion was sceptical about the future of Manchukuo:

> The fact is Japan has bitten off more than she can chew and if left alone circumstances will be too strong for her. With a hostile China boycotting her trade, with a hostile and resentful population in Manchuria and continual guerrilla warfare, the draining of her resources will be terrific and already her economic position is on the verge of collapse.[17]

However, the British establishment view was reflected in a War Office memorandum of October 1932 declaring that 'A friendly Japan is the best antidote to a hostile Russia,' while General Edmond Ironside who had opposed the Bolsheviks from the beginning was to insist in October 1934 that if the Japanese should attack the Soviet Union and the Russians were to 'scream to the League like suck pigs, I hope they won't get any sympathy.'[18]

Reactions to Manchukuo

The Soviet government was not dissuaded by the Lytton Commission from building up its own defences. As Kirill Kolesnichenko appropriately observes: 'The history of Russia's Far East has always been inextricably linked with the country's military forces.' The experience of the First World War and Revolution reinforced awareness of this connection via the CER to the Pacific Ocean. Accordingly, after an order of 27 December 1933 from the USSR Revolutionary Military Council and the People's Commissariat of Railways, a special railway corps was sent to Vladivostok to develop the Far Eastern network. In May 1935, the corps consisted of eight brigades employing a total of 35,000 men.

In late 1935, the Comintern gave special attention to Japan, while the Chief of Staff of the Kwantung Army noted that 'Japan is destined sooner or later to clash with the Soviet Union' as border confrontations had already begun. Reacting to the Japanese threat, the Soviet government took steps to build up its armed forces against any threat from Manchukuo along with large-scale defensive construction and development of military infrastructure. The number of troops in the Far East increased from 44,000 in 1931 to 232,250 in 1934; between January 1932 and January 1935, tanks from 16 to 1,900, aeroplanes from 88 to 1,437 and artillery weapons from 360 to 1879. Because of the strategic importance of the region as well as its sparse population, the relations between military and civil administration were tightly organised in order to promote maximum efficiency, in for example the construction of defences and airfields, the allocation of food, fuel, transport and building materials. The use of land and local facilities was strictly controlled. Civilians were given military training, while soldiers sometimes worked in agriculture and industry. Needless, to say, the Party exercised wide powers and the NKVD (People's Commissariat for Internal Affairs) along with the GULAG (chief administration of the camps) were in operation from 1934.

In the spring of 1932, the Soviet Pacific Fleet was created, and soon became the fastest expanding Soviet fleet, the number of sailors increasing from 6,807 in January 1932 to 43,000 by the end of 1934, reaching a peak of 83,000 by November 1938. Since there was little shipbuilding in the Far East, priority was given to what were called 'Light Naval Forces,' submarines and torpedo boats carried by railway growing in quantity from 7 to 64 and from 12 to more than 100 respectively between 1932 and 1938. There were 53 navy planes early in 1932, 500 by the middle of 1938. Fortifications were strengthened along the coast.[19]

While the Soviet government emphasised its policy of strict neutrality in its rejection of a League of Nations request for cooperation, Communist parties everywhere offered their support for the Soviet policy of general disarmament.[20]

In the spring of 1933, Japan agreed to an armistice with China to stay north of the Great Wall. At the same time, recognising that the Japanese and their White Russian allies were in effective control of the CER, the Soviet government moved towards the sale of the railway to the enemy, also making an accommodation on fishing rights (to be extended in 1936 until 1941). Its confidence boosted by improving economic conditions at home and recognition from the USA from outside in November 1933, it joined the League of Nations in the autumn of 1934 as a precondition for a pact with France in May 1935 for mutual security in Europe. In the Far East in March, it had completed the sale of the CER to Japan. About 100,000 Russians returned to their homeland, only for nearly half of them to be arrested as Japanese spies. More than 30,000 of these were shot and the rest sent into exile.[21] The Soviet Union continued to build up its armed forces while incidents along the border with Manchukuo increased rather than diminished in number.

Soviet apprehension grew as Japanese military expansion in Northern China pressed against Outer Mongolia in 1936 while the Japanese government signed the anti-Comintern Pact and a trade agreement with Germany in the same year. In 1937, full-scale war broke out between Japan and China. In retaliation, the Soviet government did what it could to collaborate with both the Kuomintang and Communist Chinese, arousing Comintern opposition to Japanese aggression while the League of Nations remained inactive.

Part of the struggle was via propaganda. A Soviet publication on so-called 'Independent' Manchuria asserted that: 'preparing for war against the Soviet Union, Japanese imperialism was determined to use Manchuria and Northern China as a bridgehead for an attack on Soviet territory and Mongolia, as well as for war against the USA.' Look at it, the author sneered:

> a paradise created by the armed fist of Japanese imperialism, a paradise in which during less than two years [1931-1933] the population had decreased by four million people perishing from bullets and shells, hunger, floods, epidemics and illnesses, and fleeing from Manchurian 'bliss.'

In response from Japan came a work in English entitled 'Answering Questions on Manchuria.' Manchukuo had been created on 1 March 1932, it pointed out, officially becoming Manchoutikuo, or the Empire of Manchuria, on 1 March 1934, when the Chief Executive Pu Yi had been enthroned as the Emperor Kang Teh. Larger than Germany and France and with a population of nearly 33 million of which 80% was Han Chinese, the Empire was moving from feudalism to 'a strictly modern, rational and unified economic system,' producing more than 60% of the world's soya beans among other crops and manufactures. There were about 200,000 bandits – political, professional, religious and just plain poor, but order had been maintained. With the sale of the North Manchurian Railroad [the CER], Soviet Russia had lost its extraterritorial rights and any reason for intervention.[22]

Certainly, Japan established a stable currency and embarked upon a programme of industrialisation which would make use of coal and iron ore in addition to oil. In relation to other powers, Japan professed adherence to the Open Door policy, although maintaining a monopoly on oil and showing more interest in recognition than in overseas trade.[23]

Among foreign residents in Manchukuo, the US Consul-General in Harbin, George C. Hanson, observed a new level of lawlessness, often on the part of the Japanese military police. Travelling north, he found, in Kathryn Meyer's words, 'a multiethnic border situation of shifting alliances, naked power grabs, and unspeakable violence.' Meyer tells us much about the degradation to be found at the lower levels of society in Harbin in particular. She concludes by expressing her sadness at the depth of what she calls 'the tragedy of Manchukuo,' adding that it was not just that the system was brutal, but that the quest for power brought out the worst in some men while wasting the talents of others.[24]

When the Japanese first entered Harbin in February 1932, they were enthusiastically welcomed. But most leaders of the community held aloof from collaboration. In 1934, the Japanese set up the Russian Bureau of Emigrants' Affairs, with which all local residents had to register, and a self-styled General V. A. Kislitsyn was appointed head. Among collaborators with the Manchukuo government was K. V. Rodzaevsky, the principal organiser of the Russian Fascist Union, on which John Stephan has written an illuminating study. At its peak, the Union had a membership of no more than 10,000, mostly in the cities, while Ataman Semyonov, viewed as an anachronism by the Fascists but much favoured by the Japanese, was influential among rural communities along the Amur although based in Dairen. (He was executed in 1946 as 'a most vicious enemy of the Soviet people.') With the sale of the CER in 1935, most of the Russian nationals departed.

In December 1935, the Police Department of the British Municipal Council of Tiansin [Tianjin] submitted a report in which there was a section on the Japanese programme of 'Asia for the Asiatics' observing:

> Even before the acquisition of the Northern Manchuria the idea of founding in Siberia, especially in its maritime provinces, a Russian 'puppet state,' in parallel with Manchuria, had been contemplated by Japan ... . Tactics of Japanese on the way to annexation of Siberia are now based on the presumption that the population of Siberia at the present have very strong anti-communistic tendencies, and that Russian emigrants bringing with them deliverance from the communistic aggression with the help of Japan should, in the opinion of the Japanese, create a strong moral impression on the anti-communistic population of Siberia.[25]

However, the Police Department also considered that there was suspicion of Japanese motives on the part of the Russians in Manchukuo.

What actually happened there? John Stephan tells us how the All-Russian Fascist Party operated on four levels: as a propaganda machine; as an administrative body assisting the Japanese via the Russian Bureau of Emigrants' Affairs; as a 'Manchurian Mafia' providing narcotics and prostitutes as well as arranging kidnaps; as a recruitment agency for spies and saboteurs. Early in 1938, a 'White Army' unit called the Asano Brigade after a Japanese Colonel 'adviser' was formed. It was active along the frontier with the Soviet Union and participated in various incidents before heavy losses at the battle by the River Khalkin Gol at Nomonhan. Taken aback by the Nazi-Soviet Pact, the Russian Fascists regrouped in 1940, but several of them were shot under suspicion of espionage and germ warfare on behalf of the Soviet NKVD.

The Russian Fascists continued to operate in Manchukuo and elsewhere (Figure 9), but in Stephan's view, 'Spellbound by the mirage of a National Revolution,' they could not afford to open their eyes to the reality of themselves as 'expendable tools' of their employers because they had nowhere else to turn. In

Figure 9 The *Russkii Klub* at the All-Russian Fascist Union branch headquarters in Manchouli, north-western Manchukuo in 1940. As John Stephan says: 'A brilliantly lit swastika tauntingly faces the Soviet frontier, just two miles away.' (John Stephan)

general: 'Rootless and impotent in expatriate limbo, they anesthetized themselves to the futility of their cause by living in a world of illusions.' Ironically, they came to revere Stalin as 'the ultimate fascist.'[26]

Among foreign visitors to Manchukuo was the travel writer Peter Fleming. In 1933, armed with a letter from Stalin himself to his brother Ian, the later creator of James Bond, Peter Fleming set out from London via Moscow to the Far East. After an eventful journey on the trans-Siberian Railway including a derailment, he reached Manchouli, the border town of Manchukuo. Drawn-out formalities followed. At first, Fleming had to complete a lengthy application for a Manchukuo

Conflict with China 109

visa (recognised as legal by Japan and El Salvador only). He was then transported to the passport office in 'a tiny decrepit drozhky' accompanied by 'an enormous coolie' who described himself as a 'visaporter.' A CER train had been held up to take him 'across the wastes of North Manchuria' to Harbin, whose claim to be called 'the Paris of the Far East' would not in his opinion be supported by anybody who had lived there for any length of time.' In fact, in outward appearance at least, Russian influence was almost as strong as American influence in Shanghai. However, he continued:

> The Red Engineer working on the Chinese Eastern Railway: the White Russian lady in exile, grown fat on the luxuries of nostalgia, for ever fantastically scheming the downfall of the Soviet: the Chinese coolie and the Chinese merchant: the British taipan [foreign businessman] on his way to lunch at the Yacht Club – all these form a shifting curious pattern in the crowded streets. But none of them are the master of Harbin: few of them are the masters of their own destiny there.

Although the Japanese were indeed the masters of Harbin, they had their hands full: armed soldiers and police were everywhere, constantly on the lookout for bandits as well as keeping order, itself a difficult enough task in a largely lawless city.[27]

Fleming took the train to Hsingking [Changchun], the capital of Manchukuo, where he met its Emperor, formerly Emperor of China, Pu Yi. Like most of the inhabitants of Harbin, Pu Yi was not master of his own destiny, but rather 'a privileged spectator' if 'a charming though reticent young man.' Nevertheless, Fleming found him 'the most romantic of the rulers of the world,' dismissing others with the common prejudices of his time:

> The strong men in funny shirts: the dim presidents in top hats: Moscow grubby Jews in 1910 Rolls Royces: the rajahs and the emirs and the shahs, the big kings and the little kings – all these we have seen before.

Fleming was not sorry to leave Hsingking, however, having been obliged to read 'a few kilogrammes of the Ministry of Information and Publicity,' arguing for example that 'all the thirty million inhabitants of Manchukuo are Manchus by birth.' (In addition, there were about 300,000 Japanese.)[28]

Arriving in Mukden, he experienced 'an anti-aircraft practice,' noting:

> Japan, like other nations, is terribly afraid of attack from the air. At Vladivostok, and westwards along the Amur frontier, Russia (and who shall blame her?) maintains powerful air bases, said to be well-equipped. In the event of hostilities, the crowded and combustible cities of Japan would be within the cruising range of the biggest bombers, while the towns of Manchuria and Korea would be still more easily vulnerable. In all three countries, therefore, sham air-raids are periodically staged, and the civilian population is put through its paces against the day of wrath.[29]

But Fleming's greatest adventure in Manchukuo was still to come in the shape of an expedition against bandits who constituted the greatest problem faced by the Japanese in Manchukuo. They fell into four main categories, he discovered: (1) Pseudo-patriotic 'political' forces – about 69,000; (2) Bands of religious fanatics – 16,000 (3) Old-style bandits seeking ransoms and pay-offs – 62,000; (4) Bandits of despair, mainly poor peasants – 65,000. [Cf. above] Indeed, poverty was the main cause of banditry, which in its turn was the main cause of poverty. Horses were provided for Fleming and a companion by one 'Davidoff,' a White Russian who was the sole survivor of eight brothers, the other seven having been killed in the sequel to the Revolution. A tsarist sympathiser, he had moved to China and served in the army for a time before marrying a Chinese woman and opening a stable. The expeditionary force, a mixture of Japanese and locals, enjoyed little success against the bandits, mostly because these criminals were often difficult to locate because they could not easily be distinguished from the mass of the people.[30]

After this interlude, as Fleming called it, he paid a brief visit to Dairen which reminded him of a garden suburb, before travelling on 'Red China.' A year or so later, the American journalist, W. H. Chamberlin, who had just completed a still highly-rated history of the Russian Revolution, followed in Fleming's footsteps, so to speak, to Manchukuo. He found Harbin 'unmistakably Russian,' adding:

> Two persons whom I noticed talking on a street corner, a bearded middle-aged Russian in an engineer's uniform and an animated fair-haired woman, might have walked out of a Turgenev novel or a Chekhov play

while another glimpse of former days was 'when large numbers of worshippers filed out of the bulbous-domed Orthodox Cathedral.' But more than 20,000 Soviet Russians, mostly railway employees and their families, had left after the sale of the CER to Japan, which was busy adding four thousand miles of track to three offshoots of the CER leading to the Soviet frontier and other lines to the east and south.

Japan's expansionism, a mixture of materialism and mysticism, had led to an offer to buy the northern part of the island of Sakhalin which met with a 'freezingly negative' response from a Soviet government that was most concerned with the threat to its remote borders. Chamberlin asserted:

> If Japan had not seized Manchuria, the Soviet Union might not have considered it necessary to send a powerful army, with a large complement of tanks and aeroplanes, to the Far East and to create a flotilla of submarines in Far Eastern waters. But now that the Soviet troops and aeroplanes and tanks are there, the Japanese military leaders feel that it is an elementary requirement of national security to scale up their own military and air forces to meet the threat.[31]

Certainly, after the Japanese full-scale invasion of China in 1937, the Soviet government agreed to a mutual non-aggression pact with Chiang's Nationalist government, also supplying arms, while taking further steps to increase the strength of its forces in the Far East. By now, the regional army comprised 13 infantry divisions, one cavalry division and a mechanised brigade: about 25% of the USSR's ground forces, 22% of its tanks and up to 17% of its artillery were now stationed near the frontier with Manchukuo.[32]

From border clashes to the Second World War

The frontier, we need to remember, was almost as long as that between Canada and the United States. But most of the serious conflicts broke out at the frontier's eastern and western ends, where it was not as clearly defined as in the line between them defined by three large rivers, the Aigun, the Amur and the Ussuri. The main problem along the rivers was a dispute about the ownership of some islands near where the Ussuri flows into the Amur. (We shall have more to say in our final chapter about these islands as a subject of disagreement between the Soviet Union and the Chinese Peoples Republic.)

After years of tension along the border, hostilities between the Soviet Union and Japan finally erupted. From 1931 to 1936, Chamberlin records that, according to the Japanese Premier, there had been 2,400 disputes: from 26 March to 9 April 1936, more than half a dozen incidents mainly on the Mongolian border but also to the east – indeed the first major clash was to occur there.[33] Encouraged by Stalin's purge of the Red Army, Japanese forces moved forward in the summer of 1938. A large-scale engagement ensued at Lake Khasan on the border of the Soviet Union with Manchukuo and Korea. The Japanese withdrew after heavy fighting and accepted the Soviet demarcation of the border. On the other side of Manchukuo, Mongolia could have provided a route to Siberia for the Japanese army. Fully aware of this possibility, the Soviet Union had consolidated its influence in Mongolia with the confirmation of a mutual assistance treaty in March 1936.

A big battle along the River Khalkin Gol in the Nomonhan region ensued in the summer of 1939. The immediate cause was the Japanese claim that the border ran along the river versus Mongolian insistence that it was located some way to the east. As Geoffrey Roberts appropriately asserts:

> Given that the dispute concerned the ownership of a few square miles of inhospitable and sparsely populated terrain, it was not intrinsically important to either the Soviets or the Japanese. But the troubled history of Soviet-Japanese relations in China magnified its importance. At stake was the power relationship between Japan and the Soviet Union in the Far East and the question of who was likely to prevail in the event of a broader military conflict between the two states.[34]

The Soviet commander in a conclusive victory was G. K. Zhukov, later the leading general on the USSR's European Front in the Second World War. In a decree of 13 July, he called upon his soldiers 'to show courage, manliness, audacity, braveness and heroism' and threatened death 'to despicable cowards and traitors.' About 5,000 casualties out of a total force of 57,000 men ensued, as Zhukov implemented a plan for a pincer movement drawn up in collaboration with his staff and completed by the end of August. As a consequence of their defeat, the Japanese were obliged to give up the idea of advancing into the Soviet Union and to adopt the 'southern strategy' that would lead them into war with the UK, then the USA. In the opinion of a leading authority Alvin D. Coox, 'There is little doubt that if the Soviet Union had had to fight on two land fronts simultaneously, the Germans would have won the war on the Eastern [European] front.'[35]

Furthermore, the Nazi-Soviet Pact, drawn up at the same time as the Battle of Khalkin Gol, dashed any Japanese hopes for a joint attack with Germany on the Soviet Union, hopes made even more remote by the declaration of war on Germany by France and Great Britain that followed early in September.

In December 1939, the USSR was expelled from the League of Nations after invading Finland. Then Japan signed a neutrality pact with the Soviet Union in April 1941, even if it would not agree to any revision of the Portsmouth Treaty concluding the war with tsarist Russia in 1904–5. In mid-June Germany launched Barbarossa on the Soviet Union and, early in December, Japan attacked Pearl Harbour. World war had begun, and the settlement of the Far Eastern question would have to wait until its end.

Neutrality did not mean harmony. Indeed, throughout the world war, emphasis was given in the Far East to military requirements, with increasing expectation that there would be a showdown between the Soviet Union and Japan before the great conflict came to an end. To quote Kirill Kolesnichenko:

> When the Great Patriotic War began, the economy of the Far East adapted to wartime requirements. The most economically developed areas of the USSR were occupied ... . Without the European link, Russia's civilian and military needs in Siberia and the Far East had to rely heavily on each other to achieve military, economic, and social development goals of the regime.

In fact, as Kolesnichenko points out, civilian construction virtually ceased in the Far East as, from 1939 to 1943, about two-thirds of total capital investments were directed towards military requirements. With the mobilisation for service, women, teenagers and older people were called up to work in industry and agriculture. Meanwhile, at least some servicemen played a part in keeping the civilian economy going, and GULAG prisoners were employed in such tasks as the construction of airfields. The necessity for fishing boats to be adapted for fighting meant smaller catches, and food shortages were exacerbated by a disastrous flood in 1943. However, throughout the war, tight party control prevented a social breakdown.[36]

After the Battle of Khalkin Gol or Nomonhan, a close watch was kept on the border with Manchukuo, although the neutrality pact of the Soviet Union with Japan of April 1941 meant that all was mostly quiet on its Eastern Front. There was some reconsideration by Japan of its 'northern strategy' in the summer of 1941 when Nazi Germany launched its attack on the Soviet Union, but by this time its forces were heavily committed in the Pacific and South-East Asia. Therefore, a considerable proportion of the Soviet Far Eastern forces were sent to the higher-priority European Front, while the frontier defence was concentrated in 14 fortified regions containing artillery and anti-tank battalions. Most of these had been formed between 1938 and 1941, and most of them were deployed along the eastern Manchurian border, where a Japanese attack was considered most likely. For their part, the Japanese recognised the defensive nature of these fortified regions and were preoccupied with hostilities elsewhere. However, this was a lull was before a great storm in August 1945.

During the early years of the war, Dudley Cheke was a British consular officer in Shenyang (previously Mukden), part of a British community that consisted of employees of the Hongkong and Shanghai Bank and a subsidiary of The British American Company, among others. Although Britain had not recognised Manchukuo, Cheke was able to perform his duties without major hindrance, although foreigners were increasingly suspected of 'dangerous thoughts,' especially from the middle of 1940 onwards.

Cheke twice visited Harbin observing the train that carried the mails across Siberia taking up to a fortnight to reach Britain. 'Harbin,' he noted,

> had the air of a Russian city and I remember celebrating Easter there with all the pomp and exuberance of the Orthodox midnight service. But the Russians were given a hard time by both the Chinese and the Japanese, especially after the 'Nomonhan Incident' of 1939.

Cheke perceived that however White the Russians were, 'they tended to look rather wistfully towards even Soviet Russia as their great homeland.' There were also British fur merchants in the North, and Cheke believed that 'Manchuria was then a major source of pheasants for the London Christmas market.'[37]

Conclusion

During Allied Conferences towards the end of the war, some significant preliminary steps were taken towards collaboration in the Far East. In the Cairo Declaration of 30 November 1943, Roosevelt and Chiang Kai-shek committed themselves to the return to China of all the territories occupied by Japan including 'Manchukuo.' At the Teheran Conference from November to December, Stalin applauded Allied successes against Japan but insisted that, until victory in Europe, Soviet forces in the Far East would have to be used for defensive purposes only. While committing himself in principle to Soviet support of the Allied cause, he was evasive on the questions of preliminary joint planning for Soviet entry into the war in the Far East and the grant of bases for the US Air Force in Eastern Siberia, while giving a guarded welcome to Roosevelt's suggestion that Dairen become a free port after the war. At a meeting in Moscow in October 1944 between Stalin and Churchill, American observers led by Ambassador

114 Conflict with China

Averill Harriman pressed the case for Soviet entry into the war in the Far East. In response, Harriman was assured that preparations were being made for the transfer of 30 divisions in 1,000 military trains, but this would take up to three months, and the fragile resources of the Trans-Siberian railway were being stretched to the limit. Therefore, vital American supplies should be sent via Petropavlovsk on Kamchatka and Vladivostok. By June 1945, through the agency of Lend-Lease, a vast amount of food and weapons, including 500 Sherman tanks, was ready for transport to the Far Eastern Front.

In 1945, the Big Three concentrated heavily on the European theatres of war at the Yalta and Potsdam Conferences. Little was said by them about the termination of the war in the Far East, partly for security reasons. Nevertheless, the USA made clear its wish for the USSR to share the burden of bringing the Japanese forces to submission, and the USSR exacted large concessions in return.

These were enumerated in the Agreement concerning the Entry of the Soviet Union into the war against Japan, signed at Yalta by the Big Three on 11 February 1945 and released simultaneously in London, Moscow and Washington on 11 February 1946:

1. The *status quo* in Outer Mongolia (The Mongolian People's Republic) shall be preserved;
2. The former rights of Russia violated by the treacherous attack of Japan in 1904 shall be restored, viz:
   (a) The southern part of Sakhalin as well as all the islands adjacent to it shall be returned to the Soviet Union,
   (b) The commercial port of Dairen shall be internationalised, the pre-eminent interests of the Soviet Union in this port being safeguarded and the lease of Port Arthur as a naval base of the USSR restored,
   (c) The CER and the South-Manchurian Railroad which provides an outlet to Dairen shall be jointly operated by the establishment of a joint Soviet-Chinese Company it being understood that the pre-eminent interests of the Soviet Union shall be safeguarded and that China shall retain full sovereignty in Manchuria.
3. The Kurile Islands shall be handed over to the Soviet Union.

The agreements concerning Outer Mongolia, the ports and the railroads would require the concurrence of Generalissimo Chiang Kai-shek, which President Roosevelt would seek to obtain with the advice of Marshal Stalin, who also expressed his readiness to conclude a pact of friendship and alliance with the Nationalist Government for the purpose of liberating China from the Japanese yoke.[38]

Notes

1 Kathryn Meyer, *Life and Death in the Garden: Sex. Drugs, Cops, and Robbers in Wartime China* (Lanham: Bowman and Littlefield, 2014), pp. 86–7.

Conflict with China 115

2 FRUS (Foreign Relations of the United States), 1929, II, 186–9.
3 FRUS, 1929, II, 296–7; Ian Nish, *The History of Manchuria, 1848–1948: A Sino-Russo-JapaneseTriangle*, 2 vols. (Folkestone: Renaissance Books, 2016), Vol. 1, *Historical Narrative*, pp. 129–30.
4 Marina Fuchs, *Regional'naia elita Dal'nego Vostoka v mekhanizme sovetskoi vneshnei politiki: Dokumental'naia istoriia voennogo konflikta na KVZHD mezhdu SSSR i Kitaem, 1929* (New York: South Eastern Publishers Inc, 2020), pp. 41–2.
5 Ibid., pp. 53–4; English Language Summary, pp. 8–62.
6 Lampson quoted by Nish, *The History*, Vol. 2, *Select Primary Sources*, p. 98. See also Nish, *The History*, Vol. 1, pp. 130–1; Akira Iriye, *After Imperialism: The Search for a New Order in the Far East* (Cambridge: Harvard University Press, 1965), pp. 222–3, 264–7; Peter S. H. Tang, *Russian and Soviet Policy in Manchuria and Outer Mongolia, 1911–1931* (Durham: Duke UP, 1959), p. 257; Max Beloff, *The Foreign Policy of Soviet Russia, 1929–1941, vol. 1, 1929–1936* (Oxford: Oxford University Press, 1947), pp. 72–4.
7 Beloff, *The Foreign Policy*, pp. 74–5; John J. Stephan, *The Russian Far East: A History* (Stanford: Stanford University Press, 1994), pp. 182–3; Jonathan Haslam, *Soviet Foreign Policy, 1930–33: The Impact of the Depression* (London: Macmillan, 1983), pp. 72–3, 142–3.
8 Owen Lattimore, *Manchuria; Cradle of Conflict*, Revised edition (New York: Macmillan, 1935), pp. vi, xiv, 28, 40, 96, 212, 285.
9 David M. Glantz, *The Soviet Strategic Offensive in Manchuria: 'August Storm'* (London: Cass, 2003), p. 60.
10 Both *Pravda* quotations from Jonathan Haslam, *Soviet Foreign Policy, 1930–1933: The Impact of the Depression* (London: Macmillan), 1983, pp. 74–5.
11 Ibid., pp. 75, 79–81. 87.
12 Quoted by Ian Nish, *The History of Manchuria*, Vol. 1, p. 150.
13 Haslam, *Soviet Foreign Policy*, p. 149.
14 *Preliminary Report on Conditions in Manchuria from the Commission of Enquiry Appointed by the Council of the League of Nations*, Mukden, April 30, 1, China No. 2 (1932), Cmd. 4078 (London, 1932), pp. 1–6. The signatories of the Nine-Power Treaty were USA, China, Japan, France, UK, Italy, Belgium, Netherlands, Portugal.
15 *Appeal by the Chinese Government; Report of the Commission of Enquiry: League of Nations*, Geneva, October 1st, 1932, as in Nish, *The History of Manchuria*, Vol. 2, *Select Primary Sources*, pp. 168–9.
16 Ibid., p. 243; Rana Mitter, *China's War with Japan, 1937–1945: The Struggle for Survival*
  (London: Allen Lane, 2013), pp. 57, 59.
17 Nish, *The History of Manchuria*, Vol. 1, p. 162.
18 Antony Best, 'We Are Virtually at War with Russia: Britain and the Cold War in Asia, 1923–40', *Cold War History*, Vol. 12, No. 2 (2012), pp. 21–2.
19 Kirill Y. Kolesnichenko, 'Civil-Military Relations in the Soviet Far East during World War II (1939–1945) By the Example of Primorsky Krai', *Journal of Slavic Military Studies*, Vol. 29, No. 3 (2016), pp. 407–12; Rana Mitter, *China's War with Japan*, p. 67.
20 Haslam, *Soviet Foreign Policy*, pp. 83, 93–6.
21 Li Ian'lin, 'O literature russkoi emigratsii v Kitae', in Li Ian'lin, ed., *Liubimyi Harbin – Gorod druzhby Rossi ii Kitaia: Materialy mezhdunarodnoi nauchno-prakticheskoi konferentsii, posviashchennoi 120-letiiu russkoi istorii g. Kharbina, proshlemu i nastoiashchemu russkoi diaspory v Kitae* (Kharbin-Vladivostok: VGUES, 2019), p. 13.
22 V. Avarin, *'Nesavisimaia' Man'chzhuriia* (Moscow: Partizdat, 1934), pp. 3, 39; *Answering Questions on Manchuria* (Tokyo: South Manchurian Railway Company, The Herald Press, 1936), pp. 1, 3, 4, 12, 29, 60, 72.
23 Nish, *The History of Manchuria*, Vol. 1, pp. 169–70.

24 Meyer, *Life and Death in the Garden*, pp. 84–5, 107, 204. After further brushes with American officialdom and demotion, Hanson shot himself on board ship en route for the USA early in September 1935. Ibid., pp. 178–9.
25 FO371/22157/47-48
26 F. C. Jones, *Manchuria since 1931* (London: Royal Institute of International Affairs, 1949), pp. 77–9; John J. Stephan, *The Russian Fascists: Tragedy and Farce in Exile, 1925–1945* (London: Hamish Hamilton, 1978), pp. xvi, 63, 66, 145, 179, 187, 196–9, 204, 208, 354, 373.
27 Peter Fleming, *Travels in Tartary: One's Company and News from Tartary* (London: Cape, 1941), pp. 19, 51–3.
28 Ibid., pp. 58–9, 73.
29 Ibid., p. 61.
30 Ibid., pp. 99–102, 113–4.
31 William Henry Chamberlin, *Japan over Asia* (London: Duckworth, 1938), p. 17.
32 Kolesnichenko, 'Civil-Military Relations in the Soviet Far East', p. 408; Mitter, *China's War*, p. 98.
33 Chamberlin, *Japan over Asia*, pp. 58–60.
34 Geoffrey Roberts, *Stalin's General: The Life of Georgy Zhukov* (London: Icon, 2012), p. 52.
35 Ibid., pp. 54–64; Alvin D. Coox, *Nomonhan: Japan against Russia*, 2 vols. (Stanford: Stanford UP, 1985), Vol. 2, p. 1079.
36 Kolesnichenko, 'Civil-Military Relations in the Soviet Far East', pp. 413, 414–22; Roberts, *Stalin's General*, p. 65.
37 Nish, *The History of Manchuria*, Vol. 2, pp. 126–9.
38 As reproduced in Max Beloff, *Soviet Policy in the Far East, 1944–1951* (Oxford: Oxford UP, 1953), p. 25.

7 The Soviet invasion, the Chinese Revolution and the Korean War, 1945–56

The Soviet invasion

As the Soviet Union made preparations for the invasion of Manchuria promised at Yalta, the Japanese High Command while fully expecting an attack, nevertheless believed that by playing the USSR off against the USA, there could be a way of limiting the American dominance over their empire. Since the defeats by Soviet forces on the frontiers of Manchukuo in 1938 and 1939, the Japanese had abandoned their northern strategy and aimed at the promotion of stability in Eurasia through the Tripartite Pact of September 1940 with Germany and Italy and the Soviet–Japanese Neutrality Pact of April 1941. To repeat the point, the Nazi invasion of the Soviet Union in June 1941 and the Japanese attack on Pearl Harbour followed by Germany's declaration of war on the USA in December changed the situation radically. While the Soviet and Japanese forces were preoccupied with events remote from the border between them for some years from 1941 onwards, arguments that the Soviet and Japanese peoples could maintain peace and friendship as part of their shared Eurasian affiliations and destinies were somewhat contrived on both sides and already wearing thin by the end of 1944. Indeed, Stalin's Russian Revolution anniversary speech of 9 November included a denunciation of Japan as an aggressor, a clear warning that the Neutrality Pact had become a scrap of paper.

While the best way of securing maximum advantage for Japan would be to play one side off against the other, this stratagem would involve at least some resistance to the expected Soviet invasion of Manchukuo as well as to the ongoing American attacks from the Pacific. When Molotov announced on 5 April 1945 that the Soviet–Japanese Neutrality Pact would not be renewed after it had run for five years by April 1946, a Soviet attack was indeed expected later in 1945.

On 23 April 1945, George F. Kennan wired from Moscow to Washington his assessment that the Soviet Union would continue to exert pressure on its Asian frontiers in direct proportion to its strategic interests. Specifically, it would aim at:

1) acquiring in substance, if not in form, all the diplomatic and territorial assets previously possessed on the mainland of Russia under the Czars;

DOI: 10.4324/9781003161769-7

2) domination of the provinces of China in Central Asia contiguous to the Soviet frontier. Such action is dictated by the necessity of protecting in depth the industrial core of the USSR; and
3) acquiring sufficient control in all areas of North China now dominated by the Japanese to prevent other foreign powers from repeating the Japanese incursion. This means, to the Russian mind, the maximum possible exclusion of penetration in that area by outside Powers, including America and Britain.[1]

Kennan seems to have summarised accurately the foundations of Soviet conduct in the Far East in 1945 and after. Stalin's concern to recover what the tsars had lost, specifically mentioning in the Yalta agreement that 'The former rights of Russia violated by the treacherous attack on Japan in 1904 shall be restored,' was more the consequence of continuity in foreign policy than personal vainglory. Having been harried by the Japanese during the years of Manchukuo and fought them in 1939, the Soviet Union would indeed want to protect its borders in the face of any threat from beyond although, with the Japanese defeated and the Chinese embroiled in the civil war between Chiang's Nationalists and Mao's Communists, no immediate aggression from outside was at all likely.

Just as the Western powers solicited Soviet intervention in the war against Japan, so Stalin asked Mao to help out by moving some of his units near to the Great Wall; Stalin 'reportedly did not forget or forgive Mao for his lack of support at the moment of truth.'

(Ironically, however, in August 1945, 'Stalin was trying to curtail Mao's offensive actions, while Mao was eager to sound the battle cry for the men he had kept from combat during the war against Japan.'[2])

By June 1945, negotiations between Japan and the Soviet Union were already underway for a measure of compromise as the war in the Far East was not all that far behind the war in Europe in reaching the final stages. The Japanese were offering to restore all the losses incurred by the tsarist government in 1904–5, and more, surpassing (however unwittingly) the concessions offered to Stalin by Roosevelt at Yalta in February. Historian Yukiko Koshiro comments:

> While pursuing these diplomatic guessing games with Moscow, the Japanese policymakers regarded Stalin not as a revolutionary (Lenin II) but rather as a legitimate successor to Alexander III and Nicholas II, the last two tsars of the Romanovs – an imperialist with territorial ambition. They guessed that Stalin would naturally attempt to reestablish a Soviet foothold in Manchuria and also Korea and eventually expand out into the Pacific Ocean, a course that would sooner or later collide with that of the United States.[3]

Similar observations have been put forward by Western and post-Soviet analysts, but will need some modification when we come to consider the period after 1945.

In the Potsdam Declaration of 26 July 1945, the USA, China and the UK, while disavowing any intention to enslave the Japanese as a race or destroy them as a nation, called for 'the unconditional surrender' of all the Japanese forces. At the time, however, before the use by the United States of atomic bombs and the invasion of Manchukuo by the Soviet Union, a window of opportunity appeared to open for the Japanese Government to avoid unconditional surrender and to achieve peace by negotiation; partly by playing one enemy against the other, there seemed to be a real chance of saving some of the Japanese Greater East Asian Co-Prosperity Sphere.

On 6 August, the first atomic bomb was dropped over Hiroshima. On 8 August, the Red Army's invasion of Manchukuo took the Japanese army by surprise, since a force of up to 1.5 million men had been deployed as much as possible in secret, often at night, so successfully indeed that most of the Japanese commanders believed that the attack could not come before autumn 1945, even spring 1946.

On 9 August, as the invasion intensified, the Soviet Union declared war on Japan, and a second atomic bomb destroyed Nagasaki. On 10 August, Japan accepted the terms offered in the Potsdam Declaration, but with the condition that the status of the Emperor would remain unchanged. The USA rejected this condition. On 12 August, Soviet military operations began in Korea. The end of the war was then recognised by the Emperor himself in two recorded broadcasts: one on 14 August to the people as a whole making reference to 'a new and most cruel bomb'; the other on 17 August to the armed forces in particular with the explanation – 'Now that the Soviet Union entered the war, to continue under the present conditions at home and abroad would only result in further useless damage and eventually endanger the very foundation of the empire's existence.' In Tsuyoshi Hasegawa's expert opinion: 'Despite their destructive power, the atomic bombs were not sufficient to change the direction of Japanese diplomacy. The Soviet invasion was.' While some Japanese officials urged the USA to resist the Soviet takeover of southern Sakhalin and the Kuril Islands, others were still hoping for restraint of the USA by the USSR, possibly along with the Chinese Communist Party. In reality, for the time being at least, Japan ceased to be an active force in international relations.[4]

This bare account needs elaboration since, while the Soviet defeat of Germany in Europe has often been decried, with factors such as climate, geography and the sheer weight of numbers receiving more emphasis than the Red Army's accomplishment, the ensuing defeat of Japan in Manchuria has been neglected almost totally (Figure 10). Yet, as is already evident from the above summary, it forms part of one of the most significant series of events in human history, involving not only the first use of atomic weapons but also the prelude to the Chinese Revolution. For, after nibbling away at the frontiers of Manchuria by the tsarist regime and its Soviet successor, Russia found itself in complete possession of the three Chinese north-eastern provinces, if only for a brief period followed by a final withdrawal in the face of the Chinese Revolution that it had helped to promote. This sequel will be examined below. For the moment, let us look more closely at the invasion of Manchuria codenamed 'August Storm.'

While the Japanese Empire and its army were seriously weakened by the summer of 1945, they were not immediately prepared to yield to the Allies who expected great losses. Yet, in the view of the American expert on the subject,

120 *Soviet invasion and the Chinese Revolution*

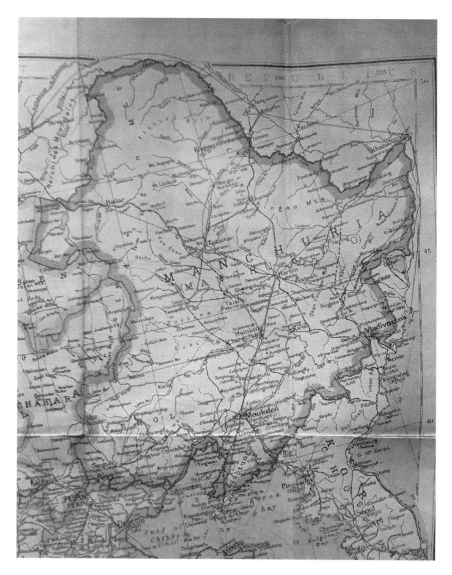

Figure 10 Manchuria (subtitled Manchukuo) from the map of China published in the 1930s in the series *Philips' Authentic Imperial Maps*, as it was still in 1945 on the eve of the Soviet invasion. (George Philip & Son, Ltd.)

David M. Glantz: 'Soviet military planners prepared an offensive plan that was as innovative as any prepared during the entire war. The superbly executed plan produced victory in only two weeks of combat.'[5]

The theatre of operations comprised an area of about 1.5 million kilometres, about as large as Western Europe, and a terrain varying from plains to mountains, with its central valley region the key to military success. The basis of the Japanese opposition to the vast invading Soviet forces was the Kwantung Army with auxiliaries from Manchukuo and Inner Mongolia. The preceding war in Europe and the Far East had taken its toll on both sides, but the Red Army was far better organised and more ready for combat than its enemy, with its leadership from Marshal A. M. Vasilevsky downwards and many of the battle-hardened rank and file in Europe. The Japanese were over-reliant on infantry and attempted too late to prepare a defensive realignment and fortification.

The order for invasion was given on 7 August, earlier than first planned. Glantz comments:

> Although Russian sources claim that the *Stavka* [Headquarters of the Supreme High Command] accelerated its offensive by two days to maximise the element of surprise, it was not just coincidental that the United States dropped its first atom bomb on the Japanese city of Hiroshima on 6 August.[6]

The invasion plan was to launch three attacks from east, centre and west to divide the Kwantung Army, then to encircle the pieces and destroy them, and thus to capture Manchukuo's vital central valley, the Liaotung Peninsula and northern Korea. Once this basic aim was achieved, the Red Army would defeat the enemy in Southern Sakhalin Island, the Kuril Islands and, if possible, the northern part of Hokkaido, the Japanese home island. The ultimate purpose of the attack beyond the defeat of the enemy and security of the Soviet borders was a mixture of new and old: 'the desire to provide assistance to the workers of eastern Asia in their liberation struggle, and the restoration of the USSR's historical rights in territory which Japan had earlier seized from Russia.'[7] Thus, as well as speaking in revolutionary terms, the Soviet government was intending, as Stalin had said at the Big Three meetings, to avenge the humiliation inflicted by Japan on its tsarist predecessor in the war of 1904–5.

By 15 August, the Red Army had penetrated Manchuria's central valley, by 2 September had not only occupied it but also northern Korea and accepted the surrender of the Kwantung Army. Japanese infantry could not counter Soviet armour, however much it tried to make use of the rough terrain and suicidal sorties. The Soviet land forces were assisted by the naval bombardments of northern Korea while amphibious operations took control of the Kuril Islands. Stiff resistance in these islands and southern Sakhalin helped persuade Stalin and the *Stavka* that Hokkaido was an island too far. The operational difficulties would have been enormous while the Allies were resolutely opposed to Soviet incursion into the Japanese home island. As Glantz points out:

Soviet control of all or part of Hokkaido would have created a situation in the Far East analogous to that which came to exist in postwar central Europe. A two- (or even three) power division of Japan would have forestalled postwar Japanese reconstruction, prolonged the military occupation of Japan, compounded future difficulties in Korea, and placed Japan as the focal point of a more intense Cold War in northeastern Asia for decades to come.[8]

Late at night on 10 August, with the Japanese surrender, Molotov stated that he was 'sceptical' about the Japanese offer which fell short of unconditional surrender in its insistence that the prerogatives of the Emperor should not be prejudiced: the Soviet offensive would therefore continue. Early on the morning of 11 August, Molotov said that he accepted the American proposal that from the moment of surrender the authority of the Japanese Emperor and government should be subject to the Supreme Commander of the Allied forces, but he also proposed that this role be shared. Ambassador Averell Harriman objected that this last suggestion amounted to a veto on American action, reminding Molotov of 'America's four-year effort in the Far East in contrast with Russia's two-day excursion into Manchuria.' Molotov insisted on the key role played by the Soviet forces in Europe.

Still, on 11 August, the US Government sent Japan the terms of surrender on behalf of the Four Powers (the Big Three plus China) including limitations on but not the removal of the Emperor, partly following British advice. However, the United States government did not consult their British, Chinese or Soviet Allies about the act of surrender nor the appointment of General MacArthur as Supreme Commander. Still less was there any reference to a partition of Japan between the Four Powers as had been discussed previously. After the Japanese Government had accepted the terms of the surrender on 14 August, Truman ordered the cessation of offensive operations on 15 August. The formal Instrument of Surrender was signed on the USS *Missouri* in Tokyo Bay by the representatives of the Four Powers and Japan on 2 September. The Soviet armed forces completed their takeover of the Kuril Islands two days later, having received the surrender of the Japanese opponents in Sakhalin on 26 August. A terse note from Truman helped to dissuade Stalin from an invasion of Hokkaido. Tsuyoshi Hasegawa suggests that, since the Hokkaido operation would clearly have violated the Yalta agreement, Stalin may have realised that it would weaken his claim to the Kurils, based on the same agreement. Certainly, he made sure that the other Yalta terms would be fulfilled by a speedy occupation of Dairen and Port Arthur.[9]

It is worth emphasising that the Western Allies did indeed discuss an Allied division of Japan before the final victory when the preponderant US power kept out not only the Soviet Union but also the United Kingdom, which could only achieve the restoration of Hong Kong, and that with some difficulty. And US forces remain in Okinawa today. On the other hand, the Soviet takeover of Manchuria, the offshore islands and North Korea meant that the Soviet Union could mount a challenge to the USA as well as contributing to the Communist victory in the Chinese Revolution.

Throughout war and peace, the Russians in Harbin and elsewhere in Manchuria did what they could to survive. Of course, the Red Army soldiers were welcomed with cheers, flowers and embraces as they drove out the Japanese in August. But as the NKVD and the counter-espionage agency SMESH arrived and re-registration began, the realisation quickly grew that one kind of oppression was being replaced by another. The press, the schools and centres of entertainment were all subject to rigid controls while churches were closed. One I. I. Serebriannikov wrote in his diary in 1945:

> from Manchuria – as usual, evidently, no news from the country occupied by the Soviets, people not arriving, birds not flying in, animals not running about, clouds not passing by, all reminiscent of the great fear of Islam in Muscovy in the sixteenth century.[10]

Of the 81,000 inhabitants of Harbin and district, some were executed and many were sent to the camps. Those who could surmount the difficulties involved emigrated, to China beyond the Wall, Korea, Japan and further, to the USA and Australia in particular.

A word on Japanese prisoners of war: it has been estimated that 600,000 of them (20% of a total of 3 million) were sent to the Soviet Union to help cope with labour shortages there. About 50,000 worked on the new Baikal-Amur railway, while others were employed in forestry or the coal industry. In 1949, a trial was held in Khabarovsk of those involved in wartime research making use of Soviet prisoners of war, and those found guilty were sent to 'labour correction camps.' Repatriation for others was very slow, while some former 'colonists' committed *hara-kiri* in order to avoid the humiliation that repatriation would have entailed. A number of Japanese decided to collaborate with the Chinese Nationalists. As for the former Emperor Pu Yi, he was kept in a Soviet labour camp until 1949, when he was sent to the newly created People's Republic of China. After carrying out a sentence of ten years from a war crimes court, he worked as a gardener and also wrote his memoirs.[11]

Postwar readjustment

Needless to say, the fulfilment of the agreements of 1945 would depend on the vicissitudes of the Chinese Civil War and other circumstances. The withdrawal of Soviet troops from Manchuria was delayed at least partly by the seizure of what was claimed as war booty in conditions of widespread ruin. Until his death in 1953, the Soviet leader was Stalin, described by Alfred J. Rieber as 'a Marxist man of the borderlands,' including Manchuria. In Rieber's view, Stalin's early years in Georgia had taught him about 'the pressure of russification' which persuaded him to accept Russian hegemony, while a second influence was 'his evolution as a professional Marxist revolutionary also shaped by the socioeconomic peculiarities of the undeveloped borderland.' More generally, Rieber suggests that:

124 *Soviet invasion and the Chinese Revolution*

> In Russian and Soviet history, four persistent factors have shaped the making of foreign policy together with implications for domestic policy: ... a multinational social structure; porous or permeable frontiers; cultural alienation; and relative economic backwardness.[12]

Let us see how these factors played out in Manchuria from 1945 to 1946, then from 1946 to 1956.

As the USA assumed control in the Japanese islands, keeping out the UK as well as the USSR, seeds of the Cold War were already being sown. As far as the mainland was concerned, Soviet agreements with Nationalist China were signed on the very day of the Japanese surrender, 14 August. These included a Treaty of Friendship and Alliance concerned with the possibility of renewed Japanese aggression, followed by a Soviet commitment 'to render to China moral support and aid in military supplies and other material resources, such support and aid to be entirely given to the National Government as the central Government of China.' In particular, the Soviet government confirmed 'its respect for China's full sovereignty over the Three Eastern Provinces'[13] (that is 'Manchuria,' let us remember, a concept never accepted by Chinese of any political persuasion.) There would be no interference in China's internal affairs including unrest in Sinkiang but the 'independence' of Outer Mongolia under actual Soviet influence would be guaranteed.

The Treaty of Friendship of August 1945 between the Soviet Union and Nationalist China was as significant for what it did not say as for what it did say. In particular, little was said about economic issues. The Soviet Union was keen to extract reparations from Manchuria while Nationalist China feared wholesale seizure of valuable resources. The Chinese insisted on the withdrawal of Soviet troops three months after the Japanese defeat while not making the same demand on American forces. Stalin and his government held back from the support of the Nationalists against their Communist opponents, asserting neutrality in what they said was an internal Chinese matter and refusing the Nationalists exclusive rights to move their troops along the Changchun branch of the South Manchuria Railway.

Stalin insisted that his government intended to maintain an interest in Manchuria while opposing American ambitions to develop their own interest in the Chinese North-East. For example, he strongly objected to the use of American ships to transport Nationalist troops to Dairen, which the Treaty of Friendship designated as a commercial port, 'subject to the military supervision or control established in the zone only in case of war with Japan.' Port Arthur, in contrast, was to be 'an exclusive naval base to be used only by Chinese and Soviet military and commercial vessels.' Stalin had sought a Soviet lease on the Liaotung Peninsula as a whole during the Treaty negotiations, but the USA had exerted pressure to deny this while extracting from a reluctant Stalin the application to Dairen of the Open Door. While continuing to oppose the use of US ships to bring Nationalist forces to Manchuria, the Red Army commander Malinovsky said that he had no objection to American aircraft being used for this purpose as his own forces withdrew. But Malinovsky denied access to American specialists for the preparation of airfields, while Chinese Communist forces occupied the important airfield at Changchun. Rieber comments: 'Stalin was not closing the door on Manchuria to Chiang, he was merely reminding him who the doorman was.'[14]

The Chinese Eastern Railway, which had been sold to Japanese Manchukuo in 1935, and the South Manchurian Railway, which had been Japanese since 1905, were according to the Treaty of Friendship of 1945 to be combined with the name of the Chinese Changchun Railway and administered jointly as in the Chinese–Soviet agreement of 1924. Moreover, while the old agreement would have expired in 1961, the new one was extended to 1975. Half of the board of ten directors and the chairman were to be Chinese, the other half and the vice-chairman Russian. (In 1924, the majority of the board of directors had been Russian.) One of the Russian directors was to be a manager of the railway, his deputy Chinese. Actual control, as in 1924, would be Soviet, while responsibility for security, which had been Russian, was now to be Chinese. Red Army troops were no longer to be transported on the railway after the war with Japan came to an end, but lands acquired by the railway and most subsidiary lines were to be jointly owned, as were subsidiary enterprises including forests, coal mines, power stations and various industrial works.

The naval base of Port Arthur or Lushun and surrounding area, more or less as leased by Russia before 1924, were to be at joint disposal for 30 years under a military commission with three Russian and two Chinese members, while civil administration would be Chinese with Russian military agreement. The commercial port of Dairen was to be open for use to all countries, but the Harbour Master would be Russian while docks and warehouses would be leased to the Soviet Union. Stalin said that a maximum of three months after the Japanese surrender would be necessary for the withdrawal of Soviet troops from the region.

Needless to say, the fulfilment of these agreements would depend on the vicissitudes of the Chinese Civil War and other local circumstances. The withdrawal of Soviet troops from Manchuria was delayed at least partly by the seizure of what was claimed as war booty in conditions of widespread ruin. The Soviet government then attempted to make the best use of the agreements with the Nationalist government, while coming to accept that the Communist opposition was growing in strength, especially among the peasants. However, while Stalin withdrew support from Chiang, he did not give wholehearted support to Mao, especially at the beginning. Western beliefs in a close Red alliance later becoming a Moscow–Beijing conspiracy to overthrow world capitalism were far from the mark. We must also recall that the Soviet Union's last years in Manchuria, 1945–56, saw turbulence in Europe as well as in the wider world in what was soon to become the Cold War.

In the immediate aftermath of the war, Chinese Communist forces managed to exert their control in Kirin and other parts of Manchuria and Chiang feared that the Soviet withdrawal would be managed in such a way that this control would be extended. The Nationalist leader sent a mission to Changchun to discuss means of sending his own troops to Manchuria with the Russians, who made legal objections, arguing, for example that Dairen was a commercial port and not appropriate for military entry. In October 1945, an American fleet escorting a Nationalist force found its way barred to all seaports. A launch from Vice-Admiral Daniel Barbey's flagship was fired upon by the Communists. But on 29 October, the Soviet Marshal Malinovsky said that Nationalist troops could enter through the port of Yingkow (formerly Newchang) which his troops would evacuate by 10 November. In fact, the Soviet forces left on 5 November, allowing the Communists to take over so that their Nationalist enemies had to land south of the Great Wall and make their way overland. Some of them indeed managed to land at Yingkow but found that there was no railway rolling stock for them to move inland.

Who did and said what in the ensuing weeks is difficult to establish. It seems that, on the one hand, Chinese Communist forces blocked the Nationalist entry into Mukden with Soviet Russian help, while on the other, in Changchun and elsewhere, the Nationalists managed to continue their regime with Russian acquiescence. Possibly, the local Soviet regime made some effort to adhere to the agreements made in August in order to prevent giving the Americans a clear excuse for intervention. We need to remember, too, that the eventual Communist victory was far from evident towards the end of 1945. Indeed, at the end of September, Moscow radio had announced that the agreements of August had played an important part in persuading Chiang and Mao to form a unified central government.[15]

The Soviet government pressed for American withdrawal from China throughout the last months of 1945. When Foreign Minister Molotov brought the matter up at a meeting of the Conference of Foreign Ministers in Moscow on 16 December, Secretary of State Byrnes responded that the remaining American troops were primarily occupied in completing the surrender of their former Japanese enemies. For his part, Molotov refused to discuss the question of the Chinese Nationalist takeover of Manchuria. Byrnes had a meeting with Stalin, and, according to the Secretary of State's own account, the Soviet leader expressed concern that the Chinese government would lose the confidence of its own people if it continued to depend on foreign support. The official communiqué stated the three Foreign Secretaries (Molotov, Byrnes and Bevin)

> were in agreement as to the need for a unified and democratic China under the National Government, for broad participation by democratic elements in all branches of the National Government, and for a cessation of civil strife. They reiterated their adherence to a policy of non-interference in the internal affairs of China.[16]

Molotov and Byrnes would each interpret this statement in their own way. There was no opportunity for further official clarification since this was the last formal agreement on China between the former Allies.

The Chinese Revolution

Early in 1946, General George Marshall was sent on a mission aimed at consolidating Nationalist control of China. At first, Soviet agreement about this seemed possible but then, on 18 February, increasingly confident of American support, the Nationalists protested in their press and in a series of demonstrations against the policies of the Soviet Union and its support for its Communist clients, complaining in particular about the continued presence of the Red Army in Manchuria and ongoing Soviet economic demands. In response, the Soviet command asserted that the delay in departure from Manchuria was caused by remnants of the Japanese forces and their puppets as well as bandits, adding that the Red Army would leave China earlier than its American counterpart.

On 19 May 1946, Nationalist troops took Changchun for themselves, but could not consolidate their position owing to continued confusion in the surrounding area. In June, General Marshall announced a truce. Still complaining vehemently about the continued American presence, and denying that they were receiving Soviet aid, the Chinese Communists launched a personal attack on Marshall soon after he had declared his mission a failure. By now too, the Chinese Communists were beginning to denounce their domestic enemy as the 'Kuomintang' rather than as the Nationalists. On 28 June 1946, a Lend-Lease agreement between the Nationalists and the USA was extended, and the American Seventh Fleet arrived at the port of Tsingtao. The Soviet press attacked the USA for its military aid to the Kuomintang, and its ambition to take over the Chinese economy. Suspicion was increased by an American–Chinese trade treaty of 4 November. On 8 December, *Izvestiia* published an article asserting: 'American policy in China is inspired by those reactionary circles in the United States who want to turn China into a semi-colony and a military-strategical jumping-off ground in the Far East.'[17] Meanwhile, relations between the Soviet Russians and the Chinese Communists were far from smooth, Russian railway staff having left Mukden late in November with the complaint that their situation had become untenable.

In 1947, the Chinese Communist army nearly made the breakthrough to Mukden from the south, cutting off Nationalist troops in Manchuria. Still denouncing American aid to the Nationalists, the Communists were probably still receiving support from the Russians even if, patently, Mao and Stalin did not see eye to eye on every issue. In March 1947, at a Conference of Foreign Ministers in Moscow, the Soviet side proposed discussion of the Chinese question, but the American was opposed. Nevertheless, the two sides agreed to exchange information concerning their adherence to the Moscow Agreement of 1945. In his note of 31 March, Marshall reiterated the previous American assertion that the US troops remaining in China were there to make sure that the Japanese troops disarmed while asking what had happened to the 700,000 Japanese taken prisoner in Manchuria. A Soviet note stated that Red Army forces had been withdrawn from Manchuria in conformity with the Moscow Agreement on 3 May 1946.

Throughout the rest of 1947, the Soviet side continued its criticism of the continued US presence in China, arguing that it was part of the long-held American ambition to dominate the Far East going back to the nineteenth century which ended with the annexation of Hawaii and the Philippines. On 25 December, Mao made a speech bitterly accusing the USA of responsibility for the Chinese Civil War.

The year 1948 saw more serious reverses for the Nationalist cause in spite of the continued US support accompanied by an increased denunciation of the Communists. The Soviet Union had not yet broken officially with Chiang but gave its support to Mao. A key moment was the Communist capture of Mukden early in November 1948. The US ambassador reported:

> Only a few days before Mukden fell, the government had five well equipped, supplied and trained armies in the Manchurian field, the most formidable striking force at its command, and within a few days these armies were lost. They were not lost from battle casualties, but from defection, although among their commanders were numbered officers long associated with the Gimo [Generalissimo Chiang KaI-Shek], and on whose loyalty he trusted implicitly,

Concerning the 'Gimo', the ambassador added:

> It was his fate that there should develop in China another revolution in competition with his own, and that, in the broader view, the KMT [Kuomintang] has become to the communist revolution what the old, war-lord regimes were to Chiang as he rose to power. The Gimo does not understand this, and so, to some extent, he regards himself as the protagonist of a revolution which must in the end succeed because all men must recognize that it is essentially right. To that extent he must regard his triumph as inevitable and his reverses as her setbacks incidental to the perversion of natural order. These are, in general, the reasons which constrain him to continue the struggle when it has become apparent that it is a lost cause.[18]

Not only did many thousands of Kuomintang troops surrender at Mukden, but a considerable quantity of American supplies was lost also. Changchun was taken too and Manchuria could now become the stepping-off point for the takeover of North China as a whole. However, as if not believing in Mao's final victory, Molotov and other Soviet spokesmen were still guarded in their observations about the Chinese Civil War, insisting on their observance of the principle of non-intervention.

Even after the Communist forces took Beijing on 31 January 1949, the Soviet government did not immediately break its relations with the Chinese Nationalists. However, from April, there was a distinct change of tone, with *Pravda* writing of the end of the 'reactionary rule of the Kuomintang' and the arrival of 'New China.'[19] With the proclamation of the People's Republic of China on 30 September 1949, the Soviet government soon recognised the new regime and withdrew recognition from the Kuomintang. In their turn, the Nationalists claimed that their Communist enemies had granted great concessions to the

Russians and repeated their assertion that the Soviet government was aiming at the creation of a puppet regime in Manchuria. They might well have believed that substance had been given to their claim with the arrival in Moscow in July 1949 of a trade delegation from the 'Manchurian people's democratic authorities.' A one-year agreement included delivery of soya beans, vegetables, fats, maize, rice and other produce in exchange for industrial equipment, motor vehicles, petrol, textiles, paper and drugs. In August, using the more orthodox title for the region, a 'People's Congress of the North-East Provinces of China' met at Mukden. The secretary of the North-East Bureau of the Communist Party became chairman of the People's Government for the North-East, declaring:

> In order to carry out these historic tasks and speed up reconstruction, it is necessary seriously to study the experience of the Soviet people in their struggle against the imperialists' blockade following the Great October Socialist Revolution as well as their experience in economic construction, the development of technique and administrative methods.[20]

On 16 December 1949, after a long train ride, Mao arrived in Moscow and soon met Stalin. The Chinese leader said in an interview on 2 January 1950 that he had come to cement the alliance with the Soviet Union and to develop economic relations. But on 12 January 1950, the US Secretary of State Dean Acheson talked of other motives:

> The Soviet Union is detaching the northern provinces of China from China and is attaching them to the Soviet Union. This process is complete in Outer Mongolia. It is nearly complete in Manchuria and I am sure that in Inner Mongolia and in Sinkiang there are very happy reports coming from Soviet agents in Moscow .... I should like to suggest at any rate that this fact that the Soviet Union is taking the four northern provinces of China is the single most significant, most important fact in the relations of any foreign power with Asia.[21]

The beleaguered American consul in Mukden, Angus Ward, supported the argument of the Secretary of State, giving an economic emphasis and comparing Soviet policy in East Asia to that in Eastern Europe. Expansion towards ice-free ports was accompanied by the wish to exploit Manchuria's rich supplies while circumventing the need for lengthy overland transport. The Deputy Soviet Minister for Foreign Affairs Andrei Vyshinsky responded to Acheson's assertions on 20 January, arguing that the independence of Outer Mongolia had been agreed upon at Yalta and adding: 'It is common knowledge and normal people cannot doubt that Manchuria, Inner Mongolia and Sinkiang remain within the territory of China, constituting a component part of it.'[22] Acheson repeated his accusations on 26 January, and the State Department supported them with the publication of 'background material' on Manchuria in particular:

130 Soviet invasion and the Chinese Revolution

> The USSR is utilizing the 1945 Sino-Soviet Treaty to penetrate and extend its economic and strategic domination. Soviet troops occupy Dairen and the Port Arthur naval base. Soviet control of the railroads there has reportedly gone much further than was contemplated in the 1945 Treaty, both as regards the railroads themselves and collateral interests.
>
> Soviet influence in the native military force in Manchuria is generally recognized; Chinese Communists have openly admitted this Soviet participation. Soviet participation in the secret police has also been reported.
>
> The USSR has obtained special navigation and fishing rights in Manchuria; operates the only civil air service in Manchuria; controls and operates industrial facilities in Dairen, Harbin and Chia Massu (Kiamusze); controls the power transmission from the Yalu hydro-electric plant; controls and operates several coal and gold mines … . Munitions factories in the area are also reportedly being operated by the USSR. The Soviet Union has placed the richest industrial area of China firmly behind the Far Eastern segment of the Iron Curtain.[23]

The State Department asserted that the agreement on trade between the Soviet government and the Manchurian administration of July 1949 obliged each farmer to hand over 60% of his produce and was causing shortages in the locality and contributing to famine in other provinces of China. Moreover, allegedly, most of the machinery and industrial equipment received in return had originated in Manchuria itself. Needless to say, the Russian interpretation would be more positive, arguing that the Soviet Union supported Manchurian progress in agriculture and industry while encouraging trade with favourable terms.[24]

Surprisingly, some support for Soviet policies came from a departing Scottish missionary in a report of 1950: Russians were not generally thought of as foreigners, and the strategic importance of Manchuria to the Soviet Union was widely recognised, it said. Moreover, the report conceded, as the Christian message was being denounced for its superstition, an alternative argument was taking its place: 'In true virtue, Stalin far surpasses Gandhi, or even St. Francis.'[25]

Meanwhile, other ideological followers of Stalin, Mao and his comrades, were negotiating for two months with their Soviet counterparts in Moscow. Finally, three agreements based on those concluded with Chiang in 1945 were signed on 14 February 1950 and published the next day. The first, 'of friendship, alliance, and mutual assistance,' was aimed at preventing 'a repetition of aggression and violation of peace on the part of Japan or any other State which should unite in any form with Japan in acts of aggression.' The most likely identity of 'any other State' was of course the USA. The two sides would strive for a peace treaty with Japan and other participants in the Second World War. They would collaborate for 30 years in matters of defence, economy and culture. The second agreement was concerned with the Changchun Railway, Port Arthur and Dairen. Basically, the Soviet Union would give up all its rights in Manchuria except for those in Dairen at the conclusion of a peace treaty with Japan or at the end of 1952, when the fate of Dairen would also be considered. But Port Arthur could be used as a joint naval base in the case of attack by Japan or any other State in conjunction with Japan. The third agreement was to promote the revival of the Chinese economy through the extension of credits amounting to $300 million which would be used for delivery of industrial and military equipment in particular. China would pay annual interest of one per cent and make repayments in raw materials, tea, gold and American dollars over a ten-year period beginning in 1954. The terms were not all that generous: for example, the credits amounted to less than the $450 million extended to Poland in 1949.

A question mark hovered over Manchuria. Stalin at one point asked Mao if he should sign separate agreements with Xinjiang as well as Manchuria, whose special status was indicated by the fact that the Deputy Chairman of the Manchurian Provincial Government remained in Moscow after the conclusion of the Moscow agreements, having been accorded precedence over the Chinese ambassador at a celebratory banquet. There was speculation that the two-year period for the implementation of the terms of the agreements would allow room for further manoeuvre. Meanwhile, as a sign of its apartness, Manchuria retained its special currency. On 25 April, a new Chinese-Soviet Company was inaugurated for the Changchun Railway. Although the administration was to remain Chinese, the General Manager, like many of the engineers, would continue to be Russian. There was also a secret agreement that 'the citizens of third countries' would be excluded from working in Manchuria as well as Xinjiang, Stalin no doubt having in mind Americans in particular.[26]

In February 1950, as one of the further agreements between the Soviet Union and the People's Republic of China, the Chinese Changchun Railway was transferred exclusively to the PRC gratis; Port Arthur likewise, but with compensation to the USSR; Dalny would be jointly administered by both powers although recognised as the property of the PRC. This agreement was to depend on the conclusion of a peace treaty with Japan.[27] It was also to depend, of course, on the outcome of the Korean War, which broke out in June 1950. Soviet troops were to leave Manchuria finally in 1955.

The Korean War and withdrawal

We need to recall that there is a short boundary between the Russian Far East and Korea with a longer boundary between Manchuria and Korea. Therefore, the Korean peninsula had been of interest to successive Russian governments, especially from the end of the nineteenth century onwards, although not as great as the interest in the nearby Liaotung Peninsula, which provided a warm-water port and one of the last locales for a Soviet presence in Manchuria.

During the Second World War, Korea received little attention from the Allied Powers. The Cairo Declaration of 30 November 1943, signed by the USA, UK and China, stated that the three powers were 'determined that in due course' Korea should become free and independent, while an international trusteeship for it had been favourably mentioned by President Roosevelt. At the Yalta Conference in February 1945, Roosevelt suggested that any trusteeship should be international.

Stalin did not disagree but asked if such an arrangement necessitated the presence of foreign troops, and approved of Roosevelt's answer that it would not. At Potsdam, when trusteeships were discussed on 22 July 1945, the Soviet side brought up the Korean question, then on 24 July, asked if there would be 'an invasion.' The US response was that this question could not be answered until after a landing in Japan. Adhering to the Potsdam Declaration on 8 August, the Soviet government committed itself to the trusteeship of Four Powers, with itself added to the original three of the Cairo Declaration.

The sphere of operations allotted to the Soviet Union included the whole of Korea. On 12 August, Soviet troops effected landings at points about a hundred miles and more from Vladivostok. Before this invasion took place, the US Supreme Commander had provided that the Japanese forces south of the 38th Parallel should surrender to him, those to the north – to his Soviet counterpart. An isolated American garrison was located on the west coast Onjin peninsula to the north of the 38th Parallel.

The North–South division, which came to mean so much in later years, appears to have come about almost by accident, as a suggestion by one of Macarthur's subordinates. However, it also conformed to a historical division. The North, with a population of about 8 million, had larger, mostly privately owned agricultural units but was also more industrialised; the South, which numbered about 20 million, was based on rice cultivation practised predominantly by small tenant-farmers. The Northern government, fostered by the Soviet Union, came to be led by Kim Il Sung, a Communist who had formerly led anti-Japanese partisans in Manchuria as well as Korea. In the South, the USA decided to support the conservative Dr Syngman Rhee.[28]

In April 1947, the American Secretary of War Robert P. Patterson wrote to the Acting Secretary of State Dean Acheson that he was convinced that the USA should get out of Korea at an early date, while not abandoning Korea to the Soviet Union. At the same time, however, he considered that, from the standpoint of US security, 'our policy in the Far East cannot be considered on a piecemeal basis, and logically the policy concerning Korea must be viewed as part of the integrated whole which includes Manchuria and China.' In August 1947, General John R. Hodge, the US commander in the south, wrote to Acheson from Seoul that the Soviet aim remained to set up a Communist-controlled state on the border of the USSR which could not become a base for an attack on the Soviet Union and would act as a flank for Communist Manchuria.[29] Hence, a serious clash of interests was already apparent in negotiations about the future of Korea. However, on 16 January 1950, Secretary of State Acheson explicitly excluded Taiwan and South Korea from the USA's defence perimeter in the western Pacific.[30]

Earlier, at the beginning of October 1949, Dr Rhee gave the impression that he was restrained from an invasion of the North only by his American sponsors and their fear of a new world war. On 1 March 1950, he argued that, despite advice from the USA not to attack the 'foreign puppets' in the North, he could not ignore the cries of his 'brothers in distress' and should be given heavy weapons. In fact, Kim Il Sung launched an attack on the South without warning on 25 June 1950. His forces had received the necessary equipment and training from their Soviet counterparts, while the Soviet press portrayed the Northern attack as pre-emptive in the face of Southern provocation.[31]

Stalin, 'a Marxist man of the borderlands,' to quote Rieber again, was also always mindful of the geopolitical considerations that had driven his tsarist predecessors and were explicitly recalled by him at the Yalta and Potsdam Conferences in 1945. Realising that the Soviet Union had agreed to leave Manchuria, he looked upon North Korea as a client state that could provide alternative warm-water ports and a barrier against Japan. However, playing a canny hand as ever, in April 1950, a couple of months before the North Korean invasion, he warned Kim Il Sung: 'If you should get kicked in the teeth, I shall not lift a finger. You have to ask Mao for all the help.'[32]

During the ensuing conflict, Soviet 'volunteers' made full use of bases in Manchuria, which prompted the much-debated question of bombing them, even with the atomic bomb. To anticipate such an attack, air raid shelters were constructed, some industrial establishments evacuated and Soviet forces, both ground and air, augmented. Had the US-led coalition intervened in Manchuria, the Soviet Union would probably have joined more fully in the war, a step that Stalin otherwise was keen to avoid.[33]

The armistice of July 1953 after the death of Stalin in March brought to an end the bloody conflict after the North had paid a price of up to 3,000,000 deaths for its initial aggression.

Then, Odd Arne Westad argues:

> The Korean War influenced the Sino-Soviet relationship by creating a sense of accomplishment on the Chinese side and a sense of fraternity with the Soviet Union that had stood by them. Mao felt very strongly that the Chinese Communists had proved their worth to Stalin and their Soviet comrades – and such a feeling was not uncommon even in Moscow. Yet Stalin's policy of keeping the war simmering could have created havoc in the alliance, as the terrible cost for China kept growing. Stalin, whose constant manoeuvering had led to the Korean War, ended his reign with a fatigued policy of low-grade war at Chinese expense.[34]

The cost of Soviet assistance to the PRC for its action in Korea, calculated at $2 billion, was not cancelled. However, after Stalin's death, the Soviet government under Khrushchev promised to help China.

Khrushchev blamed the former Leader for giving too much emphasis to the navy because the Soviet Union's two most likely adversaries, the UK and the USA, were significant sea powers. The Soviet situation had been made worse at the end of the Second World War, he claimed, as the Lend-Lease came to an end and much-needed transport ships were sunk before Soviet eyes. Stalin was determined to catch up but failed to recognise the importance of submarines and aircraft carriers, in the opinion of Khrushchev, who was able to see the condition of the Far Eastern forces in particular for himself after his visit to China in 1954.[35]

In spite of certain suspicions, Mao had always shown great respect for Stalin, Khrushchev suggested, for example asking for a Marxist-Leninist theoretician to help edit his speeches and articles before publication. Stalin sent F. F. Yudin, a philosopher, for this purpose, and he spent many hours with the Chinese leader. A. V. Panyushkin was detailed to supervise the reconstruction of the Manchurian railway and to become the Soviet plenipotentiary representative in Manchuria. Stalin passed on to Mao Panyushkin's reports about the Chinese governor in Manchuria, who duly disappeared.[36]

In October 1954, Khrushchev and Bulganin visited Beijing, promising aid in economic development and armaments. They agreed with their hosts that the USA continued to pose a threat to the socialist camp. There was also further full agreement that Soviet forces should be withdrawn from both Port Arthur and Dairen by the end of May 1955, albeit with some reluctance partly occasioned by the fact that the Soviet Union had spent a lot of money on fortifications in the Liaotung Peninsula. No doubt, too, there was an element of regret as an era of Russian involvement in Manchuria was coming to an end after centuries of interest and more than a hundred years of partial occupation. The Chinese, too, had some misgivings about defence in the case of American aggression, but they were assured that the forces withdrawn would be ready for action in nearby Vladivostok. Some time later, according to Khrushchev, Chou En-lai asked his Soviet comrades to leave their heavy artillery behind in Port Arthur without payment. Khrushchev offered a low price, explaining: 'Comrade Chou ..., please understand the awkward position in which we find ourselves. We haven't yet recovered from a terribly destructive war. Our economy is in shambles, and our people are poor.' The subject was dropped.[37]

Conclusion

Early in 1956, a US National Intelligence Unit evaluated the relations between the USSR and the PRC:

> Since late 1950 Soviet writers have accorded Mao special honor for his contributions to the 'Treasury of Marxism-Leninism' in the field of strategy and tactics for revolutions in 'colonial and semi-colonial' countries. There were indications in the late summer of 1954 of unusual Soviet solicitousness towards the Chinese Communists in Malenkov's public reference to the 'new situation in Asia' created by the emergence of Communist China and in the unprecedented visit to Peiping (Beijing) of Khrushchev and Bulganin. Communist China's stature in the Bloc was further enhanced by Molotov's subsequent reference in February 1955 to the 'world camp of socialism and democracy' as 'headed by the USSR – or more correctly said – headed by the Soviet Union and the Chinese People's Republic.'

However, the US National Intelligence Estimate also suggested:

> Traditional Sino-Russian territorial rivalries along their 1,400-mile common border are a potential source of friction between the Allies. Since the 18th century, China has regarded Tannu Tuva and Outer Mongolia as Chinese Territory. Although the Chinese Communists now appear to have accepted Soviet control of these areas, they may still be apprehensive about Soviet influence in Sinkiang and possibly about the recent Soviet interest in developing previously neglected regions adjacent to Sinking and Manchuria. However, the well-publicized Soviet withdrawal from Dairen and Port Arthur indicates that the Soviet leadership has taken steps to reduce Chinese Communist sensitivity in the border areas.

The CIA and its fellow agencies suggested that 'Sino-Soviet economic relations are another area of potential friction.'[38]

In 1956, there was already a hint of the split between the USSR and the PRC that was to be more open by the time of the Twenty-Second Congress of the CPSU (Communist Party of the Soviet Union) in 1961. As we shall see in our concluding chapter, dissension was to lead to an acrid dispute over the possession of Damansky Island in the Ussuri River in 1969.

In 1956, too, there was a spiritual closure to Russia in Manchuria, with the decision of the Moscow Patriarchate to bring to an end its official presence in China. By 1967, there were no more than 150 Russians left in Harbin.[39]

Notes

1 Quoted in Max Beloff, *Soviet Policy in the Far East, 1944–1951* (London: Oxford University Press), p. 30.
2 Sergei N. Goncharov, John W. Lewis and Xue Litai, *Uncertain Partners: Stalin, Mao, and the Korean War* (Stanford: Stanford University Press, 1993), p. 8.
3 Koshiro, Yukiko, 'Eurasian Eclipse: Japan's End Game in World War II', *American Historical Review*, Vol. 109, No. 2 (2004), p. 426.
4 Tsuyoshi Hasegawa, *Racing the Enemy: Stalin, Truman, and the Surrender of Japan* (Cambridge, MA: Belknap Press, 2005), Chapters 5–7, and quotation, p. 298; Yukiko Koshiro, 'Eurasian Eclipse'; David M. Glantz, *The Soviet Strategic Offensive* (London: Taylor and Francis, 2003), pp. xxv, 7, 8, 37, 43. See also Anatolii Koshkin, *Iaponskii front Marshala Stalina: Rossiia i Iaponiia: Ten Tsusimy dlinoiu v vek* (Moscow, 2004), pp. 270–98.
5 Glantz, *The Soviet Strategic Offensive*, p. xix.
6 Ibid., p. 140.
7 Ibid., p. 141. Glantz quotes a Russian source from 1999.
8 Ibid., p. 305.
9 Hasegawa, *Racing the Enemy*, pp. 225–6, 270–3.
10 A. A. Khisamutdinov, *Russkie volny na Pasifike: Iz Rossii cherez Kitai, Koreiu i Iaponiiu v novyi svet* (Rubezh: Pekin-Vladivostok, 2013), p. 464.
11 Ian Nish, *The History of Manchuria, 1840–1948: A Sino-Russo-Japanese Triangle*, 2 vols. (Folkestone: Renaissance Books, 2016), Vol. 2, *Select Primary Sources*, pp. 199–201.

136 *Soviet invasion and the Chinese Revolution*

12 Alfred J. Rieber, *Stalin and the Struggle for Supremacy in Eurasia* (Cambridge, 2015: Cambridge University Press), pp. 3, 8.
13 Ibid., p. 32. See also Nish, *The History of Manchuria*, Vol. 2, pp. 130–3.
14 Rieber, *Stalin*, pp. 399–401.
15 Max Beloff, *Soviet Policy*, pp. 41–4.
16 Ibid., p. 45.
17 Ibid., p. 53.
18 Nish, *The History of Manchuria*, Vol. 2, pp. 133–4.
19 Beloff, *Soviet Policy*, p. 65.
20 Ibid., p. 70.
21 Ibid., p. 71.
22 Ibid., p. 72.
23 Ibid., p. 72.
24 See, for example, V. L. Larin and others, eds., *Istoriia Severo-Vostochnogo Kitaia XVII–XXvv.*, Vol. 3, *Svero-Vostochnyi Kitai v 1945–1978gg.* (Vladivostok: Dal'nauka, 2004), pp. 39, 48, 61–3, 199, 206–7.
25 Edinburgh University Library Special Collections, CSCNWW 40/1/2, Report by Mr Alexander Webster.
26 Max Beloff, *Soviet Policy* (London: Oxford University Press, 1953), pp. 75–8; Odd Arne Westad, 'Introduction', in Odd Arne Westad, ed., *Brothers in Arms: The Rise and Fall of the Sino-Soviet Alliance, 1945–1983* (Stanford, 1998), pp. 11–12; Sergei N. Goncharov, John W. Lewis, and Xue Litai, *Uncertain Partners: Stalin, Mao, and the Korean War* (Stanford: Stanford University Press), pp. 123, 211.
27 For text of agreement, see Beloff, *Soviet Policy*, pp. 262–4.
28 Ibid., pp. 155–62.
29 FRUS (Foreign Relations of the United States), *1947*, Vol. VI, *The Far East*, pp. 625, 759.
30 Shen Zhihua, 'Sino-Soviet Relations and the Origins of the Korean War: Stalin's Strategic Goals in the Far East', *Journal of Cold War Studies*, Vol. 3, No. 2 (2000), p. 53.
31 Beloff, *Soviet Policy*, pp. 180–1, 183.
32 Shen Zhihua, 'Sino-Soviet Relations', p. 63.
33 William Stueck, *The Korean War: An International History* (Princeton: Princeton University Press, 1995), pp. 146, 351, 396 n. 43.
34 Westad, *The Rise and Fall*, pp. 14–5.
35 *Khrushchev Remembers: The Last Testament*, trans. and ed., Strobe Talbott (London: Andre Deutsch, 1974), pp. 19–21.
36 Ibid., pp. 242–4.
37 Ibid., pp. 246–7; Stueck, *The Korean War*, p. 363.
38 FRUS, 1955–1957, Vol. III, China, p. 246.
39 Khisamutdinov, *Russkie volny*, p. 537.

8 Conclusion

Empire and after – Manchuria past, present, future

Russia and China

From the late 1950s onwards, relations between the Soviet Union and the People's Republic of China (PRC) deteriorated. Tension came to a head in March 1969 at Damansky Island in the Ussuri River as a consequence of the collapse of the friendship between the two communist powers. By then, the PRC had published textbooks and maps asserting the historic existence of a greater China, complaining of 'unequal treaties' imposed by Russia seizing a million and a half square kilometres of Chinese territory. In 1964, Chairman Mao declared:

> About a hundred years ago the region to the east of Baikal became the territory of Russia, and from that time Vladivostok, Khabarovsk, Kamchatka and other locations have been the territory of the Soviet Union. We still have not taken account of this list.[1]

The crisis was indeed the consequence of not only hundreds but also thousands of years of previous developments. From ancient time, the lands adjoining the Amur and Ussuri Rivers had been populated, if thinly and beyond the possibility of labelling the inhabitants either 'Chinese' or 'Russian.' The Great Wall marked a frontier of almost 4,000 kilometres in length at a distance of more than 1,000 kilometres from those rivers.

When the Amur region was first being settled by Russians in the seventeenth century, the Qing dynasty, establishing itself in 1644, promoted a series of campaigns against the Russian presence. It also infiltrated Mongolia and Turkestan. Demarcation of spheres of influence was indicated by the Treaty of Nerchinsk in 1689 pushing Russia back. But further colonisation and a swing in the balance of power between the two sides meant a move in the other direction in the nineteenth century before other empires were actively involved.

The Aigun Treaty fixing the frontier along the River Amur, signed on 16 May 1858, stated in its preamble: 'by common consent for the sake of greater, eternal, mutual friendship of the two states, for the benefit of their subjects.' The Tientsin Treaty of 1 June 1858 provided for an examination of the frontiers by both sides, adding: 'Upon the demarcation of the frontiers, a description and maps of the

DOI: 10.4324/9781003161769-8

adjacent expanses shall be made and these shall serve the Governments for the future as indisputable documents demarcating the frontiers.' The Peking Treaty of 2 November 1860, confirming its predecessors of Aigun and Tientsin, was to 'consolidate the friendship between the two empires still further, to develop trade relations and prevent misunderstanding.' A protocol was added on the exchange of maps and demarcation in the Ussuri territory.[2]

A hundred years or so later, according to a Soviet source, the PRC government claimed that the map appended to the Peking Treaty was compiled by tsarist Russia unilaterally, allegedly adding that Damansky Island had been 'Chinese territory since time immemorial' and that, up to 1860, the Ussuri had been 'China's internal river.'[3] Criticising this and other Chinese claims towards Turkestan, the Soviet side commented:

> If the principle put forward in the PRC Government were accepted, namely, that the state identity of territories is determined not by the people inhabiting them, but by memories of past campaigns, then, evidently, Latin America should revert to the Spanish crown and the United States to the British fold, while Greece, heir to Alexander the Great, could probably lay claim to present-day Turkey, Syria, Iran, India, Pakistan, the United Arab Republic, etc.[4]

Indeed, the march of the empire had produced domination of the weak by the powerful throughout history.

The Damansky Island incident in 1969 followed from an argument between the PRC and USSR about their frontier. Four, even three centuries previously, Damansky Island would have barely been in the Russian consciousness of a remote area known as Tartary. Later, dreams of an El Dorado did not come true, but the economic as well as the strategic potential of what was becoming known as Manchuria, was clearly discerned with the arrival of the railway in the late nineteenth century. It was soon to become a centre of imperial rivalry through the two world wars and the Cold War before being recognised as the Chinese had always seen it – consisting of provinces integral to their republic as a whole.

In the estimation of Odd Arne Westad:

> The geo-ideological divergence between Communists in Moscow and Beijing, having begun under Stalin as a dispute on how to make socialist revolution in an Asian peasants society and Soviet 'rights' in Manchuria, by 1964 had divided the world's leftist movement into pro-Moscow and pro-Beijing factions and raised the question of a complete geopolitical repartition in the East.[5]

In 1969, neither the USSR nor the PRC was powerful enough to dominate the other in a trial of strength. There was an exchange of fire on Damansky Island, and soldiers were killed on both sides before a truce was agreed (Figure 11).[6]

The rapprochement was followed by great hopes for the economic development of the Far East, the Soviet Union collaborating with China and Japan. These

Figure 11 Damansky Island: The Border Conflict of March 1969: A Military Affair, to give a translation of the front cover of the book by D. S. Riabushkin. The disputed island in the River Ussuri near its confluence with the River Amur forms a background for the watchful Soviet soldier. (Russkie Vitiazi)

hopes were far from fully realised in the Soviet period of Russian history and beyond, partly because what was once known as Manchuria became no longer as important a region as before. Although the three north-eastern provinces remained economically significant both for their agriculture and industry, their rice and their armaments, for example, they also gained a reputation for stagnation compared with the more dynamic provinces to the south of the Great Wall. Moreover, the Chinese Eastern Railway has lost most of its importance as the main Chinese landward drive was westward along what used to be the Silk Road as part of the Belt and Road campaign. Meanwhile, the population of the Russian Far East declined and its economy fell short of many of the targets set for it.[7]

Significantly, however, geopolitical circumstances, especially rivalry with the United States, have influenced China's alignment with Russia as both powers put forward the view that the future world order will be founded on multilateralism.[8] These new circumstances have led to a new emphasis on economic and other forms of collaboration. Harbin has been hailed as 'a city of friendship.'[9]

Empire and after

The relationship between Russia and China must be considered in its imperial and post-imperial context.

The year 1945 saw not only the end of the Second World War but also the beginning of a new era in human history marked by the first explosion of the atomic bomb. Meanwhile, empires were losing their former global pre-eminence to two superpowers, the USA and the USSR, each coming to possess enough atomic weapons to destroy the world along with an all-embracing ideology, capitalist or communist. Economically, however, the Soviet Union was less developed than the USA, and its comparative weakness would lead to a collapse in 1991. After 1945, Britain and France in particular found it difficult to accept the eclipse of their grandeur, while Japan and Germany were to recover quickly with the help of their former enemies. China would enter the final stages of its civil war leading to the Revolution of 1949 which would be followed by its own rise to worldwide power. India was also to make a distinctive mark internationally after its independence in 1947.

The Cold War was global, including all parts of the world. It came nearest to hot in 1962, with the Cuba Crisis in the Caribbean. However, much of the writing and thinking on the subject was Eurocentric, concentrating on the division of Germany and the whole continent. In this chapter, appropriate to the subject of the book, there will be at least some discussion of the concept of Eurasia in its global setting.

In earlier chapters, we have observed the growth of empires from the sixteenth century through to the twentieth, pointing out their inter-relationship as described by writers from Russia and the West, with a focus on Manchuria. Empires were developed for a number of interlocking reasons, economic, political and cultural, varying from one to another. For example, at the beginning of the process, England and the Netherlands gave more emphasis to trade than Spain and Portugal; France and especially Russia attempted to maintain bureaucratic control; Catholic, Protestant and Orthodox held different views on Christian missionary activity. Timing was also important, as would be shown by the later entry into the race for an empire of the USA, Germany and Japan; by seaborne and overland variations; and by successive stages of the Industrial Revolution.

So, before we proceed further, let us summarise the process of imperial development in its context.

In the sixteenth century, the Spanish and Portuguese empires led the seaborne way, especially in Latin America. In the seventeenth century, the Dutch empire enjoyed a period of wide predominance. Then, Britain overtook the Netherlands and outstripped France as an imperial power in the eighteenth century, although the American Revolution of 1776 marked a reverse and the French Revolution of 1789 presented a new challenge. Britain continued to rule the waves as it led the industrial revolution throughout much of the nineteenth century. Meanwhile, we must not forget, the seaborne empire was accompanied by overland, by Prussia in Europe for example, while Russia swept through Siberia to the Pacific and also into Central Asia, where it was to vie with Great Britain in the 'Great Game' of Empire.

By the middle of the nineteenth century, the Russian Empire was strong enough in the Far East to push back China, which was weakened by internal rebellion as well as by British and other imperial infiltration. In 1860, Vladivostok (which means Rule over the East) was officially founded on the Sea of Japan, with access to the Pacific. Alexander Herzen was encouraged to take an even broader view, let us recall: 'The North American States and Russia represent two solutions which are opposite but incomplete, and which therefore complement rather than exclude each other.' Herzen was among those who saw the Amur as a counterpart to the Mississippi. Together, he suggested, Russia and America could outstrip Europe and make of the Pacific Ocean the new Mediterranean. They would each have a vision of a 'manifest destiny.'[10]

Let us recall, too, that in 1864, Russia's Foreign Minister Prince Alexander Gorchakov wrote to Russian representatives abroad:

> The United States in America, France in Algeria, Holland in her Colonies, England in India – all have been irresistibly forced less by ambition than by imperious necessity, into this onward march, where the greatest difficulty is to know where to stop.

Towards the end of the nineteenth century, the race for empire accelerated, the number of competitors increased and the venue expanded in a second stage of the Industrial Revolution replacing wooden sailing ships with steam-driven ironclads while extending the use of railways. The imperial powers continued to lead the world in firepower with the introduction of the machine gun and other weapons. 'The Scramble for Africa' was soon followed by a scramble for China, involving the USA and Japan as well as Britain, Russia and other European powers. Alarm at Russia's expansionist plans increased after March 1891 when its government announced plans for the construction of a railway from Moscow to Vladivostok,

142 *Empire and after*

followed in 1896 with the beginning of the Chinese Eastern Railway, a shortcut through Manchuria.

In 1894, as the Trans-Siberian Railway was under construction, the last tsar Nicholas II came to power. In the same year, after a dispute with China centred on influence in Korea led to war, Japan invaded Manchuria. In May 1895, however, under pressure from Russia, Germany and France – all alarmed about the threat to their own growing interests in the region, Japan received an indemnity but was obliged to withdraw. Manchuria as a centre of imperial interest was born.

Russian expansionism in Manchuria, including the beginning of the Chinese Eastern Railway from 1896, as well as encroachment elsewhere by Britain, Germany and other powers, added to Chinese resentment, leading by 1900 to an anti-foreign movement known as 'The Society of Harmonious Fists' or the Boxers. The imperialist powers responded, with the USA keen to establish its 'Open Door' policy as opposed to concessions made to individual empires.

Japan's ambition to extend its influence on the Asian mainland was encouraged by the conclusion of an Anglo-Japanese Alliance in 1902. Increasingly disturbed by Russian infiltration into Korea as well as Manchuria, Japan began the war in February 1904 with a naval attack on Port Arthur and a military invasion of Korea. Further disasters for Russia at sea and on land would have led to greater humiliation if the USA had not restrained Japan in the Treaty of Portsmouth of August 1905. Russia was spared an indemnity but Japan was able to establish a protectorate over South Manchuria and a hold on Korea.

The impact of the Russo-Japanese War of 1904–5 was huge, leading to the 1905 Revolution in Russia and the political awakening of Asia. Thereafter, Russian policy was for the most part to collaborate with Japan to the detriment of China, giving emphasis to the maintenance and development of the Chinese Eastern Railway through Northern Manchuria with its headquarters in Harbin. Other powers remained interested in the region. For example, the American railroad magnate Harriman attempted to enlarge his influence. British politicians and businessmen alike hoped that the renewal of the Anglo-Japanese Alliance in 1911 would be to their benefit on the mainland. In 1911, too, Revolution in China involved the collapse of the Manchu or Qing dynasty and the arrival of a republican regime hoping to restore Chinese sovereignty.

The outbreak of the First World War in 1914 distracted the other great powers, allowing Japan in 1916 to make demands on China which could offer little immediate resistance to Japanese encroachment in Manchuria and elsewhere. However, while the Russian Revolution of 1917 encouraged Japan to intervene further in the Far East, the other great powers were alarmed while Chinese ideas of sovereignty were stimulated further.

After the February Revolution overthrowing the tsarist regime was followed by the October Revolution installing Soviet power, the intervention of the Japanese in Russia was followed by the British, Americans and others. The Versailles Conference of 1919 attempted to impose order on the world, especially in Europe. Then, in the Washington Conference of 1921–2, a concerted attempt was led by the USA to limit in particular the naval armaments of the UK and Japan along with its own, and to stabilise the situation in China through re-assertion of the Open Door and restraint of Japan. Excluded from Washington as it was from Versailles, Soviet Russia declared its fundamental opposition to imperialism at the same time as regaining its hold on as much as possible of the former tsarist empire.

Harbin developed as a cosmopolitan centre for a wide range of emigrants with views ranging from pro-Bolshevik to Fascist before the Soviet regime managed to gain a measure of control. The 1920s were the heyday of Harbin.

In 1929, a brief war took place between Russia and a resurgent China unhappy at the threat to its sovereignty posed in Harbin and its hinterland. Soon, however, the Great Depression distracted the attention of Western imperial powers, and in 1931, for economic as well as political reasons, Japan took the opportunity to seize all Manchuria as the state of Manchukuo, with the former Chinese Emperor at its puppet head. This event has often been seen as an important milestone on the road to the Second World War. Certainly, in 1939, just before hostilities broke out in Europe, the Red Army pushed back the Japanese from the implementation of a northern strategy aiming at encroachment into Manchuria, Mongolia and beyond.

Through most of the Second World War, Soviet forces had to concentrate on defeating the Nazi invader in Europe. But towards the end of the global conflict, the USA pressed the USSR to join in the Far Eastern war with an attack on Japan, which it duly launched in August 1945.

The rapid Red Army advance through Manchuria alarmed both the Japanese and the Americans and influenced the manner in which the war came to an end, including the use of the atomic bomb. The Soviet Union was anxious to restore its sphere of influence and made full use of the opportunities presented by the collapse of Japan to return to take over Manchukuo and appropriate much of the Manchukuo industry. With the decline and fall of the European empires, the USSR and USA faced each other as emerging superpowers.[11]

Certainly, the Soviet Union maintained a presence in Manchuria as well as in Eastern Europe after 1945. But the situation was to change with the momentous communist Chinese Revolution in 1949. The ensuing Korean War marked the last gasp for the Soviet presence in Manchuria, whose death was heralded by the end of hostilities in 1955 as the People's Republic of China, at last, assumed full control over its north-eastern provinces and most Soviet citizens departed. A period of distrust between the two Communist powers ensued, coming to crisis with the Damansky Island dispute of 1969.

The collapse of the Soviet Union in 1991 left Russia with only one qualification for superpower, its ability to destroy the world, as its economy lay in ruins and its ideology was largely discredited, except in China, which was rising as a replacement communist superpower. Then, Russia's alignment with China helped to shore up its former status in an updated form of Eurasianism.

The first Eurasian was Chinggis Khan, demonstrating in an all too practical a manner the interconnectedness of the great landmass under the infinite sky. In the twentieth century, after a long gestation, Eurasia became the basis for a geopolitical concept and a cultural interpretation. Manchuria was to play an important part in two main waves of Eurasianism, the first after the Russian Revolution, the second after the collapse of the Soviet Union.

144 *Empire and after*

The basic argument of Eurasianism was that Russia was neither European nor Asian but an amalgam of both. We have described some of its origins in earlier chapters, including those arising in or stimulated by imperial expansion into Manchuria.

After the Second World War, the perspective on the subject shifted through the Cold War to the present period, when, in the works of Lev Gumilev and others, Neo-Eurasianism emerged as the significance of the Mongol invasion of the thirteenth century was viewed positively in the light of more recent writing on its place in Russian development. Paradoxically, however, the more the term entered the state and popular discourse, the more the founding fathers of Eurasianism were forgotten.

If ultimate objectivity is to be found in a global approach, however, more might be said not only about Europe and Asia but also about the world beyond, especially as it was taking shape after the First World War and Russian Revolution. Eurasianism was one among a number of responses to the challenge in the failed Russian Empire. While other failed European empires, German, Austrian and Turkish, also promoted new ideas, the victorious empires, notably the British and French, made noteworthy adjustments. In Asia, Japan and China reasserted their distinctive varieties of nationalism. Above all, the USA realised its 'manifest destiny' in the Washington Conference of 1921–22, asserting American influence in the Pacific Ocean and on the Chinese mainland in addition to its dominance of the Western Hemisphere.

Finally, on legacies, Neo-Eurasianism is partly responsible for putting Russian President Putin's fief in an enclave, however vast, through its alignment with China. In this case, it may be asked, which influence came first, Russian neo-imperialism or Western neo-Russophobia? As for Russia's neighbour, the American geostrategist Zbigniew Brzezinski suggested in 1997, 'China is already a significant regional power and is likely to entertain wider aspirations, given its history as a major power and its view of the Chinese state as the global center.'[12]

Manchuria past

What can one say about a country that perhaps never existed? The question is posed by a leading Russian scholar Vladimir Sokolov, who reminds us that the term 'Manchuria' did not fully replace Tartary until the confluence of the nineteenth and twentieth centuries. While the Manchus paid special attention to their ancestral area in the seventeenth century, this covered only part of the region that came to bear their name. Their relation to neighbouring peoples was complex and controversial.

Sokolov describes the four-hundred-year history of Manchuria with his own italics as the journey *of a dream of one's own in someone else's* (*mechta o svoem v chuzhom*).[13] The dream, Sokolov continues:

> comprises a mixture of representations of the dangers of Tartary, of the merciless conquerors of the thirteenth century flooding through to Europe, the search for signs of the secret kingdom of Prester John – the lands of Tendyk

from the tales of Marco Polo, published in European maps of the seventeenth century, and towards the end of the century turning into the *Nikanskoe tsarstvo* ('Nikan kingdom'), then at the beginning of the nineteenth century into the reveries of runaway Old Believers, accepting the hazy appearance of White Water. The Russian image of Manchuria was also connected with a memory of the abundant lands of the Amur … . In addition to all this, the liberal utopian ideas of inclusion in peaceful development by way of seaborne trade and for the good of the country (in spite of the evident powerlessness for many years in the administration of huge possessions stretching beyond the Pacific Ocean – along the northwest coast of the American continent!).[14]

Taking a broad view of Russian imperial development, Sokolov makes seven points. First, while many foreigners talked of a sinister 'Russian threat,' many Russians themselves believed that their activity was part of an open worldwide development. Second, withdrawal from North America in 1867 meant a clearer focus for activity along the Amur and in Manchuria. In 1853, Count Nikolai Muravyov, governor-general of the Far East, had already suggested to Nicholas I that the Russian Empire was over-extended in North America and would have to pull back sooner or later. Third, because of Russia's Orthodox mission in Peking, and long experience of dealing with the Chinese, Russians understood the Qing Empire 'from the inside.' Fourth, dealings with Japan as well as China had been intimate for many years in Northeast China, creating a special region of interaction if not without misunderstanding. Fifth, propaganda and 'image' played an important role. Foreign diplomats often presented a negative picture of China as well as of Russia in 'Manchuria.' Sixth, the Qing dynasty sought exclusive control of the region, drawing on both its ancestral rights and the more recent potential of the railway. Seventh, Japanese intellectuals already talked in the late nineteenth century of a Great East Asia in which their country would play a leading part.[15]

After the Russian Revolution and Civil War from 1917 to 1921, there were significant developments in all seven points made by Sokolov. First, almost needless to say, the 'Soviet threat' seemed more sinister than the Imperial. The Comintern attempted with little success to gain international support for the Soviet Union which was obliged to adopt a policy of Socialism in One Country. Second, the loss of former parts of the Empire to the West, in particular a large slice of Poland, the Baltic States and Finland, encouraged a fortress mentality in the Soviet Union which was reinforced later by the expulsion from Japanese Manchukuo in the Far East. Third, ties with both Nationalist and Communist forces in China drew on previous experience. Fourth, interaction with Japan was limited in Manchukuo until the battles of 1939, then encouraged with China by the collapse of Manchukuo and Soviet takeover in 1945. Fifth, propaganda and 'image' from communist and capitalist alike played at least as important a part as before. Sixth, the north-eastern provinces became a significant theatre in the Chinese Civil War leading to the Chinese Revolution of 1949, soon after which Soviet forces finally withdrew. Seven, ideas of the Japanese Empire dominating a Great East Asia became even more ambitious after the creation of Manchukuo before the comprehensive defeat in 1945.

146 *Empire and after*

Many of these points concerning Imperial and Soviet Russia have been touched on above in the context of global international relations, in particular with Great Britain and the USA from Hakluyt and Howell to Mahan and Mackinder and beyond. Both these great powers began their expansion on land before extending overseas in the context of successive phases of the Industrial Revolution.

Moving on from the suggestions on Manchuria before the Russian Revolution and our projection of them into the Soviet period, let us turn to the evaluation of the late Rosemary Quested, one of the most significant Western writers on the subject, who provided a further overview of the international context of Russian Manchuria which she described in 1982 as:

> the only complete multi-class European community which has ever existed in Southern or East Asia, or indeed in any part of Asia since the fall of Byzantium, outside the bounds of the Soviet state. All other European colonies in Asia from the beginning of modern times consisted almost entirely of planters, seafarers and businessmen, military and officials superimposed on lower classes of the subject nationalities. Such European working class and peasant elements as existed in the British, French, Dutch and German, even Spanish and Portuguese Asian colonies, were minute, fragmented and usually transient. The Russians in Manchuria were the only ones at any time to possess both a working class and a peasantry of their own, numbering several tens of thousands. Yet the Russian colony in Manchuria passed, like others before it, from pioneering origins through a phase of power and dominance to ultimate extinction, pointing the road which Hong Kong and Macao, the surviving European toe-holds in Asia, must some day follow.[16]

(Indeed, Hong Kong reverted to Chinese jurisdiction in 1997 and Macao in 1999.)

As her title indicates, Quested investigates the question: 'Were the Russians indeed "matier" than the true Westerners, not to mention the Japanese, as was believed by a number of observers at the time?' She also asks whether 'Russian and Soviet policies and ethnic relations in Manchuria can be compared with the same in China proper and other parts of Asia, such as Persia, Turkestan, Mongolia and the Caucasus.' In this regard, she quotes the American traveller to Turkestan in 1876 Eugene Schuyler: 'The Russians ... have not so much of that contemptuous feeling towards the natives which is marked in the dealing of the Anglo-Saxon race with people of lower culture and civilization.'[17] The attitude of the Russians was born of centuries of experience of meeting other peoples in the broad context of Eurasia, she suggests.

Quested goes on to assert that:

> nationalism of modern type, not feelings of cultural superiority, provided the cement of the Russian people, with Orthodox Christianity a bond already failing in the educated classes. Russian nationalism rested in feelings that the Great Russians, masters of the Empire, were a unique people with a unique

capacity for goodness and greatness, if also evil. ('We are better than they are, even if some of us sometimes behave worse.') In this it did not differ from that of other European nations, except perhaps in the greater recognition of its own evil capacities – a product both of the dissatisfaction of the intelligentsia with the political system and of the survival of some of the intense religiosity of earlier Europe, from which the West had somewhat smugly departed. It did differ, however, from the feelings of superiority of the traditional Chinese, which as often noted rested on the assumption that they were the fount of civilization, the only fully civilized people in the world, and hence to be judged by an entirely different measure from the rest. ('We are so far above them that there is no comparison at all. Of course, it is not their fault.')[18]

Quested adds:

If the outlook for the Russians simply as conquerors was rather poor, their best hope lay in offering to the Chinese the economic advancement and modernity which the latter were soon to want more and more with every passing year.[19]

At the beginning of the twentieth century, there were thoughts in this direction of developing a 'Yellow Russia' making use of favourable Far Eastern circumstances. Quested comments:

If that strange foetus had ever been born, Yellow Russia, whether including all or any large part of Manchuria, would clearly have been a plural society, with a racial class structure something like that of colonial Malaya or premodern Poland. There would have been a Russian higher officialdom, with Chinese and Russian clerks, a business class and town population mainly Chinese, but including many ethnic groups, whilst the peasants would have been overwhelmingly Chinese.'[20]

The Russian Revolution marked the end of the Russian colonial period in Manchuria 'in fact, if not perhaps in intention' according to Quested, who suggests that the idea of a satellite state in the north of Manchuria or even the whole might have occurred to Stalin, that is before the Japanese created their own in Manchukuo.[21]

In conclusion, Quested suggests that tsarist Russia in Manchuria passed through stages of imperialism in general consonance with what have been described above as the Great Game of Empire and the New Imperialism along with a particular emphasis on the significance of the construction of the Chinese Eastern Railway. The Soviet period brought an official missionary fervour for the advancement of all Soviet peoples, however imperfectly realised.[22]

Later, after a period of enmity almost leading to war, an even 'matier' relationship which Quested did not live to see developed between Russia and China.

148 *Empire and after*

Manchuria present

The Chinese Eastern Railway began to lose its significance when new Silk Roads were developed to the West as the PRC adopted the Belt and Road Initiative taking in Central Asia and much else besides. Peter Frankopan has written a book on the New Silk Roads in a global context without any mention of the Northeast Provinces.[23] In 2012, I found that Russia in Manchuria appeared to be indeed a thing of the past. Yet the memory lingered on in Harbin. The cathedral (Figure 12) and synagogue were still there, although as museums. Many of the shops and other buildings from earlier days were still there, too, albeit in different guises. Surprisingly, there were Russian souvenir shops with MAGAZIN in Cyrillic to

Figure 12 St Sophia Cathedral, first built in 1907 in wood, then reconstructed from 1923 to 1932 in stone, has become a feature of the scenery and a museum in Chinese Harbin today. (Wikipedia)

identify them, and a park named after Stalin. But there was no Russian person in evidence, although appearances were to prove deceptive.

There is a poignant photograph of a half dozen or so surviving Russians in Harbin at the end of the twentieth century, one or two of them possibly half-Chinese (Figure 13).[24] However, a second wave has come to Harbin, and a Russia Club was formed for them and sympathetic Chinese in 2005, the year before the last of the old generations, Efrosiniia Andreevna Nikiforova, died. The Club organises festivities for the New Year and other occasions, while devoting itself to the conservation of Russian culture (Figure 14). It has revived an old Soviet custom, the *subbotnik*, unpaid voluntary work on Saturdays, taking care of cemeteries,

Figure 13 The last old Russians in Harbin in the year 2000: photograph from the journal of the Russian Society in Ekaterinburg published in collaboration with State Archive of Sverdlovsk province. The final survivor Efrosiniia Andreevna Nikiforova died in 2006. (Nikolai Kuznetsov)

150 *Empire and after*

Figure 14 Children of the new Russians in Harbin celebrate Golden Autumn in October 2017 and Reading Day in 2015 as events in the calendar of the Russian Club. (VGBOU VO, VGUES, Vladivostok)

for example.[25] Meanwhile, at the Amur State University in Blagoveshchensk, a Centre for the Study of the Far Eastern Emigration was instituted in 2013. The Centre has set up a museum, 'Russian Harbin: History, Culture, Literature' and publishes a series on this subject entitled 'Russian Harbin Captured in the Word,' among a wide range of activities (Figure 15).[26]

A recent visitor to Harbin has been Ed Pulford in his wide-ranging book entitled *Mirrorlands: Russia, China, and Journeys in Between* and published in 2019. As Pulford reminds us, if not as great as that of several other Chinese cities, Harbin's population of more than 10 million vastly exceeds that of the entire huge

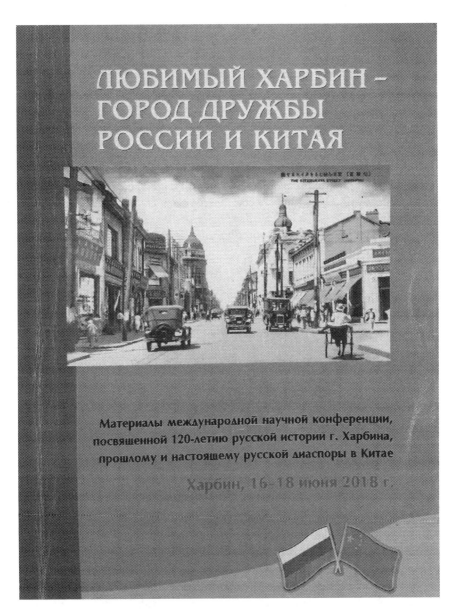

Figure 15 Beloved Kharbin: A Town of Friendship between Russia and China: Materials of an International Academic Conference devoted to the 120th Anniversary of the City of Kharbin, the Past and Present of the Russian Diaspora in China, Harbin 16–18 June 2018, translation of the front cover complete with a photo of Kitaiskaia Ulitsa (China Street) from the interwar period and crossed flags. (FGBOU VO, VGUES, Vladivostok)

152 *Empire and after*

Russian Far-Eastern Region, the size of Europe excluding Russia, but amounting to less than 7 million.

Of Manchuria as a whole, Pulford observes:

> Since the region's colonisation by Russia and Japan early in the twentieth century, and continuing through the Mao years, Manchuria has been home to vast industrial complexes churning out steel, automobiles and other machinery. But many of these have struggled to modernise following the post-Mao end to the socialist command economy, and, mired in financial scelorosis, the north-east has sought a new direction.[27]

There has been emphasis in particular on tourism, Harbin taking advantage of its harsh winter to mount an annual Ice Festival. In summer, one of the Ice Festival's major venues, Sun Island, becomes 'a kind of Russian-oriented theme park' where Chinese tourists may enjoy a 'European' experience, administered in part by recent immigrants from Vladivostok.'[28]

Wherever he travelled along the frontier between Russia and China, Pulford found attempts to attract tourists as well as evidence of economic decline. In Manzhouli, for example, where Peter Fleming had entered Manchukuo in 1933, he found a church built for tourists and giant dolls, 'cosy emporia' and 'more illicit nocturnal attractions' as well as neglected dwellings. In Southern Manchuria, at Hanchun, in a triple borderland, there were attempts to cater for Chinese, Russians and Koreans alike, aided by the investment of tens of billions of dollars by the central Chinese government.[29]

Pulford uncovered evidence of the past stretching back into the years of old Tartary and before, although here too the dominant theme of the present could be found in the aspiration to foster memories of ancient peoples in 'a joint Sino-Russian Hezhe-Nanai ethno-tourism park' on an island in the Amur by Khabarovsk, for example. Most striking, however, for Pulford were the dilapidation and detritus of the Soviet period.

He comments:

> Although it is now often too late to remember what was once shared among these divided cross-border groups, since the 1990s almost all the inhabitants of the borderlands have existed in a kind of mirrored mutual dependency, relying on one another for trade, and more recently marketing one another's perceived Asianness or Europeanness to attract tourists. Much mutual ignorance persists despite this greater contact, but whether they know it or not, local populations share a trove of common experience.'[30]

This 'trove of common experience' includes the rise and fall of the Russian Empire in the context of the rise and fall of other empires, followed by the rise and fall of the Soviet superpower in the context of the rise of its American and Chinese counterparts. Hundreds of years of history have left their mark on relations between Russians and Chinese, sometimes as mutual suspicion, sometimes as now in rapprochement. Friends or not, neighbours along a frontier as long as that between the USA and Canada will never be able to ignore each other. As far as the West is concerned, still in the twenty-first century, the 'threat' posed by Russia has wide currency as in many previous times. The historical investigation provides at least a perspective on both positive and negative aspects of the contemporary situation.

Conclusion

An authority on the earlier period when Russia was expanding throughout Eurasia and beyond, Nancy Shields Kollmann, adopts the model of an 'empire of difference,' which relied like several of its contemporaries on rule from the centre but also allowed 'diverse languages, ethnicities and religions of their subject peoples to remain in place as anchors of stability.' Up to the year 1801, the closing year of her work, Tartary was demarcated as the region to the south of the River Amur but was yet to take on the identity of Manchuria. There was as yet no question of substantial Russian infiltration, and any diversity was not so much allowed as beyond any control from the centre. Nevertheless, in its relations with the peoples of the Far East, there was some recognition of an 'empire of difference' beyond a certain amount of extermination.

John P. LeDonne gives a geopolitical emphasis to the pre-revolutionary modern years, developing Mahan's ideas of seaward expansion and Mackinder's on the Eurasian 'Heartland' to conclude that 'The sea separates, while the land binds.' Therefore, in his view, before 1917 the Russians tried to create 'a ring fence to support a fortress-fleet strategy' against both naval attack and subversive ideas. LeDonne catches nicely the increase of Russian influence in Manchuria from the second half of the nineteenth century culminating in the establishment of the Chinese Eastern Railway as an integral facilitator of the 'ring fence.'

In his overall assessment from the sixteenth century to the twenty-first, Dominic Lieven writes: 'The Russian Empire was a hybrid. It combined aspects of modern European empire and of the tradition of autocratic land empire.' He suggests: 'The rise and fall of the Russian and Soviet empires were owed to many factors but the international context was of immense importance.'[31] In particular, Lieven asserts that Manchuria was of more significance for Japan than Russia, that Manchukuo was an essential hinterland in the Japanese grasp for supreme power in Asia before the balance swung in favour of China. Lieven's description of the rise and fall of the British Empire as an accompaniment to his main theme is illuminating indeed, especially on its implications for the future of the United Kingdom as a possible parallel to the past of the Soviet Union.

To turn to Russian evaluations, from their vantage point in the Urals, Academician V. V. Alekseev and his colleagues conclude:

> The particularity of the eastern regions (distance from the centre of the country, the weakness and extent of communications, the sparseness and low density of the population, the relatively low level of the development of economic

links, the variation in levels of the development of the peoples and the lands they inhabit) has exerted its influence on the character on the politico-administrative culture of the country and strengthened the tendency towards the growth of its heterogeneity (for example, the consequence of the absence or late arrival of certain legislative norms, of governmental institutions; the long continuance of different, especially traditional, forms of administration.)

The vastness of Russia, eluding comprehension, they say, has given to the Russian mentality both the demand for self-sacrifice and a feeling of security.[32]

In Tomsk, further to the east, the late Anatoly Remnev wrote widely on Siberia and the Far East with special reference to regionalism before coming to the conclusion that

despite considerable evidence of separatist feelings, along with the government's fears and its persistent search for Siberian independence (or autonomy), Siberians' discontent with their humiliating conditions never grew into a real danger of Russia losing Siberia.[33]

Russia did of course lose Manchuria to Japan in the 1930s and then returned it to China, the rightful owner, in the 1950s. From the vantage point of the outside spectator, it seems that, as mirrored in the fate of Harbin, the loss has not been critical and is of major interest to those living in Vladivostok and elsewhere in the Far East.

Such observations add perspectives to Russia in Manchuria as a problem of empire in the past. In the future, regional strategic problems involving the Chinese north-eastern provinces and their neighbours, the Koreas and Japan, might well arise after a period of quiescence. If so, the explanation will come largely from history. Yet in the year 2020, which has brought this book to completion but also introduced to the world all the complexities of Covid-19, our communal sense of one small world has been strengthened. And so today, with environmental disaster threatening us all, Eurasianism and other regional ideologies must give way to globalism, to the salvation of the planet.

Notes

1 D. S. Riabushkin, *Ostrov Damanskii: Pogranichnyi konflikt Mart 1969 goda* (Moscow: Russkie Vitiazi, 2015), p. 8.
2 *Statement of the Government of the USSR, 13 June 1969* (Moscow: Novosti, 1969), pp. 5–6.
3 Ibid., p. 7.
4 Ibid., p. 13.
5 Odd Arne Westad, *Brothers in Arms: The Rise and Fall of the Sino-Soviet Alliance, 1946–1953* (Stanford: Stanford University Press), p. 239.
6 Riabushkin, *Ostrov Damanskii*, pp. 35–7, suggests that over 30 Russians died, up to a hundred Chinese.
7 Ibid., pp. 136–7; information gathered during author's visit to Vladivostok in 2017.
8 See, for example, Wang Li, 'An Inquiry into China's Alignment with Russia', *Vestnik MGIMO-Universiteta*, Vol. 3, No. 60 (2018), 48–58.

9 Li Ian'lin, ed., *Liubimyi Harbin – Gorod druzhby Rossii i Kitaia: Materialy mezhdunarodnoi nauchnoi-prakticheskoi konferentsii, posviashchennoi 120-letiiu russkoi istorii g. Kharbina, proshlomu i nastoishchemu russkoi diaspory v Kitae, 16–18 iiunia 2018g.* (Harbin-Vladivostok: VGUES, 2019), pp. 20–2.
10 Paul Dukes, *The Superpowers: A Short History* (Routledge: London: 2000), pp. 22–3; Mark Bassin, *Imperial Visions: Nationalist Imagination and Geographical Expansion in the Russian Far East, 1840–1865* (Cambridge: Cambridge University Press, 1999), pp. 2, 166–7.
11 See, for example, Odd Arne Westad, *The Global Cold War: Third World Intervention and the Making of Our Times* (Cambridge: Cambridge University Press, 2007).
12 Zbigniew Brzezinski, *The Grand Chessboard: American Primacy and Its Geostrategic Imperative* (New York: Basic Books, 1997), p. 44.
13 Vladimir Sokolov, 'Tropoiu Arsen'eva: k istoricheskoi antropologii voennogo vostokovedeniia DV Rossii nachala XX veka', *Vladimir Klavdievich Arsen'ev, Sobranie sochinenii v 6 tomakh*: Tom III, *Nauchno-prakticheskie publikatsii, otchety, doklady, 1906–1916gg.* (Vladivostok: Rubezh, 2012), p. 741.
14 Ibid., pp. 741–2.
15 Ibid., pp. 742–5.
16 R. K. I. Quested, *"Matey" Imperialists? The Tsarist Russians in Manchuria, 1895–1917* (Hong Kong: Centre of Asian Studies, University of Hong Kong, 1982), pp. 3–4.
17 Ibid., pp. 4–5, 15.
18 Ibid., pp. 12–3.
19 Ibid., p. 16.
20 Ibid., p. 157.
21 Ibid., p. 326.
22 Ibid., pp. 329–31.
23 Peter Frankopan, *The New Silk Roads: The Present and Future of the World* (London: Bloomsbury, 2018).
24 *Russkie v Kitae: Russians in China*, No. 23 (Ekaterinburg, 2000), p. 1.
25 M. S. Kushnarenko, 'O Russkom Klube v Kharbine', in Li Ian'lin, ed., *Liubimyi Kharbin: gorod druzhby Rossii i Kitaia* (Vladivostok: VGUES, 2019), pp. 21–31.
26 A. A. Zabiiako, 'Tsentr izucheniia Dal'nevostochnoi emigratsii' Amurskogo Gosudarstvennogo Universiteta: Itogi i perspektivy issledovaniia istorii, kul'tury i literatury vostochnoi vetvy russkogo zarubezh'ia', in Ian'lin, ed., *Liubimyi Kharbin, gorod druzhby Rossii i Kitaia* (Vladivostok: VGUES, 2019), pp. 339–51.
27 Ed Pulford, *Mirrorlands: Russia, China, and Journeys in Between* (London: Hurst, 2019), p. 189.
28 Ibid., pp. 204, 206–7.
29 Ibid., pp. 79–81, 218–20.
30 Ibid., p. xvii.
31 Nancy Shields Kollmann, *The Russian Empire, 1450–1801* (Oxford: Oxford University Press, 2017), p. 2; John P. LeDonne, *The Russian Empire and the World, 1700–1917: The Geopolitics of Expansion and Containment* (Oxford: Oxford University Press, 1997), pp. xii, 367–8; Dominic Lieven, *Empire: The Russian Empire and Its Rivals from the Sixteenth Century to the Present* (London: Random House, 2003), p. 419.
32 V. V. Alekseev, E. V. Alekseeva, K. I. Zubov, and I. V. Poberezhnikov, *Aziatskaia Rossiia v geopoliticheskoi i tsivilizatsionnoi dinamike XVI-XX veka* (Moscow: Nauka, 2004), pp. 585–6.
33 Anatolyi Remnev, 'Siberia and the Russian Far East in the Imperial Geography of Power', in Jane Burbank, ed., *Russian Empire: Space, People, Power, 1700–1930* (Bloomington: Indiana University Press, 2007), pp. 450–1.

Index

Page no. followed by n represent Notes
Page no. in *Italics* represent Figures

Acheson, D. 129
Afghanistan 28, 56, 99n5
agriculture 68
Aigun Treaty 137
Aisin Gioro 3
Alekseev, V.V. 153
Arsenev, Vladimir 57, *58*
Arthur, W.C. 25
Atkinson, T.W. 26
atomic bombs: Hiroshima 119; Nagasaki 119

Bax, Captain B. W. 29
Bezobrazov, Captain A.M. 45
Bland, J.O.P. 60
Boxer challenge 41
British Government 1n2
Brzezinski, Zbigniew 144n12
Bullitt, W.C. 77, 78

Carlyle, Thomas 7
Catherine the Great 20
Chamberlin, W.H. 110
Cheke, D. 113
Chekhov, A. 30
Chiang Kia-shek 98, 128
children of Harbin Russians *150*
Chilikin, V.A. 86
China, inventions 2
Chinese Cake (cartoon) *53*
Chinese Eastern Railway 39, 83, 142
Chinese Revolution 127
Chinggis Khan 143
CIA 135
Cochrane, Captain J.D. 21
Cold War 122n8, 124, 125, 140
Communist International (Comintern) 78

Daily Telegraph 66
Dairen 13, 124, 130
Damansky Island 138, *139*, 143
Denikin, A.I. 59
Dersu Uzala (1976) 57

Eastern Provinces (Fungtien, Kirin, Heilungkiang) 4
Eastern Tartary, map *20*
Edict of Toleration (1773) 21
Esperanto 87

Fleming, P. 108, 110
fortress mentality, Soviet Union 145
Frankopan, P. 148
Friendship Treaty 124

General Dmitry Khorvat, military engineer *81*
Glantz, D.M. 101, 121
globalism 154
gold 6
Grave, V.V. 65
Great Northern War 18
Great Wall of China 21
A Guide to the Great Siberian Railway 42n16

Hanson, G.C. 97, 106
Harbin 40, 61, 87, 97, 123, 143
Harriman, E.H. 57
Haslam, J. 101
Herzen, A. 141
Hiroshima, atomic bomb 119
Hodge, General J.R. 132
Hokkaido 122
hunhutsy (redbeards) 40, 59

158 *Index*

ideology, Harbin 88
The Influence of Sea Power upon History 1660–1891, Mahan, A.T. 37
International Workers' Day 62
inventions, China 2
iron 6
Izvestiia 127

Japan 44, 100, 105, 142
Jesuits 19

Kankrin, Count E.F. 22
Kennan, G.F. 117
Kharbinskii Vestnik (*Harbin Herald*) 70
Kharbin *151*
Kiakhta, Treaty of 20
Kokovtsov, V.N. 59
Kolesnichenko, K. 112
Korean War 131
Krasnoshchekov, A. M. 79, 81, 82, 95n11
Krushchev, N. 133
Kulomzin, A.N. 38
Kuril Islands 121, 122
Kuropatkin, A. 42

Lampson, Sir M. 99
Land-Lease 127
Lattimore, O. 100
LeDonne, J.P. 153
Liaotung Peninsula 3, 121, 124, 131
Lieven, D. 153
Lin Sun 3
Lytton Commission 101, 104

MacArthur, General D. 122
Mackinder, H.J. 78
magpie, sacred bird 3
Manchoutikuo 106
Manchu and Muscovite 45
Manchukuo 102, 104, 106
Manchuria, map *5, 120*
Manchurian Mafia 107
The Manchus: The Reigning Dynasty of China (Ross) 1
Mao tsi tung 126
Marshall, General G. 127
Marshall, P.J. 18
Mary, B. 4
Methodists 87
Mongolia 67
Muravyov, N. 22

Nagasaki, atomic bomb 119
Nanking, Treaty of 22

Nerchinsk, Treaty of 18
Nikolai Muravyov-Amurskii *23*
NKVD 123
Nord en Ost Tartarye 14
Novosti Zhizni 86
Nurhaci 3

Odd Arne Westad 133
Open Door (USA) 41, 57
opium 6, 24; trade 29n32
Opium War (1839–1842) 22
Orthodox mission (Peking) 19

Pall Mall Gazette 66
Patterson, R.P. 132
Pearl Harbour 117
Peking Treaty 25, 138
People's Revolutionary Army (NRA) 82
Perry, Commodore M.C. 23
Peter the Great 18
pneumonic plague 68
population 7
Port Arthur 130
Portsmouth Treaty 57
Potsdam Declaration 118
POWs, Japanese 123
Pravda 101, 128n19
Przhevalskii, N.M. 30
Pu Yi 109, 123n11
Pulford, E. 150
Putnam Weale, B.L. 45, 58, 69

Qing Dynasty 145
Quested, R. 146

Railway Construction Gang *43*
railways 1, 22, 100; *see also* Chinese Eastern Railway, SMR
rhubarb 20
Rieber, A.J. 123
River: Amur 21, 22, 25; Ussuri, Yalu 4, 45, 111; Liao 5
Roberts, G. 111
Rodzaevsky, K.V. 107
Romanov, B.A. 37, 47
root crops 6
Ross, John 1
Russian Fascist Organisation (RFO) 89, 107
Russian Geographical Society 26
Russian Revolution 71
The Russians on the Amur: Conquest and Colonisation (Ravenstein) 27
Russians in Harbin c.2000 *149*
Russkii Golos (Russian Voice) 85

Russkii Klub 108
Russo-Japanese War 47

St Petersburg 47n29, 62
St Sophia Cathedral *148*
salmon 6
Sazonov, S.D. 67
Semyonov, G.M. 79
Serebriannikov, I.I. 123
Shimonoseki, Treaty of 44
Sino-Soviet Treaty 130
Sokolov, V. 144
sorghum 6
South Manchurian Railway (SMR) 59
Soviet Invasion 117
Soviet Pacific Fleet 105
Soviet Union, fortress mentality 145
Stalin, J. 98, 117, 123
Stephan, J. 69, 82, 107
Sun Yat-sen (President) 64

tea trade 29
Tientsin Treaty 137
Tilley, H.A. 27
tobacco 6
Trans-Siberian Railway 36, 47, 142

Transom, J.M. 24
Triple Entente (1907) 56
Tsitsikar 19n4
Tsuyoshi Hasegawa 119, 122

Ustrialov, Professor N.V. 86, 89

Vasilevsky, Marshal A.M. 121
vegetables 6
Vladivostok 29, 61, 69, 141
Vologodskii, P.V. 83, 84

War, Japan and China 39
Wenyon, C. 37
wheat 6
William III 18
Wilson, W. (US President) 77
Witte, S.I. 36

Yalta Conference 114
Yellow Russia 147
YMCA 87
Younghusband, F. 30
Yukiko Koshiro 118

Zhukov, G.K. 111

Printed in the United States
by Baker & Taylor Publisher Services